3039300

D1196493

DATE DUE

DEMCO

EASTERN EUROPE:

A COMMUNIST KALEIDOSCOPE

THE DIAL PRESS
NEW YORK

EASTERN EUROPE:

A COMMUNIST KALEIDOSCOPE

JOHN DORNBERG

For Jane
who is experiencing it

Published by The Dial Press
1 Dag Hammarskjold Plaza
New York, New York 10017

Library of Congress Cataloging in Publication Data
Dornberg, John. Eastern Europe.
Bibliography: p. 299. Includes index.
Summary: Explores the history, politics, economics,
technological and artistic developments, and quality
of life of five Eastern European countries: Bulgaria,
Czechoslovakia, Hungary, Poland, and Romania.
1. Europe, Eastern—Juvenile literature.
[1. Europe, Eastern]   I. Title.
DJK9.D67   947   78-72202
ISBN 0-8037-2208-7

Contents

Note

To speak of Eastern Europe or the Soviet bloc obviously entails more than the five countries—Bulgaria, Czechoslovakia, Hungary, Poland, and Romania—treated in this book. It means Yugoslavia as well as East Germany.

Except for certain comparative references, however, I have excluded fuller treatment of them from this book for several reasons.

In the case of Yugoslavia, though certainly a Slavic and East European country, it must be remembered that it regards itself as nonaligned and is not a member of either the Warsaw Pact or the Council for Mutual Economic Cooperation (Comecon), the Soviet bloc's "common market." Though certainly a Communist country, its relations with the Soviet Union and the USSR's more loyal allies have been strained since 1948 and the form of Communism practiced there is so radically different from any other in the world that it requires fuller treatment than the limits of this book would permit. Moreover, it has so little in common—politically, economically, and in the context of world affairs—with the five "bloc" countries that it must be viewed as a separate case.

East Germany, though very definitely a part of the bloc, a member of Comecon and of the Warsaw Pact, is also a separate case and has been left out for that reason. Until 1945 it was an integral part of the German Reich. It started on the path to separate statehood—a development only reluctantly recognized by West Germany, the United States, and most of the world's other Western capitalist democracies as recently as the early 1970's—as the Soviet occupation zone of Germany. The path was uncertain and rocky, even in the eyes of East Berlin's mentor, the Soviet Union, which until the mid-1950's could not make up its mind as to whether that was the course it wanted history to take. East Germany did not join the United Nations as a separate state, and was not recognized as such, until 1972. And today its outlook is still so uncertain that it looks more toward its West German neighbor than toward Poland or Czechoslovakia, for example. A major share of its Western trade is with West Germany and is not even considered foreign trade at all, going by the name of "intra-German." West Germany does not recognize a separate East German nationhood or citizenship and automatically regards all East German citizens as its own. The question of reunification has been neither resolved nor laid to rest on either side of the border. It is a separate state, but not a separate nation, and as such its position in the context of this book would simply be out of place.

EASTERN EUROPE:
A COMMUNIST KALEIDOSCOPE

1

A World of Contrasts

It was February 1968 in Vienna. I was posted there as bureau chief for an American news magazine, covering Eastern Europe—primarily the five "satellite" countries of the Soviet bloc: Poland, Czechoslovakia, Hungary, Romania, and Bulgaria. I was about to be transferred to Moscow, and Alan Tillier, the man who was to replace me, had come to town. So had Bud Korengold, the man I would be replacing soon in Moscow. Together we set out to drive the 180 miles from Vienna, capital of neutral Austria, to Budapest, the capital of Communist Hungary, where we were to report on a high-level conference of Communist party officials from some thirty-five countries around the world—a routine assignment for foreign correspondents, but also a good opportunity for the three of us to get to know each other and exchange ideas and experiences.

To me Budapest was a familiar place. My work reporting on that part of the world had taken me there often and I regarded it as just one more Communist capital.

For my two colleagues, however, it was a brand-new experience. Alan Tillier, who up to then had been working in Paris, had never been to any Communist country before. Bud Korengold, who had spent eight years reporting from the Soviet Union, knew Moscow inside out but in all that time had never visited any of the other Soviet-bloc nations. They were about to view Budapest like men coming from two different planets.

As we drove into the city, I could see Alan on the seat next to me, his face getting grayer and more solemn, while Bud's, which I saw through the rearview mirror, was definitely lighting and brightening up. Both were studying the terrain and surroundings closely.

When we finally pulled up in front of our hotel on teeming Lenin Boulevard, Alan shook his head sadly and said: "Oh, no. It's all so drab and depressing. Don't tell me this is where I'll be working for the next few years." Bud, on the other hand, bolted out of the car and, doing something like a joy dance, shouted: "My God, it's great! Just look at all the shops and neon lights. I can't believe that this is Communism, too."

The incident, as fresh in my mind as if it had happened only yesterday, reveals much about the contrasts and contradictions of Eastern Europe.

Though inhabited by almost ninety million people, more than one third the population of the United States, it is a comparatively tiny chunk of real estate—five independent countries squeezed between the borders of Germany and Russia—which covers an area of only 344,000 square miles: somewhat larger than the state of Texas but considerably smaller than Alaska.

Its political, historical, and cultural importance, especially to America, cannot be overestimated. Not only did both world wars begin there, in 1914 and 1939, as rivalries and contests for might between the big powers, but it was the central stage of the cold war between the United States and the Soviet Union from the late 1940's to the early 1970's. Moreover, nearly five million Americans were either born in or are the second-generation descendants of emigrants from Poland, Czechoslovakia, Hungary, Romania, and Bulgaria. At least that many again can trace their family origins two and more generations back to Eastern Europe.

Yet, for the majority of Americans it is an entirely alien world—one inhabited by people with unpronounceable names, its map dotted by plains, forests, mountains, rivers, cities, towns, and villages that are equally unpronounceable— a world whose babel of languages few people outside can speak or understand, one with strange customs and mores.

Few parts of the globe have been more misunderstood or misinterpreted in recent years, and there are few about which more propaganda and sheer nonsense have been written.

True, for the past three decades or so, Communism has been the political and economic common denominator of the East European countries. They are all members of the Warsaw Pact, Moscow's military counterpart to the North Atlantic Treaty Organization (NATO); and the Council for Mutual Economic Cooperation (Comecon). And they most certainly are in the Soviet "sphere of influence"—more than the West European countries are in that of the United States.

But to regard them as a cohesive bloc marching in step to the Kremlin's tune is not only an oversimplification but has led to serious miscalculations by U.S. policy makers in years past. On the contrary, they are one of the most diversified areas of the world—a kaleidoscope of nationalities, ethnic groups, languages, dialects, religions, and cultures with less in common than the nations of Western Europe.

On the one hand, three countries—Poland, Czechoslovakia, and Bulgaria—are peopled by Slavs, but Slavs who a past thousand years have had completely different historical, religious, and cultural experiences. The Poles are Roman Catholic, the Czechs and Slovaks Catholic and Protestant, and the Bulgarians are Eastern Orthodox and Muslim. They have deep animosity toward each other, and their languages have less in common than German, Dutch, and Swedish. One, Bulgarian, is even written in a different alphabet.

On the other hand, the second largest country—Romania— has a population that is basically Latin. The people are descendants of the pre-Christian Dacians and of Roman Emperor Trajan's legionnaires who conquered and settled in ancient Dacia around A.D. 106. The language has much in common with Italian and nothing at all with those spoken in Romania's neighboring countries—the Soviet Union, Hungary, Yugoslavia, and Bulgaria. Yet the predominant religion is Eastern Orthodox. Hungary, one of the smallest but most affluent of the five countries, is peopled by an ethnic group completely different from the others—the Magyars. Their closest historical and linguistic cousins are probably the Finns who live about a thousand miles to the north.

Over the centuries the borders of all five countries have been redrawn numerous times and have been as open as a sieve, so that there are now large settlements of Hungarians in Romania, Turks in Bulgaria, Slovaks in Hungary, Czechs in Poland, not to mention the descendants of German colonists still to be found all over Eastern Europe.

Soviet economic, military, and political power does loom over all of them, but, contrary to cold war propaganda and some preconceived notions, it does not loom heavily enough to call these countries mere dependencies or "satellites." That struck me when I first began covering them as a newsman in the early 1960's, and I am even more struck by it today.

Like most people of my generation—too young to serve in uniform in World War II but old enough to watch the cold war start—I could remember the dramatic speech that Britain's Prime Minister Winston Churchill gave while on a visit to the United States at Fulton, Missouri, in March 1946.

"A shadow," he said, "has fallen upon the scenes so lately lighted by the Allied victory. From Stettin in the Baltic to Trieste in the Adriatic an iron curtain has descended across the continent of Europe."

I looked for that "iron curtain" we had all heard so much about when I became a correspondent in Eastern Europe, but did not really find it until I went to Moscow and began covering the Soviet Union itself. In a figurative sense it turned out to run along the Soviet border and it is a curtain of culture and attitudes, a psychological curtain. It has less to do with the Russian Revolution of 1917 or the USSR being Communist than with the preceding ten centuries of Russia's isolation from the mainstream of European history. But the "satellite" countries west of that border—especially Poland, Hungary, and Czechoslovakia, though also Romania and Bulgaria—were and remain very much a part of that mainstream, despite three decades of Soviet domination. Moreover, they still regard themselves as culturally superior to the Russians on whom they are politically, militarily, and economically dependent.

These facts may help explain why my two colleagues, Bud and Alan, reacted so differently when they first saw Budapest on that February day in 1968.

By American and West European standards they are poor and backward, so Alan was right when he called it "drab and depressing."

Most of the larger cities have a seedy look to them. All first-time visitors to Eastern Europe are struck by the neglected, dilapidated appearance of buildings and houses, the shoddy construction work that makes instant slums of new apartment and residential complexes before the first tenants even move in, the lack of color and cheeriness, and the darkness of the towns at night—in part because of constant energy and power shortages, in part because there is not the profusion of advertising signs to which Americans and West Europeans are accustomed. To cite just a few statistics: only one out of six families in Eastern Europe owns a car, only half the households have refrigerators, and per population there are only half as many TV sets as in the United States.

Then, too, East Europeans must work much harder and longer to eke out a living that is far less affluent than in the West. The average Hungarian, for example, must work three times as many minutes—forty-five—as the average American to earn a pound of beef and at least ten minutes longer than the average West German. In terms of time spent working, a man's suit costs three, a woman's dress four, a color television set ten, and a sub-compact-size automobile about six times what they do in the United States.

Then, too, all over Eastern Europe the choice and supply of consumer goods are so limited that obtaining them is not a problem of having the money (credit buying hardly exists), but finding the items in stock. There is a shortage of some goods all the time and of all of them some of the time—even ordinary daily things such as pins and sewing needles, rubber bands, stationery, toilet paper, and kitchen utensils.

During 1977 and early 1978, for example, meat of any kind was in such short supply in Poland that I saw hours-long lines of shoppers standing in front of butcher shops everywhere in Warsaw and other cities. The meat shortage even gave rise to strikes and riots, not to mention bitter, sarcastic jokes which people told quite openly and fearlessly to anyone willing to listen. One that I heard told of a man standing for over an hour in a meat queue and getting more impatient and livid about it by the minute. Suddenly he turned to the woman behind him and said: "I'm so angry I can't take it anymore. Would you hold my place while I go over to Party headquarters to punch Edward Gierek [Poland's Communist party chief] in the nose?" She nodded, and he stalked off to the Party building, only to return after a couple of minutes even angrier. "What happened?" the woman asked. "You won't believe it," he said. "The line outside Gierek's office is even longer than this one."

But by the standards of the Soviet Union, the East European countries are so affluent that Bud was also right when he jumped out of the car in Budapest and called it "great." He was seeing it with Russian eyes after having spent so many years working in Moscow.

Though the average Hungarian must work so much longer to buy that pound of beef than an American or West German, he or she spends fifteen minutes less on the job to earn it than the average Russian. By comparison, Soviet citizens work almost twice as long as Hungarians in order to buy suits, dresses, TV sets, or cars, and the quality, choice, and supply of merchandise in the USSR are considerably worse.

For the majority of Soviet citizens, a visit to any of the East European countries is a once- or twice-in-a-lifetime treat and not unlike a trip to a land of milk and honey. I have often watched and overheard busloads of Russian tourists in various cities of Eastern Europe. Much like little children pressing their noses to toy-store windows just before Christmas, they ogled the bustling traffic, the many cars, the comparatively well-dressed people on the streets, and the greater affluence. They always expressed amazement—and envy—at what appeared to them a dazzling array of consumer goods, a much higher standard of living, and a greater degree of personal freedom than they have in the USSR.

And, like some Americans on their first visit to Western Europe, especially West Germany, the richest country of all, I have heard these Russians in Eastern Europe express anger and resentment, saying very loudly, "You'd think it was they, not we, who won the war." It is important to remember that three of the Soviet-bloc countries—Romania, Hungary, and Bulgaria—were allies of Nazi Germany during World War II fighting against Russia, and that Poland and Czechoslovakia, having been conquered by the Germans, were liberated by the Soviet army.

But economic and living conditions in the East European countries cannot be measured only by applying—or comparing—American and Russian yardsticks. A more meaningful test is to compare life today with that before they became Communist states after World War II.

Only one country—Czechoslovakia—was highly industrialized, at least in its western, Czech-speaking regions called Bohemia and Moravia; whereas Slovakia, whose people speak a related but distinct language, was primarily agricultural.

The others, notably Bulgaria, Poland, and Romania—less so Hungary—were incredibly backward societies. A thin urban industrial-commercial class and rural landowner caste ruled over a huge, largely impoverished, illiterate, and miserable peasant majority. There was almost no industry, and farming was primitive horse and hand labor unaided by any mechanized equipment.

Since the Communist takeover, but especially since the early 1960's, there has been a complete turnaround. Bulgaria's population, which was almost eighty percent rural and engaged in medievallike farming up to 1945, is now sixty percent urban and working in industry and commerce. Romania is undergoing a similar transformation.

By far the most breathtaking case is Poland, a country approximately the size of the state of New Mexico but with a population of thirty-four million—about equal to that of Illinois, Pennsylvania, and Texas combined. It is the largest of the five countries.

Before World War II, during which it suffered proportionately greater losses than any other country, including the death of six million people, it was one of the poorest nations in Europe, with more than two thirds of its populace living on the land and eking out a bare existence from farming.

Today more than two thirds of all Poles live in cities and work in industry and trade; and Poland ranks as the seventh most important industrial power in Europe, the eleventh largest in the world. It is the world's fourth biggest producer—and second largest exporter—of high-grade anthracite coal, and the fifth largest of refined copper. It is a major manufacturer of steel, chemicals, synthetics, machine tools, engineering products, and electronic equipment. It has one of Europe's largest merchant marines, and ranks ninth among shipbuilding nations—well ahead of such traditional maritime countries as Great Britain, Italy, France, Norway, or Sweden. Since 1971, when it embarked on its industrialization drive in earnest, Poland has been turned into the world's largest single construction site. Agriculture has been modernized and the horse-drawn wagon and plow—almost a trademark of Poland when I first visited the country in 1967—are giving way to tractors and other farm machines.

The price, as in the other East European countries, has been high. Much that is newly built was built shoddily because it was built too fast with labor not yet properly trained. New apartment houses do look like instant slums, highways barely opened for traffic are already pockmarked with chuckholes. The pint-size, Italian-designed cars that are rolling off the new assembly lines and are the dream of every

Warsaw, Poland, today

Pole tend to drive, ride, and sound like trucks. Quantity comes before quality. Moreover, in order to flex their industrial muscles and pull their country up by its bootstraps, Poles have had to do without the amenities of most Western countries, and visitors from the West who judge it only by their own standards are sure to be shocked. But that was to be expected.

To my question why quality consumer goods and the thousands of minor things that make life more agreeable were still in short supply, the mayor of a Polish city whom I have known for years once said to me: "That's simple. 'A' always has to come before 'B.' In our situation, consumer goods were 'B' and the means to produce them were 'A.' But I'm sure you've noticed a change from your last visit." I certainly did.

Though the East European countries still present a very mixed and varied economic picture, with the standard of living in Czechoslovakia and Hungary much higher than in Poland, and Poland's again higher than Bulgaria's or Romania's, life in each of them, for the majority of their people, is tangibly better than it was before they became Communist. The real question one might ask, since life has gotten better all over the world, is how much better it might be in Eastern Europe had it not gone Communist. Given the course of history, it is a question with no answer.

For at least twenty years after Winston Churchill coined his famous "iron curtain" phrase at Fulton, Missouri, the West looked upon Eastern Europe as one huge prison camp where ninety million people cowered under Communist oppression. The picture drawn—and perhaps broadly true in the 1940's and 1950's, though no longer—was that of fawning satellite states trembling whenever Moscow cracked the whip, and held in near slavery by the Soviet army. In 1959 the U.S. Congress even passed a resolution describing them "captive nations." To this day it requires the President to declare something each year called Captive Nations Week.

Aside from the fact that these nations do not consider themselves "captive" and laugh at the label, the term assumes that they were "free" before entering the Soviet orbit. That was not the case. With the important exception of Czechoslovakia, a genuine democracy from the time of its creation as an independent state in 1918 until Adolf Hitler occupied and dismembered it in 1939, the others were all ruled either by autocratic monarchs or dictators of one sort or another long before the Communists came to power in them. Nor was the presence of Soviet troops—though obviously an important factor—always the force behind the Communist governments established in Eastern Europe after World War II. In Hungary, where the Red Army maintained a large contingent because it had been an enemy country allied with Nazi Germany, it took until 1947 for the Communist regime to solidify its control. In Czechoslovakia, from which all Soviet forces had withdrawn by 1946, it took the local Communists until 1948 to gain complete power.

Moreover, in the three decades since the Communist takeover, some of the countries have managed to free themselves from Soviet control to a remarkable degree, though it is a freedom that takes on different and sometimes very curious forms in each of them. It is often misunderstood and misinterpreted in the West. That was especially true in the United States during the 1976 presidential campaign when Gerald Ford and Jimmy Carter argued over whether the East European countries were under "Soviet domination" or not.

Romania, for example, does not have a single Soviet soldier stationed on its territory. It refuses to permit Warsaw Pact maneuvers within its borders, does not let its troops participate in those maneuvers elsewhere, and only allows its top generals to join in staff and command exercises. It is not fully integrated into Comecon and does more trade with Western capitalist and nonaligned "Third World" underdeveloped countries than it does with all of its Communist allies and neighbors. It conducts a highly independent foreign policy. In 1967, when the Soviet Union broke diplomatic ties with Israel, lining itself up on the Arab side, and forced the East European countries to follow suit, Romania flatly refused. To this day it is the only Soviet-bloc nation that formally recognizes Israel. But at home, in domestic affairs, it is the country that is the least free. Its ruler, President Nicolae Ceausescu, is a total dictator in command of a repressive regime with all the ugly trappings of a personality cult. There is virtually no freedom of speech. Restrictions on thought, culture, and travel are the tightest in Eastern Europe.

Hungary, on the other hand, never deviates even a fraction of an inch from the Kremlin's foreign policy line and forty thousand crack Soviet troops are still stationed there. Yet it is called "the merriest barracks in the Communist camp." Its people enjoy not only the greatest material comforts but the widest personal, political, and cultural freedoms and human rights. Budapest is one of the liveliest capitals in Europe— Eastern or Western. Hungarians can travel whenever and wherever they wish—as long as they have the money. Writers may write, artists may paint, and musicians are free to play or compose what they please without restrictions. Yet it was in Hungary in 1956 that Moscow used brutal force to put down an anti-Communist revolution. The man whom the Soviets then installed as leader and Communist party chief, Janos Kadar, was once hated and labeled the "Kremlin's enforcer." Today, after introducing a "live and let live policy" in 1961, he is considered the most liberal, openminded, and democratic ruler in Eastern Europe.

The Polish people, although they live under an authoritarian regime, also clearly have a good deal to say about who rules them and what policies their government follows. It is the only East European country where repressive Communist leaderships have twice been toppled from power and replaced by more liberal ones because of workers' strikes, riots, and demonstrations—once in 1956 and again in 1970. As recently as June 1976 public disturbances forced the reigning government of Communist party chief Edward Gierek to repeal a set of unpopular decisions to raise food and consumer goods prices.

Since the East European countries have come under Soviet influence they have managed to preserve considerably more autonomy and independence than is generally known or than Western propaganda campaigns of the cold war era, such as Captive Nations Week, led us to believe. The economies of the nine West European countries that are members of the Common Market—to cite one example—are far more integrated and dependent on each other than those of the East European countries that belong to Comecon. In fact, that makes many East European commercial and trading officials unhappy. "We would have tons less trouble if we only had a few ounces more integration and cooperation among each other," an East European banker once told me.

Because of their histories of being suppressed by their more powerful neighbors—some for decades, others for centuries—they are all fiercely patriotic and nationalistic. Although their leaders are all Communists dedicated to the cause of Communism, they are nationalists first—Bulgarians, Czechoslovaks, Hungarians, Poles, and Romanians. They place patriotism ahead of the Soviet idea of "internationalism," and the interests of their own countries ahead of those of the Soviet Union. Their aims are to stake out their own nations' independence while still remaining Communist, and to improve life at home.

Soviet military power, political authority, economic weight, and ambitions of empire in this part of Europe are real. No country with a neighbor as big, mighty, and bullying as the Soviet Union can really afford to ignore it, especially since the USSR also happens to own and control the flow of numerous vital raw materials such as oil, natural gas, and a treasure chest of minerals. Nevertheless, the trend in Eastern Europe, particularly during the past ten years, has been to ignore the reality of Soviet power or, at any rate, to pay only lip service to it. That is a risky game. But because they play it, the East European countries are becoming more important to the United States.

It is often said about them that "the only thing they hate more than each other is Russia." That is true only in part There is certainly no love lost among the five countries, but their relationship to Russia and the Soviet Union is one of both love and hate.

Soviet influence in the area did not begin with the arrival of the Red Army in World War II. Its historical roots actually go back to Russia's own medieval beginnings and are closely linked to czarist Russia's role in the area.

Ethnic and religious factors have much to do with it. Thus, some of the Slavic peoples of Eastern Europe—especially the Slovaks, Bulgarians, and Serbs of modern Yugoslavia—tended to look toward Russia as a friend and protector, particularly against other big powers and bullies in the region such as the Ottoman Turks and the Austro-Germans of the Hapsburg Empire.

On the other hand, both Slavic and non-Slavic peoples of Eastern Europe who had opted for Roman Catholicism and, after the Reformation, also for Protestantism, tended to look westward and to resent the Russians. This was true of the Poles, Czechs, and Hungarians.

Russia always had ambitions in the area, frustrated at one point or another in history by rival big powers—Poland, when it was one of the "great states" in the sixteenth and seventeenth centuries; the Ottoman Turks; Austria-Hungary; and Prussia. Over the centuries loyalties and attitudes in Eastern Europe changed often, usually based on the old adage that "the enemy of my enemy is my friend." What did not change were Russia's ambitions. They survived the end of czarist rule, the Bolshevik Revolution, and right into the era when Josef Stalin presided in the Kremlin.

And Stalin wasted no time establishing Russian authority in Eastern Europe when the defeat of Hitler's Nazi Reich gave him the opportunity. He based his claims in part on the traditional rights of the victor to his "spoils"—in this case Bulgaria, Romania, and Hungary—and in part on Soviet Russia's recognized need for a "buffer zone" of friendly countries, for it had in the past been the victim of frequent aggression from the West.

Communist ideology helped Stalin establish Soviet authority in Eastern Europe—primarily by bringing local, though usually Moscow-trained, Communists to political power. But this had nothing to do with Moscow's alleged aim of world revolution.

The threat of "world Communist revolution" made a good propaganda issue in the cold war, and some people still fear it today. In fact, it has not been a Soviet goal since the 1920's when Stalin defeated Leon Trotsky in the struggle for power in Moscow. Having won command of the Soviet Communist party, Stalin pursued a policy that has remained the policy of his two successors, Nikita Khrushchev and Leonid Brezhnev: to "build Communism in *one* country," the Soviet Union.

But neither Stalin nor Khrushchev nor Brezhnev had (or

have) any objections to using the world Communist movement and the Communist parties of other countries as tools of Soviet foreign policy and as instruments for furthering Russia's age-old ambitions of power. This was what led to strains and troubles within the international Communist movement and to open breaks with Moscow by those local Communists who had fought and won their own revolutions and had come to power in their own countries without any Russian help. The best known examples are Josip Broz Tito in Yugoslavia and Mao Tse-tung in China.

In Eastern Europe, as nationally minded, patriotic, second-generation "home" Communists have succeeded to power, replacing the leaders of the immediate postwar and cold war days, they began to challenge the Soviet Union's role, its claim to be a "model" for others to emulate, its territorial ambitions, its demand for total loyalty, and its insistence that Bulgarian, Czechoslovak, Hungarian, Polish, and Romanian interests must take a back seat to those of the USSR.

After World War II the Soviet Union also bolstered its new authority in the region by promising to defend it against any future German aggression. In the case of Poland, caught by geography between its traditional enemies Russia and Germany, and having been invaded, partitioned, and occupied by both on a number of occasions during its history, the promise sounded good. The Poles' fear of Germany, being greater than their dislike of the Russians, enabled the Soviet Union to tighten its postwar grip on Poland. Similar considerations also persuaded the Czechoslovaks to make their peace with Moscow. It was a choice between the lesser of two evils.

But in more recent years West Germany has proved peaceful (East Germany is a Soviet ally). It improved its ties with the East European countries, and gave them guarantees against aggression in various treaties. So the East European need for Soviet "protection" against West German ambitions, real or imagined, has lessened. Along with it the East European countries have become more restless and independence-minded.

Eastern Europe today is a complex world of contrasts and contradictions—neither captive nor free, not yet affluent but no longer backward and poor. It is a kaleidoscope because it is colorful, complex in its composition, and fragile: turn or shake it, and the picture you get will be completely new. The five countries have much in common and at the same time nothing. What is true for one is true for all of them and at the same time for none. It is a world that is changing fast and dramatically.

Certainly, as the next pages and chapters will show, its people do want more human rights, better wages and working conditions, higher standards of living, and a greater voice in managing their own affairs than the Communist regimes now in power—some patterned more, others less, on the Soviet model—allow them.

But the majority, if given a choice, would still prefer a socialistic or communistic society. Communism, after all, never takes root in a vacuum and certainly finds few supporters in the world's wealthier, more socially just countries. The United States and West Germany are perfect examples of relatively affluent nations where Communist ideology has almost no appeal and Communist parties are so small that the votes they get during elections barely register on the computers.

By contrast, the countries of Eastern Europe had long histories of almost unbelievable poverty, social unrest and political discontent. Communist regimes had come to power briefly in a couple of them after World War I and were then suppressed. The suppression of local Communists, though they were ruthless revolutionaries, made martyrs of many of them. By the time World War II ended, Communism in Eastern Europe, backed by the "liberating" Soviet army, was far from being an unpopular idea. Thirty years of it since then have left it deeply ingrained in the minds of most people as the only possible way of life, especially for the younger ones who have known nothing else.

They would, however, prefer a different style of Communism: less rigid and less dictatorial. One could call it a kind of "democratic Communism." It exists, for example, in Yugoslavia, also an East European Communist country, which broke out of the Soviet bloc more than thirty years ago and has managed to maintain its independence as a neutral, nonaligned nation ever since. It was also taking shape during the spring and summer of 1968 in Czechoslovakia where a new, more open-minded team of Communist leaders had come to power and where it was called "Communism with a human face." Unfortunately, that experiment was considered highly dangerous in Moscow and Soviet tanks and troops were sent in August 1968 to crush it.

Despite that invasion of Czechoslovakia in 1968, an event that has been neither forgotten nor forgiven in Eastern Europe, the majority of people, if given a choice, would also elect to remain in the Soviet orbit. What they do want, but are not likely to get, is a new deal from Moscow—changes in the spirit and letter of their contract with Russia—for at no time in the past three decades has the demand for national dignity and the hunger for human rights in all the East European countries ever been greater.

There is something that one could call the East European tragedy. It is the fact that Eastern Europe today is like a hope unfulfilled and a promise not kept because of the heavy hand of Moscow and Soviet-style Communism. In a way, it is a test tube of history that got crushed in the collision of interests and ambitions between the big powers of the world.

2

The Land–
A Crazy-Quilt Map

All of Europe is small by American standards, but Communist Eastern Europe is just a fragment of it—a comparatively tiny plot of land cut up like a jigsaw puzzle by national boundaries, none of which existed in their present form before 1918 and some of which were not officially recognized by all Western countries until 1971. From north to south it measures just barely 1,000 miles—about the distance from New York to Chicago—and the width from west to east is never much more than 400 miles. The total area—344,000 square miles—is just a fraction more than that of Wyoming, Montana, and Idaho. Yet it is inhabited by more than ninety million people, almost ninety times the population of those three states.

Following the map clockwise, one observes that it is bordered on the north by the Baltic Sea, on the east by the

Soviet Union and the Black Sea, on the south by Turkey and Greece, on the southwest by Yugoslavia, and on the west by Austria, West Germany, and East Germany.

Poland, the northernmost and largest of the five, has an area of 122,000 square miles—a little more than either New Mexico or Italy—and a population of 34 million. It is bordered on the north by some 430 miles of coastline along the Baltic, on the east by the Soviet Union, on the south by Czechoslovakia, and on the west by East Germany. The capital, Warsaw, has a population of 1.5 million. There are five other cities—Lodz, Crakow, Wroclaw, Poznan, and Gdansk —with populations of 500,000 to 1 million and twenty-six more with more than 100,000. Poland's principal river, the Vistula, bisects it from south to north and is its principal artery of life, rising in the Carpathian Mountains near the border with Czechoslovakia and flowing majestically for more than 650 miles, through such cities as Cracow and Warsaw, finally spilling into the Baltic at the port of Gdansk.

Czechoslovakia, with its almost 50,000 square miles and nearly 15 million people, is equal in size to the state of New York. It is bordered on the north by Poland, the east by a short strip of the Soviet Union, to the south by both Hungary and Austria, and on its western frontiers by both West and East Germany. Prague, its capital—often called the Golden City—has a population of 1.1 million. Four others—Brno, Bratislava, Ostrava, and Pilsen—are cities of 100,000 to 500,000.

Hungary, the smallest of the countries, has only 36,000 square miles—the size of Indiana—and a population of 10.5 million. On its northern boundary is Czechoslovakia. To the east it touches a small corner of the Soviet Union and a long stretch of Romania. On the south it is bordered by Yugoslavia, and to the west by Austria. Budapest, the capital, is the largest city in Eastern Europe with a population of more than 2 million—twenty percent of the country's total. Situated astride the Danube, it is actually two cities: hilly Buda on the right side of the river and flat, sprawling Pest on the left. They are linked by a half dozen majestic old bridges that help make the city one of the most beautiful and charming in Europe. Others with more than 100,000 inhabitants are . Miskolc, Debrecen, Szeged, and Gyor.

Romania, with its 92,000 square miles, is slightly smaller than Oregon but, with 21 million people, 10 times more populous. On the north and east it is bordered first by the Soviet Union, whose frontier makes a 900-mile curve around Romania, and then by the Black Sea. To the south lies Bulgaria, and in the west it is bordered by both Yugoslavia and Hungary. Bucharest, the capital, is often called the Paris of the East, and is a city of 1.5 million. Other principal centers with 100,000 or more population are Cluj, Sibiu, and Brasov.

Bulgaria has an area of 43,000 square miles, making it slightly larger than Tennessee, and a population of almost 9 million. Its northern neighbor is Romania. To the east is the Black Sea, which gives Bulgaria one of the loveliest and warmest coastlines in Europe. To the south lie the European parts of Turkey and Greece, and to the west it is bordered by Yugoslavia. Sofia, the capital, located in the western part of the country, is a thriving, bustling, hilly city of almost a million inhabitants. Other principal centers with populations of more than 100,000 are Plovdiv, Varna, and Burgas, the latter two being cities on the Black Sea.

Small as Eastern Europe may be, it is surprisingly varied in its topography. Its geography—coupled with its history—gives the countries and their peoples strikingly different outlooks.

The Poles, for example, look not only west toward Germany and east toward Russia, but north across the Baltic to the countries of Scandinavia, which are among Poland's major

EASTERN EUROPE TODAY

trading partners. The Bulgarians, on the other hand, sense the nearness of the Aegean and Mediterranean seas, and glance across the lands of their southern neighbors, Greece and Turkey, toward Asia Minor. From Sofia, for example, it is but a sixty-minute flight to Athens or Istanbul.

Going from north to south, the area can be divided into four distinct geographical and topographical belts that stretch across it from east to west.

The top tier is part of the great North European Plain that extends all the way from the Atlantic Ocean, the North Sea, and the English Channel to the Ural Mountains, deep in the heart of Russia, which divide Europe from the Siberian part of Asia. Here lies Poland, astride the Vistula and its tributaries—a land with no natural boundaries to either west or east, which has often made it a convenient highway for conquering armies moving in either direction. It is a flat land—often flat as far as the eye can see—which gains contours only along its southern border with Czechoslovakia, where the Carpathian Mountains rise to altitudes of more than eight thousand feet.

The Carpathians form the next belt. A complex, zigzagging mountain chain whose spurs go by various other names, it extends over a good part of Eastern Europe from Czechoslovakia and Poland in the northwest, across a corner of the Soviet Union, deep into Romania, where part of the range is known as the Transylvanian Alps. Czechoslovakia is both a hilly and a truly mountainous country, punctuated by dark forests in the west, and occasional broad valleys of gentle countryside around Prague and Brno.

One of the world's principal rivers, the mighty Danube, dominates the third region of Eastern Europe, and it does so literally because it flows through and/or divides from each other all the countries with the exception of Poland. Some 1,776 miles long, it moves in a generally southeasterly direction from its source in southwest Germany, finally emptying through its great delta estuary into the Black Sea.

The Danube is Eastern Europe's great, throbbing artery. Its valley and plain, cutting through the Alps, the Carpathians, and the Balkans, has for centuries provided a route to migrating peoples, invading armies, and traders. No other river in Europe is as scenically varied, turning from a racing alpine torrent into a teeming waterway of commerce, then again into a rushing mountain cataract, and eventually, on its delta, into a subtropical swampland. Nor has any other river in the world had as long and turbulent a history. None flows through as many lands of different peoples—West Germany, Austria, Czechoslovakia, Hungary, Yugoslavia, Romania, Bulgaria, and the Soviet Union—or echoes to as many languages on its banks.

The ancient Celts pushed their way across Europe along it, using the river as an avenue for their primitive trade. The Romans built the first roads and cities on its shores and the first bridges across it. Huns, Avars, Goths, Magyars, Slavs, Mongols, Turks, and Germans fought over and settled along it.

Hungary is located almost in the center of the Danube's plain, a land of gently rolling hills in the west which then, at Budapest and east of the Danube, opens up into the *puszta*—a steppe famed in legend and song for its Gypsies and colorful herdsmen who are Europe's only "cowboys," and as talented on their beautiful horses as any in America's Wild West.

Romania, which controls almost half of the Danube's total length—either as a river running through it or as the border with three of its neighboring states, Yugoslavia, Bulgaria, and the Soviet Union—is by far the most varied of the East European countries in landscape and geography. The western edge is still part of the *puszta* but then rises rapidly into a central mountainous region—the Carpathians and the Transylvanian Alps. Both are ranges as breathtaking and as beautiful as any in Switzerland or Austria with lush green valleys and deep canyons. In the winter they have enough good snow and slopes to keep any skiing buff happy. Moving eastward, the land flattens again until it reaches the Florida-like delta of the Danube and the fine white sands of the Black Sea coast.

Looking south on the map one sees, below the Danube, which forms most of the border between Romania and Bulgaria, the fourth and final great belt of Eastern Europe— the Balkan Peninsula, which extends from the Adriatic Sea on the west, and such countries as Yugoslavia, Albania, and Greece, to the Black Sea in the east. The Balkan range is like a dinosaur's backbone to Bulgaria, rising to altitudes of almost eight thousand feet. Toward the south rise the even higher Rhodope Mountains, part of the Balkan complex.

Some of the countries, notably Poland and Romania, are comparatively rich in certain minerals and natural resources. Others, especially Hungary and Czechoslovakia, seem to have been at the end of the line when Mother Nature distributed her wealth and must live more by their wits and skills.

Poland is fortunate, first of all, in sitting atop one of the world's greatest treasure chests of anthracite coal, considered to be virtually the best in the world because of its low sulphur content. But, because many of the deposits lie as deep as three thousand feet underground, extracting it is both difficult and expensive. Poles proudly call their coal "our black gold." The major deposits are in the southwest corner of the country in Silesia. Huge amounts of soft brown coal—lignite —have also been found and can be used by Poland for energy production, leaving more of the hard coal free for export. In 1959 the Poles also discovered an enormous store of copper ore in Silesia. There is also lead, silver, zinc, sulphur, cadmium, and iron.

Romania has the luck of owning what is Europe's largest land-based oil field, and hopes to find even more oil offshore in the Black Sea. In fact, an oil derrick is one of the symbols of the Romanian coat of arms and the national flag. Annual production from the wells around Ploesti, north of Bucharest, is more than 100 million barrels of crude oil, putting Romania in the same league with at least one of the smaller oil-rich Arab countries—Oman. Where there's oil, there is very often natural gas, and so it is in Romania, whose annual output is more than 30 billion cubic yards. It also has fairly substantial stores of brown coal, bauxite, manganese, lead, zinc, gold, and silver.

Neighboring Hungary and Bulgaria, on the other hand, have almost no important mineral resources, with the exception of bauxite in Hungary and some lignite coal, lead, and zinc in Bulgaria. Bulgaria, for example, must import almost four times what it produces in various fuels, hydroelectric, and nuclear power to meet its energy needs. The ratio for Hungary is two to one. But both countries are rich in land and agricultural potential and make good use of those resources. Hungary produces and exports some of Europe's best beef, and excellent wines and fruit, not to mention those red peppers that are an essential ingredient of its best-known dish—goulash. Bulgaria has become something like a truck gardener for many West European countries.

And then there is Czechoslovakia, the most industrialized but, in terms of natural wealth, the poorest of the five. True, it has the European continent's largest deposits of pitchblende, from which both uranium and radium are extracted, a good store of timber, and some iron ore. But its supply of manganese has been exhausted, and it has neither enough coal of any kind nor enough water power to meet its own energy needs.

Small countries even by European standards, the nations

of Eastern Europe have been conquered and subjugated by powerful neighbors and invaders, and have waged wars against each other so many times in their recorded history that it is hard to count up and remember them all. And yet none, it seems, was ever a rich enough prize to explain all that bloodshed and suffering.

Their political borders have been drawn and redrawn so often that they seemed at times as flexible as rubber bands. The frontiers that exist today are almost but not exactly those drawn after 1918 and World War I. The major changes since then—largely to the benefit of the Soviet Union but also of Poland—came during and after World War II. In theory all those boundaries were supposed to follow national and ethnic lines, so that Romania would be a country of Romanians, all Hungarians would be inside Hungary, and the Bulgarians would have Bulgaria to themselves.

Unfortunately, the theory didn't quite work out in practice. As a result, Eastern Europe today is not just a crazy-quilt map but also a boiling pot of ethnic groups and minorities, many of whom are just waiting for the first good opportunity to realign the boundaries again.

3

The Peoples–
A Bubbling Pot of Tribes

Back in the early 1960's, when Communist China and the Soviet Union first engaged regularly in armed border clashes over plots of real estate which each country considered its own, Nikita Khrushchev, then the ruler in the Kremlin, allegedly told Chou En-lai, then the Chinese prime minister, "We refuse to recognize territorial claims based on the bones of old ancestors."

There are many such claims in Eastern Europe.

There are also deep-seated animosity and resentment among the peoples of those countries caused by many centuries of tribal and religious wars as well as the arbitrary drawing and redrawing of their boundaries in ways which failed to take into account the plight of minorities living within or beyond them.

A Hungarian Communist journalist once said to me, "The

country that baffles me and that I admire the most is Switzerland. It is much smaller than ours, both in area and population. Yet it has three distinctive ethnic groups—the Germans, French, and Italians—each speaking and preserving its own language but also fluent in those of the other two. Each has its own culture and customs. They have lived peacefully with each other for hundreds of years and really consider themselves Swiss. It ought to be a model for us here in Eastern Europe."

Eastern Europe certainly needs a model. To some idealists in the 1940's and 1950's, Communism, with its lofty platform of internationalism and brotherhood among all peoples, did seem like one. Based on the hopeful theory that the downtrodden working class and peasantry of all countries and races had problems and aspirations in common which were stronger than any traditional national and ethnic differences, Communist ideology was supposed to unify the area. It didn't.

In fact today it is the nations and peoples of Western Europe that are drawing together, despite great differences of language, religion, tradition, government and economic interests; lingering suspicions; occasional friction, and long histories of waging war against each other. In 1979 they even elected representatives directly to a West European parliament.

True, they still face many problems and obstacles, but slowly the Common Market of Western Europe—a community of nine countries soon to number ten or eleven—is becoming like a "United States of Europe." Even now it is almost as easy and natural for an Italian to travel or live and work in West Germany, for a West German to move to or around Belgium, or a Belgian to France, Italy, and England, as it is for a Californian to visit and settle in New York, a New Yorker in Texas, or a Texan in New Mexico.

But a Bulgarian who wants to cross the Danube to Romania via the bridge between the cities of Ruse and Giurgiu needs a passport and a visa. Hungarians cannot just go to Czechoslovakia whenever they please or Poles to Bulgaria. There are all kinds of formalities and frontier checks. Though the countries are all members of Comecon, and even of the same military alliance, the borders between some of them are as fortified and tightly guarded as if they were at war. Only Poland and Czechoslovakia have made travel a little easier for their citizens. Since the spring of 1978 the need for visas between those two countries has been abolished.

Ethnic loyalties, resentments, friction, distrust, and suspicion, caused by centuries of struggle, have not been erased or repressed by Communism in Eastern Europe; nor have memories of old kingdoms and little empires that either once really existed or were dreams that never quite came true.

The Poles, for example, continue to hate and fear both their Russian and German neighbors for a variety of reasons, and it is only a question of which they hate and fear more. At the same time they look down upon the Czechs. If the Poles like anyone in Eastern Europe, then it is probably the Hungarians.

Yet the Hungarians have their troubles with the Slovaks, whose territory they owned and controlled for hundreds of years, and they hate the Romanians because Transylvania, once part of Hungary, is now part of Romania—after having changed hands several times. Almost 1.8 million Hungarians still live there under conditions, so Hungary says, that are discriminatory.

The Romanians, in turn, hate the Russians. The most important reason is that in 1945 the Russians grabbed a piece of territory—Bessarabia, in Moldavia—which Romania had grabbed from Russia in 1941, which Russia had taken from Romania in 1940, which Romania had taken from Russia in

1918, and which Russia had annexed in 1812 at a time when Romania did not really exist.

The Bulgarians are engaged in a continual feud with the Yugoslavs, especially the Serbs, against whom they fought three wars between 1913 and 1945, over the status of Macedonia, now one of Yugoslavia's six constituent republics, though there are also hundreds of thousands of Macedonians who live in both Bulgaria and Greece.

In fact, it can be said that if the East Europeans do agree on anything, then it is in their common dislike of the Gypsies, more than 2 million of whom live and roam in this part of the world, and the Jews, of whom only 189,000 remain in Eastern Europe. The rest were either murdered by the Nazis and anti-Semitic local fascist regimes during World War II or driven into emigration since then.

Religious traditions have much to do with all this animosity. That may seem strange since, in theory, being Communist, the East European countries are officially atheist. Actually, religious belief and practice in Eastern Europe are thriving and most of the regimes have made their peace with the churches and the clergy.

To think of Poland without the Catholic Church is like not thinking of Poland at all, and not just since the election of Cardinal Karol Wojtyla, a Pole, as Pope John Paul II, and his triumphant visit there in 1979, the first Pope ever to visit a Communist country. The country's history is so closely interwoven with that of its Church that the two are almost one. And it was this Catholic faith, as opposed to the Orthodox faith of the Russians, that served as the cause, and sometimes the pretext, for many wars and power rivalries between the two. The same goes for Hungary, which is sixty-five percent Catholic and twenty-one percent Protestant, in its long, turbulent relationship with neighboring, largely Orthodox Romania. Since both are Orthodox, one might expect the Romanians and the

Russians to get along better, but part of the trouble has been that they profess Orthodoxy in two different languages, and, what may be more important, two different alphabets—the Latin used in most Western countries and the Cyrillic used in Russia, Bulgaria, and Serbia. In fact, one of the main bones of contention between Romania and the Soviet Union is that the people of Moldavia, who speak a Romanian dialect, were forced to write and read their language in Cyrillic after the Soviet Union annexed that territory in 1945.

Shouldn't these issues be less of a cause for dispute today? Perhaps, but that is not the case.

Fortunately, for the past three decades Eastern Europe has been spared the hatred that erupts in terrorism, assassinations, murders, and bomb throwing, but it smolders right beneath a seemingly calm surface.

Fierce national pride and intense patriotism also contribute to the troubles. Most of the countries were occupied and subjugated by various conquering rulers for centuries and did not become independent nations until a hundred, in some cases sixty, years ago. And their independence has been interrupted since. Their hunger for signs and symbols of past national glory, no matter how short or long ago it may have been, is very great. Their Communist rulers today, though beholden to Moscow, are keenly aware of and eager to satisfy the hunger, sometimes even by doctoring history to make it fit current Communist ideas.

Hungary's Crown of Saint Stephen is one such symbol.

The jewel-studded, golden crown was sent to a Magyar chieftain, Stephen the Good, for his coronation as Hungary's first king in the year 1001 by Pope Sylvester II. It was a token of thanks for having Christianized his then largely pagan people. Stephen was later made a saint. Though many subsequent kings who wore it were not Hungarian but Austrian, and though since 1918 there has been no king of Hungary at all, the crown has remained a sacred symbol of Hungarian national existence for nearly ten centuries.

In early 1945, when Soviet army forces were closing in on Budapest, officials of Hungary's pro-German government and members of its pro-Nazi fascist movement removed the crown from a vault in the city's Royal Castle. They fled to Austria, surrendered, and turned the crown over to an American army unit. It was then taken to the United States for safekeeping at Fort Knox.

That is where anti-Communist Hungarian émigrés and exiles wanted it to stay, arguing that the Communist regime in their homeland had no right to the symbol. But in Hungary virtually everybody—pro-Communist and anti-Communist— wanted it back. "Returning it," an American diplomat in Budapest once told me, "is the single most important gesture we could make here. Everyone, from Janos Kadar, the Communist party chief, down to the simplest peasant on the *puszta,* has strong nationalistic and patriotic feelings that center around the crown."

Finally, in the autumn of 1977, President Jimmy Carter announced his decision to return the crown. Hungarian-Americans were so angry that they staged demonstrations in front of the White House and the Capitol. Senator Robert Dole of Kansas even appealed to the Supreme Court to try to stop the President. But in Hungary everybody was elated, especially Kadar, whose prestige and popularity skyrocketed because he had gotten back the crown. It is now on display in Budapest for all proud Hungarians to see.

Poland's Royal Castle in Warsaw is another symbol.

When the Germans invaded Poland in 1939, they had a cruel master plan. Poland, as a nation, was to disappear and become a German colony in which all reminders of Polish national identity were to be erased. Warsaw, for example, was to be torn to the ground, its people dispersed into the countryside as slave laborers, and an entirely "Germanic city" was to be built on the site as a "monument to the Germanic victory over the Slavs." That plan was never carried out. Nonetheless, Warsaw suffered heavily during its famed 1944 uprising against the Nazis. Then, having crushed that revolt in a month of fighting, the Germans went ahead, street by street, house by house, fire-bombing, dynamiting, and demolishing what remained. They took special pains to destroy and level completely the sixteenth-century Royal Castle.

After the war the Communist government of Poland faced a hard choice: rebuild Warsaw or create a new modern city? Rebuild they did—stone for stone—all the beautiful, historic buildings of the picturesque old quarter, with its cathedrals and churches, its palaces and mansions, down to the last architectural detail. But for more than twenty-five years the Royal Castle on the banks of the Vistula remained a ruin: a tragic reminder of the war and of Poland's lost glory.

A few weeks after coming to power in December 1970 as Poland's new Communist party chief, Edward Gierek pledged to rebuild the castle. That effort to restore Poland's main symbol of national unity was completed in 1978.

The huge building with its four hundred rooms has been reconstructed on the basis of old paintings, drawings, and photographs in all its gilded splendor, exactly the way it looked for almost four centuries.

To provide the eighteen million dollars that the project cost, women donated their jewelry, workers gave blood, musicians their concert fees, old people their life savings. Money poured in from all over the world, especially from people of Polish ancestry abroad.

"There has never been anything like the enthusiasm for this project," one of the officials in charge of it told me. "It has united everyone—Communists, anti-Communists, Catholics, atheists, the young and the old—for regardless of their differences, they are all Poles."

Poland is actually the East European country that has the least troubles with its neighbors or minorities. That is probably because its population is ninety-eight percent Polish today, thanks to the way its borders were redrawn after World War II.

In the east Poland turned over nearly forty-seven percent of its prewar territory—some 70,000 square miles of land— to the Soviet Union. It is a region over which the two countries had fought numerous wars, which was inhabited by a mixed population of Poles, Russians, and Ukrainians. In exchange, Poland got more than 43,000 square miles in the west and north—regions that had once been Polish centuries ago but which for at least two hundred years, and in some areas even longer, had been basically German. It was like putting a nation on rollers and moving it some 150 miles westward. About four million Germans were expelled and deported to Germany from the newly won territories and some six million Poles, most of them from the region that had gone to the Soviet Union, were brought in and resettled. It was the largest, most dramatic movement of peoples in modern times.

The plan had been worked out among the three principal wartime leaders: United States President Franklin D. Roosevelt, British Prime Minister Winston Churchill, and the Soviet Union's Josef Stalin. The idea behind it, as Churchill once said, was to avoid "the mixture of populations" that up to then in Europe had "caused endless trouble." Although it took West Germany until 1971 to accept the loss of those former German territories and formally recognize Poland's new frontiers, on the whole the plan proved good.

True, some 300,000 Russians and Ukrainians still live in Poland, and some 1.5 million Poles in what is now the Soviet

Union. Those Poles in the USSR began showing signs of unrest in 1975 with demands—backed by Warsaw—that they be allowed to leave and resettle in Poland. There are also Germans in Poland who want to go to West Germany, though the actual number is a matter of dispute between the two countries. The West Germans say there are more than 250,000, the Poles admit to only about 120,000. Since 1976 an average of 25,000 a year have been leaving. All in all, though, Poland is the country with the least ethnic problems in Eastern Europe today.

On the other hand, thirty years of being allies have not diminished the Poles' dislike of the Russians. Wherever one goes in Poland and to whomever one speaks, including high-ranking Communist party and government officials, one hears bitter anti-Russian jokes and remarks. In the sixteenth and seventeenth centuries, when Poland was a great power with its eastern boundary reaching deep into what is now Russia, it lorded it over the Russians. But for the past 250 years the shoe has mostly been on the other foot. Poles either cannot, or refuse to, forget—particularly that Stalin joined Hitler in carving up Poland in 1939.

The relationship with Germany is even more strained, and Poles will take any opportunity to tell any visitor about the terrible things the Germans have done to them in the course of history, especially during World War II. They go to great efforts to justify their claims to the areas they got from Germany in 1945. One history book even quotes a tenth-century Arab explorer as proof that the region where the Oder River flows into the Baltic had originally been Polish.

But compared to other parts of Eastern Europe, those are barely ripples on very troubled waters.

Czechoslovakia is actually not one country but two, composed of two main ethnic groups—the Czechs and the Slovaks—who, though fairly closely related and speaking languages more similar to each other than German and Dutch, have detested one another for centuries.

The Czechs once had a proud and fairly powerful kingdom—Bohemia—which lost its independence for about three hundred years starting in 1620. The Slovaks never did have a state they could call their own, and were usually under the domination of Hungary. In 1918, when the old empires that had ruled over both of them collapsed, the two peoples were formed into one country—Czechoslovakia. It was an explosive mixture, in part because the Czechs tended to look west toward Germany, the Slovaks east toward Russia, in part because the Czechs were so much more industrialized and richer than the Slovaks that economic exploitation resulted. The arrangement ended temporarily in 1939 when Hitler first annexed part of Czech Bohemia, then occupied the rest of the Czech lands and established an "independent" Slovak puppet state. At the end of World War II Czechoslovakia was reestablished, but the union was an unhappy one.

In 1969 Czechs, who account for sixty-five percent of the total population, and Slovaks, who make up thirty percent, each formed separate states that are joined together in a federation similar to those in Switzerland and the United States.

The Communist *federal* government is in charge of defense, foreign policy, and economic matters, but the two Communist *state* governments have independent control over just about everything else. Separate languages are spoken, but both are used at the federal level. Gustav Husak, the president of Czechoslovakia and chief of its Communist party, is a Slovak; Lubomir Strougal, the prime minister, is Czech, and there is fair division of offices and powerful jobs down the line.

The arrangement has worked fairly well since 1969 and has helped to pull up Slovakia's standard of living, but it has not helped the lot of Czechoslovakia's other minorities or improved relations with its neighbors, especially Hungary. Some 600,000 Hungarians—four percent of the total population—live in Czechoslovakia, while 131,000 Slovaks live in Hungary. Their status and rights, epecially concerning education, newspapers, magazines, and books in their own respective languages, are matters of frequent friction between the two countries. There are also 71,000 Poles, 51,000 Ukrainians, 10,000 Russians, and 77,000 Germans in Czechoslovakia.

The Germans are a specially sore point. There used to be three million, nearly all of whom were deported to Germany at the end of World War II. West Germany claims that the few who remain want to leave. The Czech government denies this.

Feelings toward the Russians have undergone a total change. The Slovaks traditionally felt friendly toward them because they considered them ethnic cousins. The Czechs warmed up to them in the late 1930's when Britain and France, in order to appease Hitler, sold Czechoslovakia down the river, leaving the Soviet Union as the only big power willing to stand up for Czechoslovakia's rights. That friendliness even turned to love when the Soviets helped set up a liberation army to free the country from the Germans in 1945. At that time the Slovaks were so pro-Soviet that there was even a strong movement in Slovakia to join the USSR as one of *its* republics.

But in 1968, when the Russians invaded to crush and destroy Alexander Dubcek's experiment in "Communism with a human face," love turned to instant hatred. "In one night," a Czechoslovak Communist told me at the time, "the Russians made a centuries-long enemy of what had been a centuries-long friend."

Hungary has probably done more than any other East European country to bring peace among the minorities living within its present boundaries. That may be because they account for only a small part of the population—less than six percent. There are about 230,000 Germans, 130,000 Croatians, some 40,000 Romanians, and 130,000 Slovaks. The Hungarian constitution guarantees them the right to be educated in their native languages. They have newspapers and magazines of their own and there are no known major cases of discrimination.

But Hungary's trouble is that it once was much larger than it is today. As a result, nearly 3 million Hungarians—thirty percent of the country's present population—live in neighboring countries, part of whose territory used to belong to Hungary. Besides the 600,000 who live in Slovakia, where they are discriminated against because they used to discriminate against the Slovaks, another 600,000 are in Yugoslavia's republics of Serbia and Croatia. And no less than 1.8 million Hungarians live in what used to be the Hungarian chunk of present-day Romania, making up almost nine percent of that country's total population. Most of them are in the area called Transylvania.

For a number of years they have complained that they are being suppressed, deprived of their rights, and are being forced to assimilate with the Romanians as part of President Nicolae Ceausescu's drive to "Romanianize" his country and imbue Romanians with more national pride and patriotism.

In November 1975, representatives of the Hungarian minority, some of them high-ranking Communist party officials, even asked that the United Nations set up a special watchdog commission.

The Romanians, on the other hand, argue that the Hungarians have the same rights, chances, and privileges of all Romanian citizens.

In the summer of 1977 the dispute became so heated that Ceausescu and Kadar held a special meeting on the border

Slovak Nationality Day is celebrated in Hungary.

between the two countries in an attempt to resolve it. They agreed to relax travel restrictions to allow more and easier visits between members of families on both sides of the border. The Romanians agreed to set up a consulate in the Hungarian town of Debrecen, the Hungarians one in the Romanian city of Cluj.

But by the spring of 1978 Hungary was claiming that Romania had not kept its promises. Numerous delaying tactics had been used to prevent Hungary from opening its consulate in Cluj, Romania was not letting many of its Hungarian nationals travel to Hungary, and Hungarians who came to Romania were not allowed to stay with their relatives in private homes, but had to book into hotels.

"Dealing with the Romanians," one Hungarian official complained in March 1978, "is more difficult and frustrating than [dealing] with the Chinese."

Since the argument is between two supposedly allied Communist countries, it is really serious when officials talk about it as openly as that. Much of it has been conducted in a kind of code among historians, writers, and scientists trying to prove that either the Hungarians or the Romanians were in Transylvania first. Since, in either case, it was many centuries ago, both sides have been busy making archaeological excavations to score points for or against.

Romania also has trouble with another large minority group living in Transylvania: some 400,000 Germans who can trace their origins to settlers who arrived there centuries ago. They have all preserved their German language and customs, have their own newspapers, schools, theaters, and book publishing houses, and live in cities and towns that are so Germanic in their nature and appearance that it sometimes seems they are in the wrong place on the map.

But these Germans, too, complain about discrimination and attempts to "Romanianize" them, and they were especially unhappy in the early 1970's when the Romanian government ordered that the old German names for various cities be replaced by their Romanian ones, even in the German-language press.

Moreover, many Transylvania Germans want to emigrate to West Germany. The reasons, in my opinion, formed by travels in the area, are not so much ethnic as they are economic. Life in West Germany is so much better and easier than in poor Romania—and politically much freer, too—that it works like a magnet. But the Transylvania Germans are all among Romania's better educated and more skilled workers and technicians. So the government in Bucharest is reluctant to see them leave. It is a touchy issue, especially because the right to travel and emigrate is a basic human right, more severely restricted in Romania than in other Communist countries with the exception perhaps of Czechoslovakia.

Romania's biggest problem, however, at least in the eyes of the Romanians, is with the Soviet Union over Moldavia.

Moldavia is one of the fifteen republics that—somewhat like the fifty American states—make up the USSR. With an area of about thirteen thousand square miles—somewhat bigger than Maryland—it is one of the smallest. It is made up mostly of two regions called Bessarabia and the Northern Bukovina. Its being part of the Soviet Union is a highly controversial matter.

The controversy starts with the question: who and what are the Moldavians?

According to Soviet historians, they are ethnically Slavic, consider themselves as such, and were liberated from the "yoke of occupation under the Turkish Ottoman Empire" by the Russians in 1812.

The Romanians, to say the least, see things differently. The Moldavian language is a Romanian dialect, and the Moldavians, like the Romanians themselves, are considered descendants of those ancient Dacians and Roman legionnaires. What happened in 1812, according to Romanian history books, was nothing less than annexation and occupation of the area by Russia.

Be that as it may, after 1812 it changed hands four more times, most recently in 1945. Since then it has been a sore issue between Romania and the Soviet Union. They pepper each other with propaganda and long, wordy historical studies about the matter, often referring to what various "witnesses" had to say many years ago.

Actually, Moldavia and Transylvania have something in common, though they are separated by many miles of other Romanian territories. Moldavia is somewhat like Moscow's sore toe on which Romania's President Ceausescu can step whenever he likes. But if he steps too hard, the Kremlin can tell Hungary to step on Ceausescu's own sore toe—Transylvania.

The Moldavian and Transylvanian controversies are part of a larger picture involving Romania's domestic and foreign policy problems as well as Ceausescu's personal power as virtual dictator of Romania.

His powers, as a later chapter will show, are unmatched by any politician in Europe—Eastern or Western. He also conducts the most independent foreign policy in the Soviet bloc, thumbing his nose at Moscow whenever he can. At the same time, Romania is one of the poorest and most backward countries in the bloc and the country with the least freedom and greatest restrictions on human rights. But the Romanians also happen to be an intensely patriotic and nationalistic people. Ceausescu helps to keep himself in power by appealing to and playing upon their patriotism with such issues as Moldavia and restrictions on the Hungarian and German minorities in Transylvania.

Since 1977 he has been conducting a campaign to imbue

his people with even more national pride. The official press has been filled with complaints that the schools are not teaching enough Romanian history and literature and that educators are neglecting the "purity" of the language. Romanian workers have been told to view their daily toiling as a patriotic service to the fatherland. Parents have been encouraged to lull their offspring to sleep at night with glowing tales of great exploits by the ancient Dacians. Novelists' and playwrights' works are not being printed or staged if they do not instill enough patriotism.

Bulgaria, like the others, is also a multiethnic country, but its problems are unique.

First of all, unlike Poland, Czechoslovakia, Hungary, and Romania, it has no common border with the Soviet Union. On the other hand, the Bulgarians share the same religion and the same Cyrillic alphabet with the Russians. They have a language that is closer to Russian than to Polish, Czech, or Slovak, and they feel themselves much closer to the Russians ethnically and culturally than any of the other peoples of Eastern Europe. Indeed, they have long looked to Russia as a kind of protector and "big brother."

Second, they share many hundreds of miles of border with two NATO countries, Turkey and Greece, and an equally long frontier with a country that, although Communist, is politically and diplomatically neutral: Yugoslavia.

Though there aren't many Greeks in Bulgaria, there are about one million Turks who account for more than eleven percent of Bulgaria's total population. They are not only ethnically different, but stand out because of their language and their Muslim religion in a country where the majority is Eastern Orthodox. Those factors, plus the traditional hatreds and tensions between the two countries going back centuries, make the Turks in Bulgaria a major problem. Their plight is probably the worst of any minority group in Eastern Europe.

The Turks do not want to integrate into Bulgarian life, and the Bulgarians do not really want to assimilate them. They look toward Turkey, and in their homes the radio and TV sets are usually tuned to Istanbul and Ankara, not Sofia. Tens of thousands of them would like to emigrate to Turkey. For many years the Bulgarian government refused to let any of them go, even on visits to relatives. Then in 1968 the Turkish and Bulgarian governments reached an agreement that would allow small numbers of Bulgarian Turks to leave. But it soon turned out that Turkey didn't want them because of the high unemployment problem there and refused to issue entry permits. Since 1968 only about sixty thousand have actually left and at least twice that many are on the waiting lists. They are people caught between two worlds.

Another of Bulgaria's problems is with Yugoslavia, because of Macedonia and the 190,000 Macedonians living in Bulgaria. Relations between the two countries over that issue have never been good, but they reached their lowest level in the peacetime history of the Balkans in the spring of 1978, when Bulgaria went all out to celebrate the one hundredth anniversary of its independence and the Treaty of San Stefano by which Bulgaria briefly gained control over what is today the Macedonian republic of Yugoslavia.

The dispute, first of all, is over that piece of real estate. Of all the wars fought and the blood that has been spilled in the Balkans, no wars were ever fiercer than those fought over Macedonia. And both Bulgaria and Yugoslavia still seem absolutely neurotic on the subject. Bulgarians need only mention the 1878 treaty in order to set Yugoslavia's press, political leaders, and historians on a tirade.

What irritates the Yugoslavs especially is that during World War II, when Bulgaria was an ally of Nazi Germany, it took the opportunity to occupy all of Macedonia. Even worse, in Yugoslav eyes, the Bulgarians now claim that their own anti-Nazi partisan fighters "played a key role" in liberating Macedonia and other parts of Yugoslavia from Nazi occupation. But of all the things of which Yugoslavs are proud, they are proudest of the fact that their partisans, led by President Tito, freed the country and tied down at least 250,000 of Hitler's troops with guerrilla warfare.

But besides the territorial and historical debate, a more heated issue is the status of the Macedonian minority in Bulgaria.

The government refuses to recognize they exist, claiming that they are "ethnically Bulgarian" and that their language is "nothing more than a Bulgarian dialect." Most of them live in that small part of ancient Macedonia—the ancestral home of Alexander the Great—which Bulgaria managed to keep after all those Balkan wars. Bulgarian officials now say that "this region has always been a seat of Bulgarian national spirit, of the most glorious traditions of the Bulgarian clan." In a speech in 1975 the daughter of Todor Zhivkov, Bulgaria's president and Communist party chief, said that even Spartacus, the Macedonian leader of a famous Roman slave revolt in 71 B.C., had been of Bulgarian origin. Sillier words were never spoken, considering that the Bulgarians themselves did not come out of Asia until almost a thousand years later.

Yugoslavia, which gave its Macedonians their own republic, considers all this not only nonsense but an insult to the Macedonian people, behind which it suspects "Bulgarian territorial ambitions."

Yugoslavia says that the Bulgarian government has "prohibited singing Macedonian songs, confiscated Macedonian phonograph records, expelled freedom-loving young Macedonians from schools, and transferred Macedonians from good to bad jobs because of their Macedonian feelings." According to Yugoslav sources, there are always arrests and imprisonments of Macedonian nationalists. One Yugoslav newspaper a few years back accused Bulgaria's leaders of acting "as if they had a God-given right to decide people's destiny and cut up the map of the world. They play with history as if it were a toy balloon."

Not only do feelings in Eastern Europe run strong, but so do the words that express them.

The Gypsies are one ethnic group in Eastern Europe on which all the other peoples seem to agree. They don't really like them and they don't know what to do with them. There are many superstitions about them because they are nomadic, refuse to assimilate, preserve their own language and customs, and tend not to obey laws other than their own.

They originated in India and their language is close to Sanskrit. By the year 1000 they had reached Persia from where they moved westward in two streams: the southern through Egypt into North Africa, the northern route through the Balkans to Eastern and Western Europe.

Today there are Gypsies all over the world, including the United States: at least five million according to United Nations estimates; ten million according to the Gypsies' own.

But by far the largest concentration is in Yugoslavia, the Soviet Union, and the five countries of Eastern Europe. The figures are juggled all the time and those given by Gypsy organizations are much higher than those given by the East European governments. But it is safe to say that there are about 540,000 Gypsies in Romania; 480,000 in Hungary; 360,000 in Bulgaria; 300,000 in Czechoslovakia, and 50,000 in Poland.

In the five hundred or more years that they are known to have been there, their impact on the culture, especially the music, art, and literature, of Eastern Europe has been enormous. To think of Hungary without Gypsies, for example, is almost like thinking of no Hungary at all.

However, over the centuries they have been persecuted. The Nazis, for example, treated them no differently from the Jews and 500,000 of them, possibly as many as one million, are known to have perished in the gas chambers of the concentration camps.

They are surrounded by mystery and romance as well as many superstitions, none of which have any basis in fact. Gypsies do not steal any more than any other people; they do not practice voodoo; they do not kidnap little children. But they *are* highly independent.

This characteristic makes them a special problem for the Communist regimes of Eastern Europe. No ethnic group anywhere is less inclined to conform and submit to authority than the Gypsies. On the other hand, few political systems in the world demand more conformity and submission than Communism does.

Picture a nomadic people who believe in their own laws and customs in countries where every citizen must carry an identity card and register every change of work or apartment with the police, where every building manager knows who comes and goes. Then you can picture part of the strange situation of the Gypsies in Eastern Europe.

The way the Communist governments have treated them varies greatly from country to country. All have certainly tried to raise the Gypsy living standard. In Romania, for example, one of the new Communist regime's first measures in March 1945 was to provide Gypsies not only with land but, in many cases, with completely equipped farms that had been taken from richer and aristocratic owners.

But to the disappointment of the Communist authorities all over Eastern Europe, the Gypsies preferred to remain what they had always been. After a while some governments gave up trying. Although Romania has about 540,000 Gypsies today, the regime in 1957 stopped counting them as a separate ethnic group the way it does the Hungarians and Germans. "We just swept the 'Gypsy problem' under the carpet by refusing to admit that it exists," a Romanian official once told me.

Hungary and Czechoslovakia, on the other hand, have kept trying to integrate them, with mixed results. In Slovakia, settlements with schools and other benefits of city life have been built near the old Gypsy campsites in an attempt to raise living standards and assimilate them while still allowing them to preserve at least some of their customs.

In Hungary, according to an official report, seventy percent of the Gypsies now live more or less permanently in cities and seventy-five percent of the adult men are regularly employed. But Hungarian Gypsy representatives warn that this integration must go slower. Said one in 1976: "It is a mistake to force Gypsies, not used to modern city living, into high-rise apartment houses alongside Hungarian families before both the Hungarians and Gypsies can be freed of their deep-rooted prejudices toward each other."

One thing is certain. The attempts at integration are destroying Gypsy culture. In Hungary, someday, they may no longer be playing their violins. To be sure, it is not an immediate problem. In Budapest alone there are 729 Gypsy musicians who perform each night in 575 restaurant orchestras. They are one of the main attractions of Hungary as a tourist country. But already there are too few young Gypsies willing to take up the fiddle. There may be a drastic shortage in the years and decades ahead.

The reason: forced integration.

"The trouble," according to one Hungarian social worker, "is that when a Gypsy is assimilated, he's played out—musically. The music is part of the culture, and when you destroy the culture, you end up with no music."

The dilemma is similar to that facing all of Eastern Europe

with its many nationalities and ethnic groups. In the attempt to unify them under the banner of Communism, they have drifted further apart. And the music they make is less harmonious day by day.

4

Looking Backward

To understand Eastern Europe today one must understand its past. That is easier said than done, because it is a history marked by the unusual geographic, ethnic, and religious variety of the area and by the fact that each country's development has been so strikingly different from the others, yet at the same time amazingly similar.

A number of factors apply to all the countries and run through their recorded histories like connecting threads.

The first is that, compared to Western Europe, civilization came to them all relatively late. By the year A.D. 800, when Charlemagne had already laid the foundation for his great empire embracing what is today Germany, France, and northern Italy, the tribes whose descendants today inhabit Eastern Europe had either not yet arrived on the scene or were seminomadic, wearing skins, living in thatch huts, and deifying nature.

Second, Eastern Europe's history has been strongly influenced by the breakup of the Roman Empire. Its formal division in A.D. 395 into western and eastern parts with two capitals—Rome itself and Byzantium (later renamed Constantinople and now known as Istanbul)—resulted in the emergence of two great rival centers of power. Two distinct brands of Christianity—Roman Catholicism and Greek Orthodoxy—emanated from them and came to play decisive roles in the historical development of Eastern Europe.

Even before the final break—the "schism"—between those two churches in 1054, the peoples of Eastern Europe had begun moving on two separate cultural paths influenced by their religious convictions. Thus the Poles, Czechs, Slovaks, and Hungarian Magyars looked westward, to Rome. They used the Latin rites and the Latin alphabet. The Romanians and Bulgarians turned to the East, to Byzantium. They used the Greek rites and, in the case of the Bulgarians, also a different alphabet—Cyrillic—which two Byzantine missionaries, Saint Cyril and Saint Methodius, had developed for writing the languages of the eastern Slavic peoples. These divisions within Eastern Europe became even more pronounced when Byzantium, sometimes called the "new" and the "second" Rome, declined as a political force and the Russian duchy of Muscovy—Moscow—began to rise as a power, thinking of itself as "the keeper of the true Christian faith" and as "the third Rome."

Though it all happened so long ago, the importance of this ancient separation of Eastern Europe into two great spheres of influence simply cannot be overrated. It has left an indelible mark right into modern times. The whole outlook on life in Eastern Europe, the art, the music, the literature, the concepts of law and government and society's organization were colored by this division. And much of the bloodshed was caused by it, too.

In 1604, for example, a Polish army invaded Russia and occupied Moscow. At its head marched Roman Catholic bishops and priests determined to convert the Russians and defeat Orthodoxy. That invasion played an important role in the life of Russia's Czar Boris Godunov and a key part in the nineteenth-century play and opera based on it. To this day the scene showing those priests marching, carrying their cross and being met by Russians with the Orthodox one, is repeated dramatically and emotionally on the stage of Moscow's Bolshoi Theater a couple of dozen times each season. Though it happened some 375 years ago, it hasn't been forgotten.

Third, there is the carving up and occupation of Eastern Europe by rival and neighboring powers—first by the Germanic states, especially the Hapsburg Empire of Austria; then by the Ottoman Turks, whose realm once included virtually all of what is today Bulgaria, Hungary, and Romania; finally by Prussia and Russia, which, along with Austria, divided up Poland in the early nineteenth century.

Fourth, except for Poland, which in its sixteenth- and seventeenth-century heyday was almost six times larger than it is today and had an easternmost boundary only a hundred miles or so from Moscow, none of the countries were ever great powers. Considering the might of England, France, Spain, and Sweden in those two centuries, Poland was not really what we would call today a superpower.

To be sure, there was also once a Moravian empire which included substantial chunks of modern-day Czechoslovakia, Austria, and Hungary, but it lasted barely half a century— from A.D. 845 to 894. There were also two Bulgarian "empires." The first one reached its highest point of strength and civilization from 893 to 927 under the reign of Bulgaria's Czar

Simeon; the second made somewhat of a historical splash during the first half of the thirteenth century. Bohemia was an independent kingdom for a number of periods until it was gobbled up by Austria in 1620. On several occasions Hungary was a force to be reckoned with. But even at the height of their power, all these short-lived kingdoms and empires were backward and unimportant compared to the countries of Western Europe and hardly counted in the European order of things.

Finally, by the early nineteenth century all had virtually disappeared as independent states. Two—Romania and Bulgaria—did gain some measure of independence in the late 1800's but it was not really until 1918—after World War I —that the five East European countries took on the boundaries and the approximate, though not the final, shape they have today and began to emerge as nation-states.

Of the peoples who inhabit Eastern Europe today, only the Romanians—descendants of the ancient Dacians—can say that they have ancestral origins in the area dating back as far as the Roman Empire. They were conquered, after two fierce wars, by the legionnaires of Emperor Trajan in A.D. 106 and assimilated with their conquerors, who settled in Dacia as colonists. That victory over Dacia is commemorated by Trajan's Column, which stands, practically undamaged and unchanged by more than eighteen hundred years of history, in the center of modern, downtown Rome. The headdresses of the ancient Dacians that are carved on it closely resemble those still worn at country fairs and festivals by peasant folk-dance groups in certain areas of Romania today.

By comparison, the other peoples of Eastern Europe are relatively late arrivals.

The most numerous and important are the Slavs. Their origins are very much in dispute among historians and archaeologists. According to one older theory, now rejected by many experts, they came, like so many tribes whose descendants now populate Europe, out of central Asia, moved gradually westward during the Migration of Peoples, settling in the areas they now inhabit between the third and sixth centuries A.D. But the version more generally accepted nowadays is that they were descendants of Neolithic peoples who originated in the Carpathian Mountains in what is now eastern Czechoslovakia, the western Ukraine, and northern Romania. They expanded north, east, and south with speed and determination after the death of Attila the Hun and the collapse of his barbarian empire in 453.

Their movement followed three major streams. The western Slavs, forerunners of today's Czechs, Slovaks, and Poles, migrated toward the Elbe, Oder, and Vistula rivers in what is now East Germany, Czechoslovakia, and Poland. The southern, or, to use the Slavic word, *Yugo* Slavs, ancestors of today's Serbs, Croats, Slovenes, Montenegrins, Macedonians, and Bulgarians, headed toward the Balkans, where they still live. The eastern Slavs—today's Russians, Ukrainians, and White (*Byelo*) Russians—moved toward the Dnieper River valley, the Pripet Marshes, the Valdai Hills, the upper reaches of the Volga, and as far north as Lakes Ilmen and Peipus, not far from modern Leningrad.

There probably never was a single Slavic language, but various tribal dialects which, as the tribes began to move out in different directions, developed into the present languages. They are closely related—more closely, for example, than German, Dutch, Danish, Swedish, and English, all of which had a common root. The basic ones are Russian, Byelorussian, Ukrainian, Bulgarian, Macedonian, Serbo-Croatian, Slovene, Czech, Slovak, and Polish.

Ethnically, however, the Slavs are no longer very closely related, as a result of centuries of invasions, occupation, and mixing with other peoples, including Turko-Tartars, Germans, Mongols, Greeks, and Illyrian tribes.

By the standards of the times, and compared to their various neighbors, they were remarkably peaceful people, given to agriculture and, before being Christianized either by Rome or Byzantium, they worshiped nature. Their supreme god was the god of lightning. It was not until well into the ninth and tenth centuries, following their conversion, that they began to organize themselves as duchies, principalities, kingdoms, or states of some kind, similar to those in Western Europe.

To count up and name all the many invaders who have moved in and out of Eastern Europe is a hopeless task. But two, in particular, deserve mention because their descendants are still in place and complete the ethnic jigsaw puzzle of the area.

There were, first of all, the Bulgars.

A Turkic-speaking people who had probably migrated from much farther east, they first became noticeable in the late seventh and early eighth centuries along the Middle Volga—around what is now the city of Kazan, some five hundred miles east of Moscow. The majority of Bulgars stayed there for many hundreds of years, creating a great commercial and trading kingdom that was at the height of its power in the thirteenth century when it was invaded and occupied by the Mongol hordes of Genghis Khan and his successors.

But a smaller group of Bulgars moved southwestward in the late seventh century, traveling nearly three thousand miles through present-day Russia, the Ukraine, and Romania. In A.D. 679 they invaded the region south of the Danube, subjugated the Slavs living there, and settled permanently in the country now named after them: Bulgaria. But as has happened often in history, the conquered people proved to be culturally stronger than the conquerors. The language of the area remained Slavic and by the ninth century the Bulgars had intermarried, mingled, and merged with the original Slavs completely. All that is really left of the Bulgars today is the name.

Two centuries later another important tribe arrived in what is now Eastern Europe and stayed—the Magyars. But unlike the Bulgars, they maintained their ethnic and linguistic identity for more than eleven hundred years, right to the present, for the Magyars are the Hungarians. The terms, in fact, are identical, "Magyar" meaning "Hungarian" in their language.

Because that language is so unlike any others spoken in Europe, with the exception of those in Finland, Estonia, and Lapland, historians once believed that the Magyars had some common origin with the Huns, the Mongols, and the Turks. That theory has been disproved by modern research. The only thing they seem to have had in common was their nomadic and warlike life-style.

The Magyars, in all likelihood, originated in the Ural Mountains. At least it was from there that, around A.D. 460, they migrated far south to the northern Caucasus, where they remained for about four hundred years. There they apparently did have close contacts with Turkic peoples, for there are many Magyar words of Turkish origin. During this time they gave up many of their nomadic customs and turned to agriculture. Late in the ninth century they started having troubles with another tribe in the region, the Pechenegs, who forced the Magyars out—across what is now southern Russia, into present-day Romania. There they also had problems— with the Bulgarians, whose ruler, Czar Simeon, the founder of that short-lived Bulgarian Empire, drove them, with Pecheneg help, farther west into present-day Hungary and

Transylvania, where they settled in A.D. 895 and have been ever since. Which is not to say, however, that they were happy with their new piece of real estate.

Using present-day Hungary as a kind of base camp, they spent the next century raiding in all directions and terrorizing Europe. Medieval records describe them as ferocious warriors mounted on swift horses and almost unconquerable. First they occupied the Moravian district of Czechoslovakia, then drove far west and south through Bavaria into Italy and southern France. Their power was finally broken in 955 by Germany's Emperor Otto I in the Battle of Lechfeld, a plain some thirty miles west of Munich. After that defeat they scurried back into Hungary and began consolidating the Magyar state.

Those closing years of the tenth century were also when the peoples of Eastern Europe began converting to Christianity—either Catholic or Orthodox—and the region's written history began taking shape.

Poland's beginnings are obscure. The name of the country stems from one Slavic tribe, the Polians, whose name means "dwellers in the field," who by the late tenth century had become the most powerful. Their territory, the region of Gniezno, Poland's first capital, and that of Poznań, the seat of the first bishop, became the nucleus of the Polish state under a family named Piast, whose head, Duke Mieszko I, converted to Roman Christianity in 966 and then imposed Catholicism on his people. The date is generally regarded as the birth of the Polish state.

Mieszko and his son Boleslav I extended the territory of their duchy in numerous wars against the neighboring Slavic Pomeranians; the Danes to the north; the German Empire to the west; Bohemia and Hungary toward the south; and the early Russian state of Kiev in the east. By 1025 it was big enough for Boleslav to call it a kingdom and have himself crowned. This first fling at Polish greatness, punctuated by many more wars, with conquests as well as losses of surrounding territory, lasted little more than a century—until the death, in 1138, of King Boleslav II.

Boleslav II had decreed that after his death Poland should be divided into four equal, hereditary duchies among his four sons and their sons and that the crown itself should always go to the oldest living member of any generation of the Piast family. The arrangement gave rise to endless disputes, with whoever was king trying to transmit supreme power to *his* direct descendants. It also made the other dukes envious of their brother or cousin on the throne and so impatient to get their turn wearing the crown that murder was not uncommon. At the same time, the hereditary duchies turned increasingly to their own interests, not those of Poland as a whole. The effect of all this was that the kingdom began to split apart with rivalries and civil wars.

This created a power vacuum, and, as usually happens, someone came along to step into it. In Poland's case it was the Teutonic Knights, a German military religious order that had played an important role during the Third Crusade at the end of the twelfth century. After participating in a number of sieges and victories in the Holy Land, these knights, who were more military than religious, began moving into Eastern Europe to convert and conquer pagan tribes and to colonize. They managed to subdue nearly all of what is today northern Poland, once known as West and East Prussia. Their Grand Master built a huge fortified castle at Marienburg—the Poles call it Malbork—which stands in all its medieval grimness, virtually unchanged today. From there they began exerting mounting pressure on the Polish dukes and Poland's "rotating" kings.

For Poles today this era of their history is as vivid and unhappy a memory as if it had happened yesterday. Polish

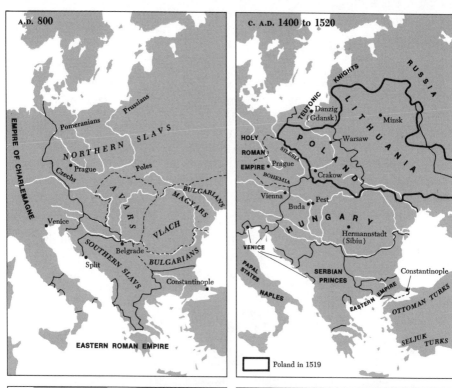

history books and legends still picture the Teutonic Knights as the embodiment of German aggression, colonization, and eastward expansion. Guides at Marienburg enjoy telling tourists how the last Grand Master became so impoverished that mercenary soldiers in his service sold the whole castle to the king of Poland and distributed the money among themselves as back pay.

There were other troubles in those days, too, notably with the Mongols, who had occupied all of Russia and frequently raided into Poland, but the Teutonic Knights remain in Polish memories as the worst.

Actually, the knights also had a beneficial effect, for the Poles were brought to their senses, stopped fighting each other, and began to reunite their kingdom.

The main line of the Piast dynasty died out in 1370 with the death of King Casimir III, an especially enlightened ruler. The crown passed to his nephew, Louis I of Hungary, and then to Louis' daughter, Jadwiga, who married Ladislas Jagello, the grand duke of Lithuania. Situated at Poland's northeastern frontier, Lithuania was a huge duchy in those days and the marriage contract joined it with Poland. With Jadwiga as his queen, Jagello was crowned as Poland's King Ladislas II, and the two of them launched the country on a new era of greatness and power. Jadwiga, who died in childbirth in 1399, was a patron of learning and the arts and founded one of Europe's earliest universities at Cracow. Ladislas, who survived his wife by thirty-five years, set out to check the Teutonic Knights, breaking their power forever at the Battle of Grunwald, not far from Marienburg Castle, in 1410.

The Jagello dynasty, which ruled Poland and Lithuania for the next 160 years, ushered in what has been called Poland's golden age. Though embroiled in countless wars—

with Hungary, Russia, the Tartars, and the Turks, who had become a major power in Europe—Poland-Lithuania constituted a huge empire that reached from the Baltic to the Black Sea. It played a key role in defending Christian Europe from the rising Muslim Turkish tide, and was a country renowned for the high state of its arts and sciences. One of the most famous figures of that era was the astronomer Nicolaus Copernicus.

When the last of the Jagello line died in 1572, a system for electing Poland's kings by the nobility was introduced. Although a step toward democracy, it led to frequent civil wars.

The following two hundred years were marked by constant strife with Poland's neighbors, its eventual decline, and finally its partition and disintegration.

There was, first of all, growing tension with Russia over religious issues, especially in the Ukraine and Byelorussia, at that time parts of Poland, which the Polish rulers tried to make Catholic but whose people preferred Orthodoxy. There were also attempts to conquer all of Russia, which first seemed to succeed, then failed at great cost. In 1587 Sigismund III, a Swedish king and member of the Vasa family, also became king of Poland. Twelve years later he was deposed from the Swedish throne and then spent the next thirty-three years trying to get it back. As a result Poland was also thrown into nearly a century of wars with Sweden.

There was one last moment of greatness, when King John Sobieski, frequently called the defender of Christian Europe against Muslim Turkey, led Polish armies to major victories over the Turks and in 1683 successfully defended Vienna from conquest by a much larger Turkish force.

"That was a great mistake," a Polish acquaintance once told me. "Poland would have been better off had Sobieski sided with the Turks instead of the Austrians, for after having helped them in their greatest hour of need and breaking Turkish power, the Austrians then began nipping at us."

The Austrians did so in alliance with Prussia and Russia, both of which had old political axes to grind with Poland.

In three partitions—1772, 1793, and 1795—arranged by Prussia's King Frederick the Great, Empress Maria Theresa of Austria, and Empress Catherine the Great of Russia, Poland was gobbled up by those three powerful neighbors and wiped from the map of Europe.

In 1794 there was one heroic revolt and last-ditch attempt to stop the course of history by Thaddeus Kosciusko, the Polish general and champion of liberty who had played a key role in the American Revolution. But he was defeated, imprisoned, and after release in 1796 returned to the United States, then went to France, where he enlisted Napoleon's help in restoring Poland's independence.

Napoleon did so, but after he was also defeated, Poland entered a century-long period of nonexistence. Its western and northern territories were integrated into Prussia, which later became modern Germany. The southwest became part of the Austro-Hungarian Empire. Although the eastern regions were set up as a nominally independent kingdom, subject to Russia, the "king" was none other than the Russian czar. Even that fiction disappeared in 1831 following a rebellion against Russian rule and the "kingdom" became a province of Russia under a governor.

The rest of the nineteenth and early twentieth century saw a great migration of Polish patriots, artists, and intellectuals to Paris, which became a major center of Polish revolutionary activity. Among the best-known figures were the composer Frédéric Chopin and the pianist Ignace Jan Paderewski, who used their musical geniuses and gifts to attract attention and win sympathy for Poland's cause.

But it was not until November 1918, after the defeat of Germany and Austria-Hungary in World War I, and a year after the Bolshevik Revolution in Russia, that there was again an independent Poland. Paderewski became its first prime minister.

Czechoslovakia's history before 1918 is actually that of two countries—one could almost say three: Bohemia, Moravia, and Slovakia—of which the latter never really existed at all as a separate state.

Slovakia formed part of the Greater Moravian Empire up to the end of the ninth century, but it was conquered by the Magyars in the tenth century and for the next thousand years was either under Hungarian rule or that of the Hapsburg dynasty's Austria-Hungary.

Moravia, which forms the central part of modern Czechoslovakia, between Bohemia in the west and Slovakia in the east, was known to have been settled as early as the sixth century by that group of western Slav people known as the Czechs. For a while it was subjugated by a fiercely warlike nomadic tribe called the Avars, but in the seventh century a Czech chieftain, Samo, defeated them and established the first known Slav state.

That state fell apart again after Samo's death in the year 658, but some two centuries later another Czech tribal leader— Rastislav—appeared on the scene and forged a duchy. He converted to Christianity and so did his people. His successor, Svatopluk, who assumed power in 870 and ruled until 894, developed the duchy into what was for those days a sizable little empire. Its territory included all of Bohemia and Slovakia, a southern section of contemporary Poland, and the north of modern-day Hungary. But the empire broke apart after Svatopluk's death. It was subsequently conquered by the Magyars, then swallowed up after Otto I, the German Holy Roman emperor, had defeated the Hungarians in the

Battle of Lechfeld in 955. From the early eleventh century on it was part and parcel of Bohemia.

Bohemia's first great ruler was Saint Wenceslaus. Though a duke, he was called "the good king." It is for him that Prague's main square is named. His statue in the middle of it is a symbol of independence and something like a national shrine for the Czechs. That Wenceslaus—there are four others with the same name who came after him—spent much of his reign fighting the Germans next door and their Holy Roman emperors, as did his successors.

It is a bit of a mystery why they had so many military troubles with the Germans, since German influence in Bohemia was growing all the time anyway because of rising east-west trade. By the time Bohemia was proclaimed a kingdom with the coronation of Ottokar I in 1198, there were German colonists everywhere, and German craftsmen and tradesmen in its developing towns, especially the capital, Prague.

It was Ottokar's grandson, Ottokar II, who during his reign, from 1253 to 1278, turned Bohemia into a major European power. It extended all the way from the Oder River, its northeastern frontier, southwestward through modern-day Austria, Bavaria, northern Italy, and Yugoslavia to the Adriatic Sea. Ottokar II was the most powerful ruler in central Europe at the time. In 1273 he competed for the title of Holy Roman emperor against Rudolf of Hapsburg, a minor Swiss princelet who had acquired some possessions in Austria. The two fought for five years until Ottokar was defeated and killed in the Battle on the Marchfeld a few miles east of Vienna. In the process he not only lost most of the territories he had gained, but gave rise to the Hapsburg dynasty of Austria which later was to play such an important role in the history of all Eastern Europe.

Bohemia itself was reduced to its original area plus that of

Moravia. Within another generation the original Czech dynasty, called the Premysls, died out and a West European duke, John of Luxembourg, was elected king. He and his successors drew the Czechs into various West European wars from which they gained little but suffering.

What Ottokar II had failed in doing, however, John of Luxembourg's son, Charles IV, succeeded in triumphantly. In 1335 he was elected Holy Roman emperor. Little Bohemia, especially its capital of Prague, suddenly found itself the center of the civilized European world. Charles was a rather remarkable ruler. A German by birth, he had been educated at the French court, but considered himself a Slav and was able to write and speak a number of Slavic languages. In Prague he founded one of Europe's greatest universities, still named for him, and turned the capital into one of the most splendid cities in the world.

But after his death in 1378, Bohemia's fortunes declined quickly. One factor was the arrival on the scene of Jan Hus, a forefather of the Protestant Reformation and Lutheranism. Hus was born to peasant parents in Bohemia in 1369, studied theology at Charles University in Prague, and was ordained a priest in 1400. Both a religious and social reformer and an ardent Czech nationalist, he used his pulpit in Prague's Bethlehem Chapel to deliver scathing sermons against privileges for and abuses by the clergy and against the commercial and land-holding penetration of Bohemia by the Germans. In the dozen years or so that he preached and wrote, until he was burned at the stake in 1415, he stirred up passions and political and religious arguments in Europe like no man had before him, and none would again until Martin Luther a century later. He gathered behind him a vast movement of followers —the Hussites—who combined Czech patriotism with social discontent and antipapal religious fervor.

"Crusading" armies recruited from all over Europe by the

pope invaded Bohemia to put down the Hussite rebels, who were led by some very brilliant generals. These Hussite Wars, as they were called, are still considered by Czechs as the most heroic period of their history. Though they laid waste to the land and triggered the end of Bohemia as an independent kingdom, the Hussite movement itself influenced intellectuals, peasants, and the lower priesthood in a number of neighboring countries, particularly Hungary and Poland.

For the remainder of the fifteenth century and early sixteenth century Bohemia was in turmoil. In 1526 a Hapsburg duke became its king and started the gradual process by which Bohemia lost its self-rule, through defeat of a Protestant army in the Battle of the White Mountain in 1620, during the Thirty Years' War.

Although there were numerous revolts and uprisings against Austrian and Hapsburg rule during the next three centuries, it was not until 1918 and the end of the Hapsburg Empire itself that Bohemia emerged again and, together with Moravia and Slovakia, formed modern Czechoslovakia.

Hungary's formal history began when those Magyar forces were defeated in the Battle of Lechfeld in 955. As a Hungarian historian puts it: "The Magyars were then faced with a choice: either they would continue their marauding campaigns throughout Europe and face the prospect of more heavy losses and ultimate annihilation, or they had to change their way of life, settle down and adopt a more advanced social pattern based on the foundation of a state."

They decided to settle down. In 972 the most powerful of the Magyar chieftains, Geza, was named the duke of Hungary. Together with his wife, Sarolta, he converted to Christianity and took the first steps to establish a Hungarian state. But it was his son Stephen, who succeeded him in 997, who completed the job and won recognition as the founder of Hungary.

Stephen put down numerous revolts by pagan nobles who objected to the action he was taking, in particular the division of Hungary into counties—the administrative division still used today—which were governed by royal officials directly responsible to him instead of to the local barons. In 1001 Stephen became Hungary's first king and, in appreciation of what he had done, Pope Sylvester II sent him the jewel-studded golden crown which has remained the sacred symbol of Hungarian national existence.

By the standards of the times, it was no small kingdom over which Stephen and his successors ruled from their first capital at Gran, a mighty fortress perched on a bluff high above the Danube. Its eastern territories included all of Transylvania, now part of Romania and a corner of what is today the Soviet Union. The southern frontier was in part the same one that Romania now has with Bulgaria and Yugoslavia. To the west it extended well into contemporary Yugoslavia, reaching all the way to the Adriatic Sea; a long stretch of the Adriatic coastline was Hungarian. In the west the Hungarian frontier extended almost all the way to Vienna. In the north Hungary bordered on Poland.

The Hungary of those days had two powerful rival neighbors—the Holy Roman and the Byzantine empires—and throughout the eleventh and twelfth centuries Hungary's kings, besides dealing with rebellious and increasingly powerful nobles at home, had to devote most of their energies to holding off invading armies dispatched by either the Byzantine or the German emperor, or playing the two off against each other.

The pressure eased somewhat when Byzantium's power finally declined at the beginning of the thirteenth century, but that was also the start of a new menace: the Mongol, or Tartar, push into Europe.

In the first three decades of the thirteenth century the Tartar hordes, trained into an invincible army by a shepherd's son named Genghis Khan, had overrun northern China, central Asia, Persia, and Russia. In 1241 Genghis's grandson, Batu Khan, invaded Europe. One branch of his army drove with lightning speed through Poland, up to the present border with East Germany, while a southern spearhead swept through Hungary, reaching the Adriatic coast. Hungary's King Béla IV tried to stop them, but the invaders won.

The Mongol threat to Europe was greater than any since the fourth-century invasion by the Huns. The fact that Hungary, and later, no doubt, the rest of Europe, escaped total destruction and occupation was due only to the fact that back in far-off central Asia the supreme Mongol leader, Khan Ogotai, had died. Batu Khan had to withdraw his forces in order to be present at the election of a successor. The Tartars then settled in Russia, where they established their State of the Golden Horde, which occupied and left an indelible mark on the Russians for 250 years. Fortunately they never repeated the invasion of 1241, but that was hardly necessary. In both Poland and Hungary it had left destruction from which it took the two countries nearly 75 years to recover.

By then, too, the last of King Stephen's dynasty had died out and a Frenchman, Charles Robert of Anjou, married to a Hungarian princess, became king and launched Hungary on a new century of greatness. It was under his son Louis I, the father of Poland's Queen Jadwiga (who married Ladislas Jagello of Lithuania), that the capital was moved to Buda. The castle that King Louis built there on a high hill overlooking the Danube still stands as one of Budapest's main tourist attractions. It was also under Louis I that Hungary made its greatest territorial gains. He fought and won numerous military campaigns, especially against the then powerful Republic of Venice, but also fostered art and learning at home, turning his new capital of Buda (Pest on the other side of the river remained a village for many more centuries) into a great cultural center.

But Louis I and a number of his successors were too busy fighting and competing with other European rulers to recognize the arrival of a new challenge and threat that was to dominate East European affairs in general, and those of Hungary in particular, for the next five hundred years: the Ottoman Turks.

The Ottoman Empire, sometimes called the Osmanli Empire after its first ruler, Osman I, was a vast state founded in the thirteenth century by Turkic peoples who had become Muslim in Asia Minor. They first landed in Europe, waging campaigns against Byzantine armies, in 1347 and kept advancing westward and northward into the Balkans and Eastern Europe, occupying all of Bulgaria, most of what is today Romania, and Serbia.

Although they almost captured Byzantium, that is, Constantinople, in 1402, no one took them very seriously in the early fifteenth century. The pope, for example, was far more interested in suppressing the Hussites of Bohemia who challenged his personal authority than in mounting a crusade against a rising empire whose ideology was the defeat of Christianity. The fact that they were threatening a brand of Christianity other than the pope's—Eastern Orthodoxy—may also have been a consideration.

At any rate, in the first half of the fifteenth century what resistance there was to the Ottoman Turks came from the kings of Hungary, a number of whom were also kings of Poland. But they weren't strong enough. In 1453 Constantinople finally fell to the Turkish ruler Muhammad II and became the new capital of the Ottoman Empire. Muhammad and his successors spent the next seventy years completing the conquest of southeastern Europe, and then overran Syria, Egypt, and North Africa. In 1526 Suleiman the Magnificent invaded Hungary, defeating the combined Hungarian and Bohemian armies and killing Hungary's King Louis II at the Battle of Mohacs.

The Battle of Mohacs is an important date not only in Hungary's history but that of other East European countries, because, for four hundred years following it, the area was dominated by three great powers: the Hapsburg and Ottoman empires and, somewhat later, czarist Russia.

After the Battle of Mohacs and ten more years of frontier fighting between Suleiman and the Hapsburg emperor Ferdinand, Hungary was divided into three parts. The east, Transylvania, kept a semi-independent status as an Ottoman puppet state. The middle, including Budapest, was Turkish, and the west, including Slovakia, became part of Austria. It retained its status as a kingdom, but in name only, for the king from then on was always the Austrian emperor.

There were many more wars between the Turks and Austrians, and Hungary was the scene of quite a few of them. In 1683, had it not been for Poland's King John Sobieski, the Turks would have succeeded in taking Vienna. That failure marked the beginning of their military decline. Three years later an allied army of Austrians, Venetians, Poles, and Hungarians drove the Turks out of Budapest, and by the end of the seventeenth century Turkey had ceded most of Hungary and Transylvania to Austria.

For all the evil deeds ascribed to them in story and legend, Turkish rule was better than its reputation. The aristocracy suffered, to be sure, but the Turkish governors, or pashas, as they were called, left the mass of the population to themselves. They also showed considerable religious tolerance. Muslims were socially, politically, and militarily privileged, but Christians—both Roman Catholic and Orthodox—were usually not persecuted. Those who converted did so primarily for opportunistic reasons.

Probably the worst part of Ottoman rule was the tribute demanded in male children. Christian boys were taken from their mothers in infancy and brought up in special schools in Constantinople as Muslims and as soldiers. They formed the elite of the Ottoman armies and were called Janissaries.

In fact, for the Hungarians themselves, life under the Turks was probably better than under the Austrians, who showed great intolerance toward Protestants, forced Germanization, and encouraged the Hungarian aristocracy to exploit the peasantry. This led to a strong nationalist independence movement which broke out in the Revolution of 1848 under Lajos Kossuth, a Protestant lawyer who declared an independent republic and became its president. It did not last long. Austrian forces, helped by those of czarist Russia coming in from the north and east, put an end to the republic in 1849. The Hungarian surrender was followed by ruthless reprisals and the end of what little autonomy Hungary had enjoyed before the rebellion.

But in 1866, after Austria had lost a war to Prussia, it made important concessions to Magyar national aims. A dual monarchy was established. Hungary, which then included Slovakia, parts of what is today the Soviet Ukraine, Transylvania, and the Croatian and Slovenian areas of modern-day Yugoslavia, became an almost equal partner with its own prime minister under the Austrian emperor in a union called Austria-Hungary.

Though there were still conflicts between Hungary and Austria, common interests—especially keeping a thumb on

the restless, underprivileged minorities—held the two together until the monarchy itself collapsed at the end of
World War I.

Bulgaria became a significant Balkan power not long after
the Bulgars streamed into the area from their original home
base on the Volga in the seventh century.

The first Bulgarian "empire" lasted from 680 to 1018 and
within a century after its establishment by a Bulgarian khan
named Asparaukh was already a threat to the neighboring
Byzantine Empire. In 809 the Bulgarians captured their present capital, Sofia, from the Byzantine emperor and two years
later laid siege to Constantinople itself, withdrawing only
after getting a promise of yearly tribute.

Later in the ninth century Bulgaria became the center of
a tug-of-war between Rome and Byzantium which was finally
resolved in 864, when the Bulgarian khan Boris I was baptized as an Eastern Christian and introduced the Cyrillic
script.

Boris, who had become khan as a pagan in 852, abdicated
in 889 in favor of his eldest son Vladimir in order to retire to
a monastery and devote the rest of his life to prayer. That
was a mistake, for Vladimir was a renegade and a reaction-
ary who tried to reintroduce paganism in Bulgaria. Boris
came storming out of the monastery four years later, deposed
Vladimir, and put a younger son, Simeon, in charge.

It was under Simeon I, who had himself crowned as czar
in 925, two years before his death, that the first Bulgarian
Empire reached its greatest power. He was highly ambitious
and waged a number of successful military campaigns
against the Byzantine emperor, and, with the help of the
Pechenegs, drove the Magyars into Hungary. Simeon was a
pious man, unlike his brother Vladimir, but one who recognized the political clout of religion in those days. He raised the
archbishop of Bulgaria to the rank of patriarch, thus making

the Bulgarian Church virtually independent. His court was of unprecedented splendor, a match for the Byzantine emperor's in Constantinople. As an able Greek scholar himself, he fostered the translation of the most important Greek works into Church Slavonic, the official liturgical language, and under his rule Slavonic literature enjoyed a golden age. But his empire did not survive him by a hundred years. It was annexed by Byzantium in 1018.

Byzantine domination, however, was weakened by internal disorders at Constantinople and various military pressures from outside, and in 1186 a new Bulgarian ruler, Ivan I, had himself crowned as czar and launched a second Bulgarian Empire which, at its height, in the early thirteenth century, ruled over nearly the entire Balkan Peninsula. But it, too, did not last long. In 1330 it became a puppet state of neighboring Serbia, and by 1396 it was absorbed completely into the Ottoman Empire. Bulgaria did not regain independence until nearly five hundred years later.

In the intervening years, there were frequent rebellions against Turkish rule, the most notable being led by Stefan Stambolov, for whom it is named, in 1876. The Stambolov Revolt was put down so ruthlessly and with so many atrocities committed by the Turks that Russia, eager to free its Orthodox Christian, Slavic "brothers" in Bulgaria went to war with Turkey—for the eighth time in a period of 170 years. That Russo-Turkish war of 1877–78 ended with the Treaty of San Stefano (over which Bulgaria and Yugoslavia are still arguing today) and the creation of a large, independent Bulgaria that included sizable portions of present-day Yugoslavia, Greece, Turkey, and Romania. Perhaps that explains why Communist Bulgaria today, almost alone among the East European countries, is so especially loyal to Moscow.

Though it was a large Bulgaria, it was obviously a Bulgaria set up to be under czarist Russian domination and as such enhance Russia's power in the Balkans, the Black Sea, and ultimately the Mediterranean. That was a development which the other big powers of Europe—Great Britain, Austria-Hungary, Germany, France, and Italy—wanted to stop. Under strong pressure Russia was forced to the 1878 Congress of Berlin where Bulgarian independence was undone again and Greater Bulgaria broken up. Portions of it were declared independent or ceded to other Balkan states, some chunks were turned over to Austria-Hungary, some returned to Turkey and the part that was left—about one-third of present-day Bulgaria—was declared a semi-independent principality with a German prince and close relative of England's Queen Victoria as its first ruler.

During the next forty-five years, until the start of World War I, which Bulgaria entered as an ally of Germany and Austria-Hungary, the principality was elevated to a kingdom and was embroiled in Balkan wars, some of which it won, others of which it lost, all more or less aimed at retrieving the real estate lost by the 1878 Congress of Berlin.

Romania, tracing its origins to the pre-Christian Dacians, can with some justification lay claim to the longest and oldest history in Eastern Europe. However, from the year 270, when Dacia was overrun by the Goths, there wasn't even a hint of a Romania for a thousand years. It was raided by virtually every nomadic and warlike tribe that ever set foot in Europe—some to stay and become civilized, some to simply disappear, and others to scurry back to Asia. There were Huns, Avars, Slavs, Bulgars, Magyars, Pechenegs, Mongols, and ultimately the Turks.

Whatever happened to the original Dacians, who had intermarried with their Roman conquerors, is hard to say and is the subject of heated controversy these days between Hungary and Romania. Hungary claims they had disappeared by the time the Magyars settled in Transylvania. Romania insists that they were not only around but played a major role in civilizing the Hungarians. What is true is that their language has survived more or less intact.

By the time the Mongols withdrew in the thirteenth century, the history of Romania became largely that of two principalities—Moldavia and Walachia—and of Transylvania, which for much of the time was a dependency of one kind or another.

And from the beginning of the fifteenth century the histories of Moldavia and Walachia were largely those of resisting and ultimately being subjugated by the Turks.

Three great historical figures stand out in fifteenth- and sixteenth-century Romania.

One was Dracula, on whom so many horror stories and movies of our time are based. He was real. His name was Vlad Dracul and from 1456 to 1462 he was prince of Walachia. He did not have fangs and he did not suck blood. But he was a bloodthirsty ruler, notorious for having twenty thousand of his enemies impaled on spears and sharp stakes during his six-year rule, which ended with his arrest by the king of Hungary. His name has lasted to the present: Vlad the Impaler.

The truth about Dracula is far more complex than writers of his time or since then have made it out to be. His cruelty both shocked and fascinated Renaissance Europe and he became a legend long before he died. But the story was spread largely by Hungarian and German noblemen who had their own political axes to grind and vested interests to defend.

The fact is that when Dracula came to power, Walachia and neighboring Moldavia were already puppet states of the Ottoman Empire. Walachia was torn by strife between the

big landowners and feudal barons, called boyars, and among
rival claimants to the principality's throne. It was a country
without even a hint of law and order.

Dracula not only tried to restore it, but refused to pay
tribute to the Turkish sultan and fought numerous successful
campaigns against the Turks.

Reports of the time describe how he killed by the thousands the nobles of Walachia who opposed his absolute
powers and how he devastated the lands of the peasants with
his scorched-earth military campaigns. Though he was in fact
terrifying, those stories fail to point out that most of those
impaled were actually Turkish prisoners of war and that
the punishments he meted out to the boyars were to curb
their abuses. He actually pursued a surprisingly enlightened
policy toward the peasant masses, promising that "nobody
shall be poor but all shall be rich in our country." One
Byzantine writer even hailed him as "a hero of Christianity"
for having defeated Muhammad II in a major battle on the
Danube.

Dracula's real trouble was that he was not very shrewd
politically. For example, he helped Stephen the Great to the
throne of neighboring Moldavia, only to be invaded by
Stephen in 1462. He angered the Hungarian and German
merchants of Transylvania by curbing their trading monopolies and economic privileges in Walachia. It was they, in
league with the boyars, who began spreading the stories of
Dracula's atrocities which led to his capture and imprisonment by Hungary's King Matthias Corvinus.

Actually he was one of the major figures of fifteenth-
century Romania and was overshadowed only by Moldavia's
Stephen the Great in his efforts to resist both Turkish and
Hungarian domination of the land.

Stephen the Great, who ruled Moldavia from 1457 to 1504,
was a smarter politician than Vlad Dracul. He also faced

greater problems. His principality was threatened not only by the Hungarians and Turks but also by the Poles, who in those days were the immediate northern neighbors of Moldavia. He tried to play all three off against each other, using Walachia as an occasional pawn.

He invaded Walachia to prevent the Turks from using it as a staging point for an invasion of Moldavia, and in one great battle with the Turks in 1475 managed to confuse and route the enemy by setting up an army of wooden dummies on the field. Moldavia reached the height of its power under him, but ultimately the Turks were too strong. Upon Stephen's death in 1504 it became a tributary state to the Turkish sultans.

A last attempt to free Romania from foreign domination was made in the sixteenth century by Michael the Brave of Walachia, who ranks as Romania's greatest hero. There is not a city or town where his statue does not stand or a square is not named for him. His greatest achievement was that for a very brief time he managed to conquer and unite all the three major provinces that make up Romania today.

He became prince of Walachia in 1593 by paying a huge bribe for his appointment, then got rid of the Turkish creditors who had advanced him the money by summoning them to his palace and having them massacred. The angry sultan sent a series of punitive armies into Walachia, each of which Michael defeated with the help of the prince of Transylvania.

In 1596 the sultan finally made peace with Michael, leaving Walachia virtually independent. Michael then turned to the conquest of Transylvania, at which he succeeded in 1599. One year later he entered and also conquered Moldavia.

It is hard to say what course Romanian—and perhaps all of Eastern Europe's—history might have taken had Michael the Brave lived to a reasonable old age. But in 1601 he was assassinated on orders of the Hapsburg emperor who wanted Transylvania back. After his death Walachia and Moldavia reverted to Turkish control, Transylvania to that of the Hapsburg rulers.

With the rise of Romanian national consciousness there were many rebellions against the Turks, but it was not until the Russo-Turkish war of 1828–29 that Walachia and Moldavia gained a little independence, though what followed was not much better. They became Russian protectorates. Authority over them shifted back and forth for another thirty years. Every kind of corruption was practiced by a series of princes, frequently foreign, who bought their thrones and had absolute power. The mass of peasants lived in mud huts, wore rags, and were enslaved by the landowners and whipped by the tax collectors.

In 1859 the two provinces were united as a single principality under a ruler, Alexandru Ioan Cuza, who was no less corrupt than any of his predecessors. He was deposed seven years later and replaced by yet another foreigner— Charles von Hohenzollern, a cousin of the German kaiser. He called himself Prince Carol I. In 1881 he proclaimed himself king.

It was a frightfully backward kingdom on which nearly two thousand years of foreign rule had left a legacy of violence, rebellion, intrigue, religious and ethnic intolerance, and corruption. And little was to change during the three decades between Romania's elevation to a kingdom and the start of World War I.

Over the centuries there had been many peasant revolts— outbursts of despair and insulted national pride—which were brutally violent. One of the most violent of all was in 1907, when eleven thousand people were killed in just a few weeks.

Romania was also soon embroiled in the complex new

Balkan politics and entered the second Balkan War against Bulgaria from which it seized a large piece of territory.

King Carol I did keep the country neutral at the outset of World War I, but died in the fall of 1914. The throne then went to his nephew Ferdinand, who in 1916 was lured into involvement on the Allied side against Germany and Austria-Hungary by an irresistible bribe—Romanian control of Transylvania as the spoils of victory. The promise was kept by the Allies, and Romania, in more or less its present form, took shape in 1918.

That war, which was actually triggered by the desire for independence and rising national ambitions in Eastern Europe, changed the course of history and the shape of the map.

5

A Dream Turned Nightmare

President Woodrow Wilson led the United States into the First World War with noble aims: the ultimate "peace of the world," the "liberation and self-determination of its peoples," and "to make that world safe for democracy."

His famous Fourteen Points, the peace program that he presented in a speech to both houses of Congress on January 8, 1918, laid the foundation for the reorganization of Eastern Europe in its modern form. Among other things, it called for the division of old Austria-Hungary and the Balkan Peninsula along ethnic and national frontiers, limiting Turkey's control to Turks, and the establishment of an independent Poland which would have access to the sea.

It was a beautiful and highly moral dream that soon turned into a nightmare and sowed the seeds for World War II.

To be sure, Wilson's Fourteen Points did change the face

of Eastern Europe. Where a century before there had not been a single independent nation there were now five, to which one should also add Yugoslavia and the Baltic republics of Lithuania, Latvia, and Estonia, which had declared their independence from Russia and remained independent until the Soviet Union gobbled them up again in 1940.

The great empires that had held sway were also gone— Austria demolished; Turkey and Germany, both new republics, more or less reduced to their own ethnic frontiers; and Russia embroiled in the chaos of the civil war that followed the November 1917 Bolshevik Revolution.

But this change did not eliminate ethnic and national conflicts. In fact, it aggravated them, and it was not long before the peoples of Eastern Europe were busily trying to settle old scores. Redrawing the map had created new nations, but with boundaries that cut through the territories of some national minorities and forced others to live under one governmental administration with peoples whom they had hated for centuries. It also reversed historical roles between rulers and ruled, for example in the case of Germans and Czechs, Magyars and Romanians. All of this was bound to produce bitterness and hatred and to create future points of friction over borders, disputed zones, minorities, and regional autonomy which were exploited as the pretext for World War II and which have still not been resolved.

The new countries, backward beyond belief, also had to face the economic problems of suddenly being independent. They had only a thin veneer of industry and urban life over a vast and primitive agricultural base. There was no reservoir of skilled labor, there were no trained technicians on whom to draw, and there was almost no capital for investment. Education was limited to a small, privileged group. In the countryside, meanwhile, the peasants continued much as before—illiterate, incredibly poor, deprived and subjugated by a class of landowners whose attitudes and ways had not changed much since feudal days. To complicate matters, the rest of the world was plunging into the worst economic crisis in history.

Given these circumstances, almost none of these small countries was able to set up a stable system of government. With no tradition of genuine democracy, troubled by severe inner conflicts among classes, minorities, and religions, and plagued by economic and social backwardness, the new East European countries simply did not have the basic conditions for a stable political community, especially a democratic one. Almost all started with the intention of becoming democracies, but, with the notable exception of Czechoslovakia, all failed to achieve that goal.

The two decades between the end of World War I and the start of World War II were disastrous. By 1939 all the countries except Czechoslovakia had been subjected to dictatorial rule of one kind or another.

Czechoslovakia, because it was the exception, suffered the cruelest fate of all.

The creation of the country had been largely the work of Tomas G. Masaryk, its first president, and Eduard Beneš, its second. Both Czechs and both highly respected professors of philosophy, sociology, and economics, they had been active in the liberation movement before World War I and then spent the war years in exile in France, Great Britain, and the United States, raising funds and support for an independent postwar Czechoslovakia. Both were liberals and thoroughly democratic in their outlook and ways.

The union of the Czech lands with Slovakia was proclaimed on November 14, 1918—three days after the Armistice and the abdication of the last Hapsburg emperor—and the country was recognized as an independent state soon after. It had a promising future. The constitution adopted in

1920 was a model for other countries to emulate. Bohemia and Moravia included the old Austro-Hungarian Empire's greatest concentration of heavy industry, so that there was a sound economic footing. The general standard of the peasantry had been raised by breaking up and redistributing some of the huge estates that had belonged to the Catholic Church and the land-owning Hapsburg nobility.

But there were also built-in troubles that paved the way to disaster in 1938.

The Czechs and Slovaks had completely separate histories and differed greatly in their religious, cultural, and social ways. Although the 1920 constitution was democratic, it also set up a highly centralized state administration which not only failed to take these ethnic differences into account but brought them to the surface, with the Slovaks claiming they were being discriminated against and deprived of their rights.

There were also growing problems over territory and minorities with neighboring Poland, Hungary, Austria, and especially Germany. Large areas of western Bohemia and northern Moravia—the Sudetenland—were inhabited by some 3.3 million Germans, who represented more than twenty-two percent of Czechoslovakia's total 1930 population.

Hitler's rise in Germany, his annexation of Austria, growing nationalism in Hungary, mounting demands for autonomy by the Slovaks, and tension with Poland brought these ethnic problems to a boil in 1938. In the Sudetenland the German nationalist minority, led by Konrad Henlein, the local Nazi leader who was strongly backed by Hitler, demanded the union of their territory with Germany. By the summer of 1938 Hitler was threatening to invade and go to war unless those demands were met. Czechoslovakia had allies and supporters—the Soviet Union, Great Britain, and France. While the Russians would have been willing to fight,

Britain and France, fearful of a new world war, wanted to appease Hitler by letting him have Czechoslovakia. That led to the infamous Munich Pact of September 1938, when Hitler, Britain's Prime Minister Neville Chamberlain, and French Premier Edouard Daladier met, without Czechoslovakia even being represented, to seal the country's fate.

The agreement called for immediate occupation of the Sudetenland by Germany, to be followed by a plebiscite among the area's people to determine whether they wanted union with Germany. The plebiscite, however, never took place. It was after signing this pact that Chamberlain flew back to London and, holding his rolled umbrella high, announced to the airport crowd, "There will be peace in our time." Ever since then the umbrella has been a symbol of appeasement.

Two months after the Munich Pact the country was renamed Czhecho-Slovakia and reorganized in autonomous units with a premier for each part. A Catholic priest, Father Josef Tiso, became premier of Slovakia. Eduard Beneš, who had succeeded Tomas Masaryk in 1937, resigned as president and went into exile. He was replaced by Emil Hácha. In March 1939 Hacha dismissed Father Tiso as premier of Slovakia. Tiso asked Hitler for help. Hitler used Tiso's appeal as a pretext for occupying the Czech lands of Bohemia and Moravia, turning them into a German "protectorate," and establishing Slovakia as an "independent" country which sided with Nazi Germany during World War II.

After the outbreak of the war Beneš set up a provisional government in London. Czechs and Slovaks who had managed to escape the occupation fought with Allied forces. In April 1944 the Soviet army, accompanied by Czechoslovak brigades, entered Slovakia from the east.

In the spring of 1945 General George S. Patton's United States Third Army drove in from the west.

Hitler drives through a victory arch in Asch,
Czechoslovakia, in the fall of 1938.

On May 12, 1945, four days after V-E Day had been celebrated elsewhere, the last of the German units in Czechoslovakia surrendered. The country was reconstituted in its pre–Munich Pact frontiers and Beneš resumed the presidency until the Communist takeover in 1948.

Poland, which was next on Hitler's 1939 "shopping list," actually began its drive for independence at the start, not the end, of World War I. The fact that the leading Polish nationalists hated Russia more than Prussian Germany or Austria-Hungary had something to do with it.

The dominant figure of the Polish independence movement and the man who directed Poland's affairs right into the 1930's was Jozef Pilsudski. Born in the Russian-occupied part of Poland in 1867, he first made news as a young man of twenty in 1887 when, together with Lenin's older brother, he plotted the assassination of Russia's Czar Alexander III. Lenin's brother was executed. Pilsudski was imprisoned in Siberia for five years. Upon his release he joined the Polish Socialist party and began publication of its underground newspaper.

Imprisoned again in 1900, he soon escaped. More or less dropping socialism, he devoted all his efforts to Polish independence by organizing various anti-Russian militant groups.

At the outbreak of World War I in 1914 he formed and led the Polish legions that fought for two years on the German and Austrian side against Russia. Late in 1916 the German kaiser and the Austrian emperor rewarded him by declaring their parts of Poland and whatever had been taken from the Russians an independent kingdom. But Germany, which was actually occupying that "kingdom," kept control over it—a fact to which Pilsudski objected so strongly that he was again imprisoned—this time by the Germans.

From then until the end of the war the independence

movement centered on the more moderate exiles in Paris, such as the pianist Paderewski.

Russia had bowed out of the war after the 1917 revolution led by Lenin. Germany and Austria gave up in November 1918, a day after Pilsudski was released from a German prison. He immediately returned to Warsaw, assumed command of the Polish forces, proclaimed an independent Polish republic, and named himself president. Paderewski subsequently became the first prime minister and Poland was launched again, after more than a hundred years during which it had not existed at all.

Its size and shape, however, remained a matter of much dispute and became a major issue at the 1919 Versailles peace conference.

Pilsudski still had a soft spot for the Germans and accepted the idea that they could keep most of Silesia, Pomerania, and East Prussia. Poland got a corridor to the sea through East Prussia. The key city of Danzig, a Baltic port, was declared an independent city, neither German nor Polish. Some of Silesia went to Poland and a small district to newly independent Czechoslovakia.

But the biggest argument at Versailles was over Poland's frontier with Russia. Britain's foreign minister, Lord Curzon, proposed a boundary line—later named after him—which would have given Russia large parts of Poland's former eastern territories, inhabited primarily by Ukrainians and Byelorussians. But Pilsudski insisted on the old borders of 1772—before Poland's first partition—including a substantial chunk of what had been the duchy of Lithuania but was then already a newly declared independent republic. It would have placed Poland's frontier less than three hundred miles from Moscow and only thirteen miles from Kiev.

When the Western Allies refused to let him have it, Pilsudski set out to get it by force. He went to war against Soviet

Russia, whose prime minister then was Lenin. The Russians, faced with counterrevolution, civil war, the breaking off of most of the czarist empire's former border regions, foreign intervention by Great Britain, France, and the United States, and famine and discontent at home, were weak. The Poles, with an army of nearly half a million, were strong. The war lasted well into the fall of 1920, and flared up again in 1921. The frontier on which Poland and the Soviet Union finally settled in the 1921 Treaty of Riga was about halfway between that of 1772 and Lord Curzon's proposal.

A third of this reborn Poland's population was made up of non-Poles—Ukrainians, Byelorussians, Germans, Lithuanians, Czechs, and Jews—all of whom were discriminated against rather severely.

In 1922, with adoption of a republican constitution, Pilsudski retired to private life. The constitution changed little for the Polish people or the minorities in the country, however. Though there were some reforms and some attempts at industrialization, the conditions of the peasants remained incredibly poor and the land-owning aristocracy retained most of its wealth.

The administration that replaced Pilsudski did attempt a land reform to which he objected so strongly that in 1926 he staged a coup d'etat which put him back in power as prime minister and virtual dictator, which he remained until his death in 1935. When he died, a group of Pilsudski's colonels led by Edward Smygly-Rydz took over and continued the fascist-style military dictatorship.

It was a regime that was not only quite friendly to Hitler but was also just about as anti-Semitic and repressive against the Jews as the Nazis were in Germany. Under the circumstances, it is a bit of a mystery why Hitler wanted to invade. The "master race" theory and age-old German contempt for the Slavs probably had something to do with it. At any rate, in the summer of 1939, a few months after having finished off Czechoslovakia, Hitler began putting pressure on the Poles by demanding the return of the Free City of Danzig to German control. The Poles refused.

The Polish colonels sensed what was coming. So, apparently, did the Soviet Union's Josef Stalin, who figured that the long-range German game plan was to use Poland as a staging point for an invasion of Russia. The Poles got guarantees of military support from Britain and France, which in turn tried to draw the Soviet Union into a pro-Polish, anti-German alliance. But the Russians, having neither forgiven the Poles for the 1919–20 war nor forgotten how the British and French had let down Czechoslovakia a year earlier, refused to play. Instead they decided to bargain with the Germans for more time for themselves. In the middle of August 1939 Stalin's and Hitler's representatives met to work out a nonaggression treaty between their two countries.

The Hitler-Stalin Pact, as it was called, was made public on August 23, 1939. What neither the Poles nor the rest of the world knew was that it contained a secret clause. It entitled the Russians to invade Poland from the east, as the Germans drove in from the west, and occupy those territories—up to the old Curzon Line—that Pilsudski had obtained in 1919 and 1920. There were also a few other secret clauses allowing Soviet Russia to gobble up the Baltic republics and to take Moldavian Bessarabia back from Romania.

One week later, in the early evening of August 31, 1939, a squad of Nazi SS men, led by Major Alfred Naujocks, emerged from a clump of trees on the outskirts of the then German city of Gleiwitz in Silesia, a couple of miles from the Polish frontier. Wearing Polish army uniforms, they surrounded the nearby German radio station, fired shots in a mock skirmish, and occupied the transmitter.

In heavily accented Polish, the "raiders" broadcast a

three-minute speech to Poles living in that part of Germany, promising them "liberation." Then they fled, leaving behind as "evidence of the attack" the bullet-riddled corpse of a Polish-born German concentration camp inmate, also dressed in Polish uniform, whom they had dragged to the scene with them.

This staged incident served as the pretext for Nazi Germany's "revenge" invasion of Poland the next morning, September 1, 1939. Britain and France, true to their promise, declared war on Germany as Poland's allies, and World War II was on. The German forces advanced with spectacular speed. On September 17 the Soviet army invaded from the east. Polish resistance was crushed by the end of the month and Poland was partitioned once more between Germany and Russia. Twenty-one months later the Germans attacked Russia and occupied all of Poland.

The country was liberated by the Soviet army and Polish underground fighters in 1944. An exile government in London, including a number of the old Pilsudski followers, had British and United States backing, but the Soviets, who were on the scene, supported a pro-Russian group of Polish Communists who came to power. The border with the Soviet Union was fixed slightly east of the old Curzon Line. In exchange Poland gained the southern half of eastern Prussia, all of western Prussia, Pomerania, and Silesia. The Germans who had lived there—some four million—were expelled and deported. Although Communist East Germany, the actual neighbor, recognized those new frontiers in the 1950's, it took West Germany until 1971 to do so formally.

Hungary ranks as the biggest loser of World War I.

Totally demoralized by the progress of the war, shaken by mutinies of its troops and leftist rebellions throughout the summer and fall of 1918, it declared itself a state independent from Austria on October 31, though it took the mon-

arch, Charles I, a little longer to accept the fact. He abdicated as emperor of Austria on November 11 and as king of
Hungary two days later. On November 16 Hungary became a
republic. But there wasn't much of it, nor did it survive long.
Transylvania joined Romania; the Slovak territories became part of independent Czechoslovakia. Croatia, including its Adriatic coastline, went to the new state of Yugoslavia.
The moderate, middle-of-the-road government, set up by
Mihaly Karolyi as president in January 1919, was overthrown in March by the Communist party of Bela Kun.

Kun was trying to imitate Russia's Lenin. He set up a
republic of Soviets, a Russian word meaning "councils," and
a "dictatorship of the proletariat," and nationalized all banks,
big businesses, and private estates, ruthlessly putting down
all opposition. He also envisioned a Greater Communist
Hungary and raised a Red Army with which he overran
Slovakia. That may have been his biggest mistake. The Allies
ordered him to withdraw and, to make sure he did, encouraged the Romanians to invade Hungary, which they did
gleefully, occupying Budapest in July 1919. Kun fled to
Vienna, where the Austrians first put him into an insane
asylum but later let him go to Russia.

What happened after Kun's departure and the fall of his
Hungarian Soviet Republic can be called a twenty-five-year
tragedy. Power was taken by a Hungarian admiral who no
longer had a navy, Miklos Horthy. He became regent of "a
kingdom without a king," and ruled Hungary until its defeat
during World War II in 1944.

Horthy was an ultraright nationalist who took Hungary
into alliances with Benito Mussolini's fascist Italy and, later,
Hitler's Nazi Germany. His regime was antidemocratic, anti-
Semitic, and authoritarian. It prevented all attempts at reform and protected the power of the feudal landowners. In
foreign affairs the main theme of the Horthy regime was the

attempt to recover the Magyar territories Hungary had lost at the end of World War I. And it got some of them—temporarily—with the help of Germany and Italy between 1938 and 1944.

Under Horthy's rule, Hungary, together with Germany, declared war on Russia in June 1941 and on the United States after Pearl Harbor. Its own fascist party, the Arrow-Cross Movement, played a key role in the years just before and during World War II.

The Soviet army invaded in October 1944, conquering all of Hungary and moving into German Austria by February 1945.

The first postwar government, democratically elected in 1945, was middle-of-the-road and reform-minded, but in 1948 it fell to a Communist coup.

Romania sided with the Allies during World War I. On Armistice Day, 1918, it stood bigger and more powerful than at any time since the age of Michael the Brave. It annexed Transylvania from Hungary, the Bukovina district of what is now the Ukraine from Austria, and the Bessarabian part of Moldavia from Russia. The Romanian army, recovered from defeats at the hands of the Austrians and Germans a year earlier, was strong enough to throw Bela Kun and his Red Guards out of power in Hungary. Moreover, the land reforms adopted by King Ferdinand in 1917, though slow and imperfect, were starting to ease some of the misery of the peasants and to break the hold of the powerful boyars and feudal barons.

But Romania was not a democracy and it never became one. Its history between the two world wars is one of endless corruption, power struggles, meaningless elections, intrigue, political murders, dictators deposing kings and being deposed in turn. The plot is thick, and it would make a better script for a grade-B movie than the story of a country.

Between 1927, when King Ferdinand died, and 1947, there were only two kings—Ferdinand's son Carol II and his grandson Michael. But they were on and off the throne so often that it was rather like watching two people chasing each other in a revolving door. On Ferdinand's death, Carol renounced the crown in favor of his son Michael, who was six years old at the time. Michael ruled with a regent. Three years later Carol came back, deposed Michael, and was crowned. In 1938 he assumed dictatorial powers. Two years after that, with a fascist dictator, Ion Antonescu, backing him, Michael returned, deposed, and exiled his father. In 1944 Michael overthrew Antonescu. And finally, in 1947, Michael abdicated and Romania became a Communist republic.

There is one theme, however, that runs through Romania's history between the two world wars: the power and terror of the Iron Guard. Originally called the Legion of the Archangel Michael, it was a viciously anti-Semitic, nationalistic, antidemocratic fascist group which first appeared on the scene in 1924 and dominated Romanian politics for nearly twenty years. It was organized like an army and operated through terrorism, assassinating more moderate politicians.

The Guard had strong supporters among students and intellectuals. It appealed to the peasants with the slogan, "One man, one acre," and by promising to clean up political corruption. Like Nazi Germany's storm troopers, its members marched through Romanian cities wearing green military shirts with little bags of Romanian soil around their necks, denouncing all that was foreign, especially the Jews.

Antonescu was their man, and it was with the Iron Guard's help that he seized power as dictator in 1940. It was Antonescu who allied Romania with Hitler's Germany and joined the Germans in the invasion of the Soviet Union. The immediate aim was to reconquer Bessarabia and the Bukovina region which Romania had ceded to the Russians under the terms of the Hitler-Stalin Pact a year earlier. But the Germans demanded full support and Romanian divisions were soon deep in the heart of Russia. When the tide turned against Hitler at Stalingrad, they also found themselves on the long, painful and costly retreat.

In August 1944 the Soviet army crossed into Romania; King Michael overthrew Antonescu, surrendered his country to the Russians, and put Romania into the Allied camp. By then it had suffered a million casualties.

Those Romanians who hoped that the end of the Antonescu regime and the end of the war might also mean an end to totalitarian rule were sadly mistaken, however. The Communist regime that the Soviets imposed became the most repressive in all of Eastern Europe.

Bulgaria sided with Germany and Austria-Hungary during World War I and was treated as an enemy country by the Allies, although not harshly. It lost some territory to Romania, its outlet to the Aegean Sea to Greece, and Macedonia to Yugoslavia. Ferdinand, the German prince who had proclaimed himself king and czar in 1908, fled back to his native Germany and his son, Boris III, was crowned.

Boris ruled continuously for twenty-five years, until his death in 1943. He exercised power originally through a series of military strongmen, and in 1935 became the absolute dictator himself. Under his rule Bulgaria remained a darkly backward country with not even a pretense of democracy.

Boris saw in World War II an opportunity to recapture some of the territory Bulgaria had originally gained through the 1878 Treaty of San Stefano. With Hitler's agreement he seized a chunk of Romania, then joined the Germans in their invasion of Greece and Yugoslavia with his sights set on Thrace and Macedonia. He declared war on Great Britain and the United States, but, oddly, not on Bulgaria's Slavic cousins, the Russians. His aim, a shrewd one, was apparently to get the most out of the war with a minimum of Bulgarian involvement. His refusal to meet Hitler's demands to also move against the Russians is believed to have had something to do with his rather mysterious death, possibly at the hands of the Gestapo.

Boris's six-year-old son Simeon was crowned in 1943, but it was a short-lived reign under a regent. In 1944 the Soviet Union declared war on Bulgaria and invaded by way of Romania. Anti-German opposition forces, including the Communists, the Democratic Agrarian party, and partisan fighters against the German troops stationed in Bulgaria, seized power in September. They arranged an armistice with the Soviets.

For a little more than a year there was a coalition government of democratic parties and the Communists, but in 1946 the monarchy was abolished, young Simeon sent into exile, and Bulgaria became a Communist "people's republic."

To say, as Winston Churchill did in 1946, that the East European countries had fallen behind an iron curtain, or to imply, as the U.S. Congress did in 1959, that they are "captive," would mean that they were free and democratic states before they became Communist.

Certainly they were free in the sense that from 1918 on they were no longer just territories or districts or provinces of some other powerful state: Russia, Turkey, Austria, or Germany. But that has been true since the end of World War II as well. They are independent. Some are limited more, some less in that independence by the Soviet Union's interests and demands. But that is no different from the 1920's and 1930's when their security and freedom, even the integrity of their borders, depended on the whims and wishes of other more powerful states: Germany, Great Britain, France, and Russia.

And with the exception of Czechoslovakia, democracy in

all of them was just a dream—as much then as it is now.

Had Hitler not gone to war with the entire world, the Soviet army, bringing ideology and politics with it, would never have entered Eastern Europe to drive the Germans back and perhaps these countries would not be Communist today.

On the other hand, if one looks at developments before all that happened, it is hard to imagine that under such leaders as Antonescu, Horthy, Boris III, or the Polish colonels, the East European countries would ever have become democracies.

In fact, it was under such regimes that the seeds of Communism were sown. Soviet bayonets can be compared to a plow that turned the soil, but that soil was already fertile, thanks to centuries of oppression.

6

Revolutions That Weren't

Covering the Communist countries has never rated as one of the glamor assignments of journalism.

One has to deal with a lot of unsafe airplanes, dirty trains, pot-holed highways, shabby hotel rooms, bad food, red tape, unreliable sources of information, and haughty government officials, in a world where Western correspondents are looked upon with suspicion, are shadowed by the secret police, and are forced to chase after nonnews with the risk of being tossed out of the country when they get it.

But there's one important compensation: the ability of the East European peoples to laugh at themselves and their leaders in the political jokes they tell.

Two of those I've heard tell a great deal about Communism and how it came to power in Eastern Europe.

In one, a couple of Romanian friends who haven't seen

each other for a number of years happen to meet on Bucharest's Magheru Boulevard. They head for one of the crowded sidewalk cafés there to talk and take stock of the political and economic situation.

"Say," asks one, "you know your history. That fellow Marx, the one with the big bushy beard, wasn't he called Doctor Marx?"

"Oh yes, he had a doctorate, all right."

"And that friend of his, the other one, Engels. Didn't people call him 'Doctor,' too?"

"Yes, certainly. He had a Ph.D."

"And Lenin, the Russian one with the pointed beard and the bald dome. Was he a doctor also?"

"I think so. I know he was studying law."

"Unbelievable! I always thought doctors experimented only on animals, but those guys were using human beings."

And then there's the one about the instructor teaching a course in "Marxism-Leninism" in a Warsaw high school who is asked by one of the students to explain the real difference between capitalism and Communism.

"Oh, that's very easy to explain because there's such a great difference," says the teacher. "You see, under capitalism there is terrible exploitation of man by man. But under Communism it is just the opposite."

Considering the experimentation and exploitation, it's a good thing the East Europeans can still laugh. Or maybe that's why they do. On one recent trip to Hungary when I didn't pick up a single new joke, I complained about it to a Hungarian friend in Budapest.

"It's just that there's nothing to laugh about these days," he explained, looking a little sad.

"Oh come, come," I said. "Certainly things were a lot worse before than they are now."

"That's the whole trouble," he replied with an absolutely

straight face. "They've gotten much, much better. So why joke about them?"

Things *have* gotten *very* much better, especially when one looks back to the early postwar days of Communism when Josef Stalin was still alive and the Soviets were using Moscow-trained East European Communists as well as their own people to model the five countries after the USSR and to run them almost like colonies.

Official East European propaganda describes that period and the Communist party takeovers as "revolutions."

They were anything but that, if by "revolution" we mean a mass uprising, with widespread popular support and approval, against cruel, powerful rulers or an unfair system, as for example in the American colonies in 1776 or France in 1789.

These takeovers were political power plays, in more or less democratic disguise. The technique varied from country to country. There are many ways to do something like that, even to make it look democratic on the surface. For examples one can look at non-Communist dictatorships around the world—in South America, in Asia, or Africa. Even Hitler was democratically elected in 1933 and then used legal, constitutional "emergency powers" to do away with constitutional rights and guarantees. In some countries of Eastern Europe it took only a few weeks or months to establish totalitarian rule; in others, a few years.

But nowhere was there a "revolution" like the one Lenin had staged in Russia in November 1917, which wasn't a real revolution either. All Lenin did was to overthrow the non-Communist revolutionary government that had overthrown czarist rule eight months earlier.

Nonetheless, even the Communist takeovers in Eastern Europe might have had more popular support and been less grim had they been staged primarily by "home," or "national," Communists, as they are sometimes called, instead of those trained in Moscow and beholden to Stalin who came in with the Soviet army.

The "home" Communists were those who had stayed in their countries during the years of dictatorship and German occupation, imprisoned or working underground if their party was outlawed. Many had been in Nazi concentration camps and many had fought in or organized anti-German resistance and partisan warfare groups where Communists and anti-Communists were comrades-in-arms against a common enemy. They had suffered. They were heroes, closer to the masses, had some idea of people's postwar hopes, and enjoyed quite a bit of local popularity.

The "Moscow" Communists, on the other hand, were those East Europeans who as professional party organizers and agents of the Comintern, the Communist International, had gone to the Soviet Union in the 1920's or had fled there in the 1930's to escape the police. They had somehow survived Stalin's Great Terror and purge of his own party as well as the international Communist movement, usually by keeping a very low profile at a time when anyone whose head stuck up too far politically had it chopped off. Some had stayed alive by betraying their comrades to Stalin's secret police in order to save themselves. All had lived in reasonable comfort in the "Comintern hotel," the Lux, on Moscow's Gorky Street, had become far removed from the problems and hopes of their own countries, and had become willing tools of Stalin and the Kremlin.

The political conflict and power struggle between those two groups had a great deal to do with what happened in Eastern Europe after 1945.

They were behind terrible purges of the East European Communist parties in the early 1950's and the scandalous show trials, executions, and imprisonments of "home" Communists that accompanied them. Two of the leading Communist party chiefs now in power in Eastern Europe—Hungary's Janos Kadar and Czechoslovakia's President Gustav Husak—were victims of those purges. Both were cruelly tortured by their own "Moscow" comrades, forced to confess "crimes" they had never committed, then imprisoned. The same thing happened to Wladyslaw Gomulka, Poland's Party chief from 1956 to 1970.

The conflict between "Moscow" and "national" Communists also was the backdrop to some of the rebellions and similar troubles that have shaken Eastern Europe since Stalin's death in 1953: the Polish uprising of 1956 which brought Gomulka to power, the Hungarian revolution of the same year which ended with Kadar as Party chief, and, in a sense, even the "Prague Spring" of 1968 which ended so sadly with the Soviet invasion and occupation.

And where any of the old "Moscow" Communists are still alive and in a position of power or influence today, the conflict is still going on.

What were Stalin's and the Kremlin's aims which those "Moscow" Communists were so willing to serve?

They are, first of all, still the aims of the Kremlin. Understanding them is absolutely vital to understanding not only what has gone on and still goes on in the East European countries but in the whole world Communist movement. Resistance to those aims is what led to the break between Yugoslavia's President Josip Broz Tito and Stalin in 1948 and that country's "excommunication" from the Soviet bloc, to the great rift between the Soviet Union and Communist China, to Moscow's break with Albania, and to the invasion of Czechoslovakia in 1968. It is also the main issue in the present conflict between the Soviet Union and the more liberal and democratic-minded "Eurocommunist" parties of Italy, Spain, France, and some of the other Western European countries.

Some people say that those Kremlin aims are, short and simply, world revolution. That is a great mistake. As far as the Soviet Union is concerned, "world revolution" is a dead issue; it has not been Moscow's goal since the mid-1920's. After Lenin's death in 1924, Stalin's greatest rival for power, Leon Trotsky, wanted to struggle for worldwide Communist revolution. Stalin's slogan and aim was to "build Communism in one country"—Soviet Russia. Trotsky lost the power struggle and went into exile in 1929. Stalin won, and the policy has remained the Kremlin's through his two successors, Nikita Khrushchev and Leonid Brezhnev.

But to "build Communism" in the Soviet Union, which was and is a policy amounting to "making Russia strong," Stalin, Khrushchev, and Brezhnev tried to get all the help possible, especially that of the world's other Communist parties.

Very early in the game Stalin began using those parties and the world movement as instruments and tools. He turned the Communist International, the Comintern (later renamed the Communist Information Bureau, or Cominform) from an organization of independent and equal Communist parties around the world into nothing more than a mouthpiece for Moscow.

Back in 1919 when it was founded and "world revolution" was really still the basic aim, the Comintern was described as "a single Communist party having equal branches in different countries." By the time the Comintern held its Sixth Congress in 1928, the Soviet Party completely dominated all the others.

"No matter how strong the individual local leaders might be," Manuél Gomez, a Mexican delegate to that meeting, wrote, "they knew they had no chance if the Russian party was against them."

And things got worse over the years.

Photograph taken in the 1930s shows Russian dictator Josef Stalin with his successor Nikita Khrushchev.

This "Russia First" policy also required creating many myths and fictions which are maintained to the present day.

One of them is that the Soviet Union is a "model" for Communism which all others must follow. Another is that the way Russia became Communist is the "right method" which all others must practice.

Another myth is that whoever rules in the Kremlin is as infallible as the pope in Rome, and his directives for Russia are supposed to apply to all Communist parties, whether they make sense or not.

If it is the fashion in Moscow to build big steel plants and dams, or manufacture huge tractors, then everybody in the Communist camp is supposed to do the same, even if they have no iron ore and no rivers to dam, or if small and medium-size tractors would be a lot better for local conditions. If running the whole economy through a top-heavy, centralized bureaucracy or creating vast collective farms with twenty thousand workers is right for the Soviet Union, then it should be right for little Hungary or Czechoslovakia where such methods will never work. The same goes for political administration, education, culture, science, and Communist ideology.

Since Moscow is supposed to be always right, the current "party line" there, whatever it may be, is law.

That attitude caused much misery for the Communists of Eastern Europe in 1939, for example, when, after having waged a years-long propaganda war against him, Stalin suddenly made his pact with Hitler. The pact bought Russia more time to prepare for the invasion that was to come. But in practice it meant that hundreds of leading German, Czechoslovak, Bulgarian, Romanian, and Polish Communists who had fled the Nazis or their own fascist governments for safety in Russia, were actually rounded up by Stalin's police and shipped back home—to prisons and concentration camps.

The Comintern officials and East European Communists in

Moscow who escaped that sudden betrayal were the ones Stalin wanted and needed. They were, for the most part, human puppets. They followed the Party line obediently by switching overnight from being anti-Nazis to pro-Nazis, then back again when the Nazis invaded Russia. They had no hopes or desires of someday leading home grown, popular, "national" Communist revolutions in their own countries. And it was with these obedient servants that the Soviet Army brought Communism to Eastern Europe.

It did so not because Stalin wanted to make the world "safe for Communism," but to make it "safer for Russia," which had, after all, been invaded three times from the west in less than half a century.

Certainly he did so under the banner of Communism. Like czarist Russia before it, the Soviet Union was and is an imperialist power, eager to extend its might and influence. And like many big empires in the past, it uses an ideology or faith as an instrument. What Catholicism was for the medieval Germans' Holy Roman Empire, Eastern Orthodoxy for the Byzantine emperors, or Islam for the Ottoman Turkish sultans, Communism became for the Soviet Union after World War II—a pretext and a useful tool.

Turning the East European countries into satellites with the help of the Soviet army and Moscow-trained Communists had a double purpose.

First, Stalin wanted and needed a "buffer" zone of countries, loyal to and dependent on Moscow, that would help protect Russia from future invasion. Making them Communist was obviously the best way.

Second, since all those countries had been, at one time or another, Russia's enemies, he wanted to make sure they would stay friendly. So their Communism had to be Soviet style. He feared the local, homegrown, "national" version of Communism which someday in the future might become a source of trouble for Moscow. For example, Poles under *their* banner of Communism might someday march into Lithuania, Byelorussia, and the Ukraine, or Romanian Communists could make claims on the Bukovina and the Bessarabian part of Moldavia.

An unfounded fear? Not really, when you remember that Polish "home" Communists in 1945 demanded not only the prewar borders that had been gained by Pilsudski in 1920, but those of 1772, or when you take a look at the current trouble between the Soviet Union and Romania over Moldavia.

For Stalin at the time, his policy must have seemed in Russia's best interests, but it proved to be short-sighted and was certainly a mistake, if friends, not just satellites, were what the Soviet Union wanted. Sooner or later, the "Moscow" men and women were bound to disappear. Now the "home" Communists and a second generation of leaders are in power almost everywhere. The most important thing to know about them is that they are Poles, Czechs, Slovaks, Magyars, Romanians, and Bulgarians first, and Communists second.

And for the peoples of Eastern Europe, many of whom welcomed the Soviet army as "liberators," Stalin's policy became a tragedy, just as it did for the "home" Communists who came out of the prisons, the concentration camps, or the mountain guerrilla hideouts with great dreams and hopes of a better future.

The roots of Communism in Eastern Europe reach as far back as they do in Western Europe—the late nineteenth and early twentieth centuries—when the ideas of Marx, Engels, and other Socialists began spreading and winning support: faster in the areas under German and Austro-Hungarian control, somewhat later in those dominated by Russia and Turkey.

Neither Lenin's older brother Sasha nor Poland's Jozef

Pilsudski considered himself a Marxist or Socialist when they attempted to assassinate Czar Alexander III in 1887. They were revolutionaries for the sake of revolution who wanted to overthrow a cruel system, but they had no system or program to put in its place had their plot succeeded. Lenin himself was only seventeen years old at the time and in his later writings, when he called himself a "scientific socialist," he criticized his brother for this lack of plan.

One thing did make the East European Socialists different from those in Western Europe: since their areas and countries were under foreign domination, they were very much caught up in ideas of national liberation and independence. Pilsudski, who turned away from Socialism in 1900, is the best example.

The rift in Socialism which led to the birth of Communism during World War I was started by none other than Lenin.

Marxist Socialism came to Russia itself in an organized form in 1898 when the Russian Social Democratic Labor party was founded secretly in the city of Minsk. One of its original leaders, though he was in Siberian exile at the time, was Lenin. By 1903 he had succeeded in splitting the new party into two factions, the *menshevik*, meaning "minority," and the *bolshevik*, or "majority," of which he was the leader. The basic differences at the time were tactical and strategic.

The Mensheviks wanted a loosely organized "mass" party, the Bolsheviks a small, disciplined one made up of professional revolutionaries. The Mensheviks also argued that because of its backwardness, Russia was not ready for a proletarian society of the type Marx had envisioned. They favored a period of interim rule by the *bourgeoisie,* as in Western Europe. The Bolsheviks, on the other hand, believed that Russia should go directly from feudal to proletarian rule, not only by workers but also by peasants, thus skipping the bourgeois, capitalist period of its historical development.

In 1912 the two factions finally split into separate parties with the Bolsheviks, under Lenin, soon calling themselves Communists. During World War I the differences between them and other arguments—for example, whether to support the war effort or not—led to similar splits in the Socialist parties of Western and Eastern Europe and the rise of the Communist movement, especially after Lenin's Bolshevik Revolution in Russia in 1917. By the end of the war Hungary's Party was already strong enough for Bela Kun to stage his own Bolshevik-style revolution. The split between Communism and Socialism became ever deeper, so that today Europe's Socialists, such as Britain's Labor party and West Germany's Social Democrats, are among the most outspoken anti-Communists in the world.

The experience and fate of the Communists in the new East European countries differed greatly between the two world wars.

Only Czechoslovakia's Communist party was legal, and though sometimes restricted in its activities, it became quite strong, gaining considerable practical political experience and popular support.

The parties in the other countries were banned most of the time, with leaders often in exile or in prison and working underground. Yet their track records are different.

In Romania the Communists were a tiny group and had almost no support. In Hungary what attraction they might have had was weakened by the reign of Bela Kun's Red Terror. In Bulgaria, although the Party was illegal during most of the period, it enjoyed peasant support and became a voice for peasant discontent. The Polish Communist party originally had some success among the ethnic minorities, but fell afoul of the Comintern in 1938, was dissolved, and many of its leaders were murdered in Stalin's purges. What remained of it was destroyed by Hitler, with most of the surviving leaders escaping to Moscow, where their fate often was also death.

The first East European country to become Communist after the war was Bulgaria. It had been at war with the Soviet Union only a few hours when the pro-German regime was overthrown by a coalition calling itself the Fatherland Front which was made up of Communists, members of the Democratic Agrarian party, and anti-German partisan fighters. In that first government the Communists had only two cabinet posts: the ministry of justice, which controlled the courts, and the ministry of interior, which ran the police.

The Communists had everything going for them, and not just because they had their hands on those two important levers of power. It was the oldest Communist party in the Balkans. Its founder, Dimitar Blagoev, was honored internationally as one of the organizers of the first Marxist circles in Russia itself when he was a student at the University of St. Petersburg in the 1880's. And it boasted an internationally famous figure as its leader, Georgi Dimitrov.

A revolutionary since boyhood, Dimitrov had been in exile in Berlin in 1933 when the Nazis came to power and soon after set fire to the Reichstag, the parliament building. Dimitrov, though he had nothing to do with that crime, was accused of it and arrested. His cool conduct of his own defense and the accusations he made against the Nazi prosecutors during the trial won him world renown. He was acquitted, went to the Soviet Union, became a Soviet citizen, and, from 1934 until 1943, when it was disbanded and renamed the Cominform, he was secretary-general of the Comintern. The most remarkable thing about him was that he was almost the only prominent "Moscow" Communist who not only managed to keep a high profile when low ones were the key to survival, but at heart he remained a "home" Communist—a Bulgarian first.

To many Bulgarians, especially the young and the underprivileged of all ages, the Communist party looked like the main hope for a better future. It also benefited from the pro-Russian feelings of the Bulgarian people. There were many who were not Communists but who were not anti-Communists either, who were ready to serve a Communist regime. They were soon to be disillusioned.

Violence and terror were nothing new to Bulgaria, a land where sooner or later old scores were always settled. But there had never been anything like what followed. With the Communists, backed by the Soviet army, in control of the police and the courts, thousands of real and imagined enemies of the new order were arrested, then executed or imprisoned. Among them, of course, were all the leaders of the prewar and wartime fascist government, but also many democratic politicians as well as innocent ordinary citizens who simply got in the way of the machinery. Bulgaria's Communists hold the record for making the bloodiest beginning of all the new regimes in Eastern Europe. And it was taking place when, in name at least, Bulgaria was still a monarchy and the Communists were not yet in full power.

That was to change soon after Dimitrov's arrival from Moscow in 1945. After a plebiscite held in 1946, King Simeon, then aged nine, was deposed; Bulgaria became a "people's republic," with Dimitrov as premier. Although elections were all rigged, there was still some democratic opposition. Continuing terror stamped out the last of it in 1947. All industry was nationalized and agriculture collectivized. In 1948 a new constitution, modeled exactly on that of the Soviet Union, was adopted.

Dimitrov, who meanwhile had fallen out of favor with Stalin, died in 1949. Factional battles, accompanied by purges and executions of "home" Communists, followed his death. In 1954 a relatively young man, Todor Zhivkov, became head of the party, then premier, and later Bulgaria's president. He still rules the country with an iron hand today.

The pattern for takeover in Romania was only slightly different. Though it took a little longer to set up total Communist control, at least Romania's "home" Communists could claim that they were the first to grab power from those who had been trained in Moscow.

Following the Soviet invasion and the overthrow of Antonescu's Iron Guard fascist regime by King Michael in August 1944, the country was at first under a mixture of Soviet military and Romanian army administration. Many fascists and pro-Germans were still around and there was total disorder. In February 1945 Andrei Vishinsky, the Soviet deputy foreign minister, arrived and ordered the king to set up a "national democratic front" government, led by the Communist party but including the Social Democrats and a number of left-wing and liberal parties. Petru Groza, a non-Communist, was named premier, though Communists held the vital ministries of justice and interior.

For nearly three years Romania was in a state of limbo. There were rigged elections which gave the Communists more and more power. There was violence, police terror, and political murder. Opposition parties were sometimes legal and sometimes illegal. And there were many protests by the Western Allies about what the Soviets were doing. Yet, all along Romania remained a monarchy with the king on the throne. Finally, in November 1947 Michael was forced to abdicate by a parliament already completely dominated by the Communists; in early 1948 Romania became a "people's republic."

During those early years the Communist party itself was a faction-torn organization. Its nominal leader was Gheorghe Gheorghiu-Dej who had joined the illegal party as a young

man in 1930 and had played a key role in a brutally suppressed railroad workers' strike in 1933. Along with other
strike leaders, nearly all of them underground Communists,
he had been imprisoned until escaping in 1944, shortly before
the fall of the Antonescu regime. But real power was held by
two sinister figures who had spent many years in Moscow
exile and returned with the Soviet army—Anna Pauker and
Vasile Luca.

Both were purged by Gheorghiu-Dej's "home" faction in
1952, and he later claimed that Romania had been the first
country "to de-Stalinize its party while Stalin was still alive."
Gheorghiu-Dej remained Romania's ruler until his death in
1965. His successor, Nicolae Ceausescu, has been in charge
since then.

In Hungary the Communist struggle for power took even
longer, and for a number of years there was a good chance
that it might fail. This may have been because of the strong
anti-Russian feelings of the Hungarians and their unpleasant
memories of the 1919 Bela Kun regime, or it may have been
that the Communists themselves, under Moscow-trained
Matyas Rakosi, were treading lightly.

In the fall of 1944 the fascist pro-German government fled,
and although a provisional government, set up in December,
signed an armistice, the Nazi Wehrmacht units stationed in
Hungary continued to put up stiff resistance, with the result
that the country suffered widespread devastation.

Though it was being run by the provisional government,
as an enemy country Hungary was under Soviet military
occupation.

In the first free election, held in November 1945, the
Communists, who enjoyed Soviet backing, did very badly.
They won only seventeen percent of the votes, as did the
Socialists. The left-wing National Peasants' partly obtained
only seven percent. But the middle-of-the-road Small Farm-

ers' party got an absolute majority—fifty-seven percent. Technically that would have been enough to form a single-party government, but the Soviet authorities demanded that the government be a coalition, with the other three major parties included. The Small Farmers' leader, Ferenc Nagy, became prime minister, while a Communist, Imre Nagy, became minister of the interior.

For the next eighteen months the chief aim of the Communists and their Soviet backers was to break the Small Farmers' party. A coalition of left-wing parties—Communists, Socialists, and National Peasants—was formed. In the summer of 1947, using trumped-up charges involving the murder of two Soviet soldiers, the Communists forced Ferenc Nagy to resign. In the following period of confusion they changed the electoral law, then called for a new election in August 1947.

In that election the leftist bloc got a sixty percent majority, though the Communists themselves still polled only twenty-two percent. In comparison with the November 1945 election it was a fraud. Communist agents rushed about the country in Soviet army jeeps and trucks voting several times in different places, and ballot boxes were tampered with. But compared to those being held in some other East European countries, it was still a free election. Hungary, it seemed, was going to hold out.

And, in a way, it did—until the end of 1948. By then the Communists had forced the Socialists to join them in a new Hungarian Workers' party and had either subverted the other democratic parties with their own agents or simply destroyed them. In April 1949 the leftist "majority" dissolved parliament and Hungary got a new Soviet-style constitution. The takeover was complete.

In the Communist party itself things were not going so smoothly as tension mounted between "Moscow" and "home"

Communists. As Rakosi and the Stalinists consolidated their power, there were frightful purges with "show trials," executions, and imprisonments. Among the victims were Imre Nagy and Janos Kadar, who had been minister of interior from 1948 to 1950. In the summer of 1956, however, the pendulum swung. Rakosi himself was deposed, Nagy became prime minister and Kadar one of the Party leaders. The upheaval triggered the bloody Hungarian Revolution that fall which was crushed by Soviet tanks. Nagy did not survive those events, but Kadar, who became Party chief, did. He eventually put the country on the road to recovery, to healing its political wounds, and is still in command.

The situation in Poland was complicated by a number of factors.

First of all, the Polish Communist party itself, illegal at home, had been disbanded on orders of the Comintern in 1938 because Stalin didn't like its leaders and their attitudes. Most of them were liquidated. It was not until 1942 that it began to reorganize itself secretly as the Polish Workers' Party in German-occupied Poland. This was done without Moscow's blessing. Wladyslaw Gomulka was one of the key figures.

The Poles hated the Russians, and the Russians hated the Poles. While the Russians had occupied eastern Poland from 1939 to 1941 they murdered more than ten thousand Polish army officers, burying them in a mass grave at Katyn.

There were Polish forces that had escaped in 1939 and were fighting heroically with the Western Allies in Italy and France. There were also Polish forces that had been rearmed by the Russians after 1941 who were fighting with the Soviet army. There was an underground Polish Home Army that was anti-Communist, and a force of pro-Communist partisans. In 1944 when the Home Army staged an uprising in

Warsaw, trying to liberate the city from the Germans, the Soviets, who were already on the outskirts, didn't lift a finger to help. Instead they watched for a month as the Nazis crushed the Home Army in bitter street fighting.

There was an official Polish government-in-exile in London, recognized by the Western Allies but not by the Soviet Union. It had broken diplomatic ties with Moscow in 1943 after discovery of the mass grave of Polish officers at Katyn. Its prime minister was Stanislaw Mikolajczyk, the leader of the Polish Peasant party.

But there was also a group in the liberated city of Lublin in eastern Poland called the Lublin Committee. It had been set up by the Soviets in 1944 with Moscow-trained Communist stooges, notably Boleslaw Bierut, and was soon joined by some of the "home" Communists, including *their* leader, Gomulka. The Soviets insisted that this was the legal provisional government of Poland. Being on the scene, it could exercise power and gain control step by step as the Nazis retreated.

At the Yalta Conference in February 1945 Stalin, Churchill, and Roosevelt agreed to broaden this Lublin government by adding some of the London exiles, especially Mikolajczyk, to it, and six months later it was recognized as Poland's provisional government. Though a number of non-Communist parties, including the Socialists, were in it, the Communists held the most powerful posts and controlled the country. Mikolajczyk was the only effective opposition, and by 1947 he had been forced to flee to the West.

Those two years were anything but easy sailing for the Communists, however. First of all, there was armed underground resistance against their rule which at times was so strong and effective that Poland was practically in a civil war. Then there was also the takeover of the Socialist party by the Communists. The two parties were joined into the Polish United Workers' party—its name to this day—with the Socialists eventually losing all identity.

But the most important event was the three-year-long struggle between Gomulka and his "home" Communists and Bierut's "Moscow" men. Gomulka's aim, as he put it in a 1948 speech, was a "Polish road to socialism based on the historic traditions of the Polish workers' movement." To Moscow and the Kremlin that was heresy, and a few weeks after making the speech Gomulka was deposed as first secretary of the party. Bierut took his place. Soviet control of Poland was well on the way. It was completed in 1949 when Marshal Konstantin Rokossovski, a *Russian* general, was named Polish defense minister. Gomulka himself was imprisoned in 1951 and not released until 1955.

Bierut died in the spring of 1956, his death touching off riots and disturbances all over the country that looked like the start of an anti-Communist revolution. Gomulka returned from private life and again became the Party's leader.

The Russians were surprised that he was even still alive, believing he had been quietly "eliminated" while in jail. But Poles have never done things that way. Nor was there anything the Soviets could do, or indeed wanted to do. It was a different era. Stalin had been dead more than three years, and the terrible crimes he had committed had been exposed in February of that year by none less than Nikita Khrushchev himself. Eastern Europe was being swept by a new spirit of liberalization—a "thaw"—and Gomulka, the only Communist who enjoyed some popularity, was the only man who in the hectic weeks of October 1956 even stood a chance of pulling Poland back from the kind of bloody revolution that was soon to sweep over Hungary. His return to power did just that.

Gomulka remained as Polish Party chief for fourteen years

until December 1970, when new unrest—workers' strikes over his plans to raise prices and lower wages—forced his resignation. He was succeeded by Edward Gierek.

What happened in Czechoslovakia after the war is the most ironic, and in a sense the saddest, story.

First of all, Prague itself could have been liberated in May 1945 by the Americans and not the Russians had President Harry S. Truman not ordered Patton to hold back the U.S. Third Army.

One joke about this, often heard in Czechoslovakia, tells of a grade school civics class in which the teacher asks little František, "Tell us why we love the Soviet Union." František says, "Because it liberated us." The teacher nods, then asks, "And do you know why we hate Americans?" Hesitantly František replies, "Is that because they didn't liberate us?"

But the irony of the situation is that the Russians did not stay in Czechoslovakia and that the Czechoslovak Communist party came to power in 1948 on its own. It installed itself by means of a brilliant takeover, supported by a strong minority of the population.

The Party's history was also different. Unlike those of the other East European countries, it had operated freely in a democratic situation, had strong voter backing, and knew all the democratic ground rules.

To be sure, during the war, especially the last year when Communists played a leading role in the Slovak uprising against the Nazi puppet regime, the Soviet Union took a strong interest in what would happen after liberation. Eduard Beneš, the exile president in London, and his foreign minister, Tomas Masaryk's son Jan, flew to Moscow for talks in the fall of 1944. There were no great problems and no reasons why there should be. After all, the Russians had offered their help in 1938 and would have forced Hitler to a showdown had the British and French not caved in. But the Soviets did insist that any postwar government would have to be one of "national unity" including the Communist party, then led by Klement Gottwald. Beneš and Masaryk agreed.

That first provisional government, established in 1945, included all parties. Beneš was confirmed as president. The cabinet of twenty ministers included only seven Communists. But they were like a Trojan horse. The prime minister was a Socialist who soon turned out to be a Communist stooge. Of the four deputy prime ministers, two were Communists. Gottwald was one of them. In addition the Communists had the ministries of interior, education, information and culture, agriculture, and social welfare—all key posts for exercising power and dispensing patronage.

In the first election in May 1946—as free and democratic as any in a Western country—the Communists became the strongest party by far, winning thirty-eight percent, more than double the votes obtained by any other party. Gottwald moved up a notch and became prime minister.

From then on it was merely a question of when, not whether. Gottwald packed the police with Communists, kept the country in a state of crises, gained control of the radio and press, and dominated the trade unions. In early February 1948 armed Communist gangs began demonstrating in the streets demanding more nationalization of industry. And there was mounting trouble in Slovakia. The non-Communist ministers resigned, and, under pressure from Gottwald, who threatened to use paramilitary Communist "action committees" that had been formed all over the country, President Beneš appointed a new cabinet that gave the Communists complete control.

In May 1948 a new constitution, modeled on the Soviet Union's, was proclaimed. Parliament was dissolved and a new election held. It was a fraud, with no opposition candidates to a single "national unity" ticket. Beneš resigned in

June and Gottwald replaced him as president. Though a few trappings of democracy remained, Czechoslovakia in practice was in as tight a Communist vise as any of its East European neighbors.

Shortly before he died in September 1948, Beneš told a friend that it had been like "Munich all over again."

The real tragedy is that if the Communists had waited they might have made it legally, for time was on their side. But in staging a coup, they destroyed much, though twenty more years were to pass before anyone realized how much. They destroyed their own public support, the traditional friendship between the Russian and Czechoslovak peoples, and to an extent their own country.

Unlike every other East European Communist party, Gottwald's took over a country that was very much a paying proposition. Czechoslovakia had an advanced industrial economy which had suffered little damage during the war and was in fine working order. But his was a totally Stalinist party which ruined that economy with Stalinist methods. The Party's leadership, even after Gottwald's death in 1953 and his replacement by Antonin Novotny, was so Stalinist that it was unaffected by the "thaw" of de-Stalinization in the 1950's and 1960's.

The mismanagement and neglect of Czechoslovakia's economy and the pent-up hopes of Czechs and Slovaks for a better life and more freedom were what finally led to the fall of Novotny as Party chief in January 1968 and his replacement by Alexander Dubcek. Dubcek and the men who surrounded him were reformers whose goal was a liberal, efficient, more democratic "Communism with a human face." But they came to power too late. The promises and hopes denied for twenty years had created a situation they could not handle. To meet the long-denied demands and desires of his people, Dubcek simply had to move faster than the conservative rulers of the Kremlin could permit. That is why they sent their tanks to crush his experiment eight months after it had begun.

I was in Czechoslovakia during part of that time and could feel the new spirit, and I saw how genuinely popular Dubcek and his "home" Communists were.

The irony and the tragedy of Czechoslovakia—and with it the rest of Eastern Europe—is this: Twenty years after Communism had come to power there without Soviet military help, Soviet troops were sent to destroy the only Communism that, brief as it was, ever really enjoyed widespread majority support anywhere. In doing so, the Russians not only made bitter enemies of the best friends they ever had, but unmasked themselves. Today, more than ten years after that invasion, Czechoslovakia is still the saddest country in Eastern Europe.

7

Jackets Versus Straitjackets

The countries of Eastern Europe are called "people's democracies."

It is an odd term, considering that power in any democracy is supposed to come from the people, or, as Thomas Jefferson tried to explain it in the Declaration of Independence, governments derive their powers from the governed.

What then is the difference between an "ordinary" and a "people's" democracy?

"Not much, comrade": so goes a joke that can be heard all over Eastern Europe. "The difference is about the same as that between an ordinary jacket and a straitjacket."

On paper, of course, all the East European countries are democratic.

That is, they all have constitutions that guarantee freedom of speech and the press, freedom of conscience and religious worship, freedom of assembly and freedom of street demonstration. Most of the constitutions actually go much further than that of the United States because they guarantee citizens the "right to work and employment," "the right to support in old age and in the case of illness or disability," and "the right to rest and leisure." They also provide for equality between men and women, have clauses against racial, ethnic, and religious discrimination, protect citizens against illegal arrest, guarantee public trials, protect against search and seizure, and protect the "privacy of correspondence."

Also, like most countries of Western Europe—for example Great Britain—the East European countries are parliamentary democracies. That is, the government, headed by a "prime minister," is elected by a parliament. The parliaments themselves, according to the five constitutions, are the highest organs of state power. Their members are elected "on the basis of universal, equal, and direct suffrage by secret ballot." All citizens who have reached the age of eighteen have the right to vote. In addition, like all other parliamentary democracies, they have "heads of state." In constitutional monarchies such as Great Britain, the Netherlands, Norway, or Denmark, the "head of state" is a king or queen. In republics such as West Germany, France, and the East European countries it is a president, although other titles are also used. Usually they are elected indirectly.

And yet, the East European countries are called undemocratic—even dictatorial and "captive" by some, and "authoritarian" by many. Well, they are and they aren't.

First of all, some of the countries are more democratic than others, and all five of them are *much* more democratic than the Soviet Union.

A widely told joke in the USSR describes how undemocratic and dictatorial that country is. Asked whether it is possible there to say openly and freely what one *really* thinks, a Communist party propaganda lecturer is said to have replied, "But of course, just as long as you don't *think* something you're not allowed to say openly and freely."

That joke is *not* told in Eastern Europe because it does not really apply. Granted, there are great differences from country to country, but in most of them people are much freer both to think and speak than they are in Russia.

I learned this in 1968 when, after having covered Eastern Europe for quite a while, I was assigned to Moscow.

I had good acquaintances and connections among East European journalists and government officials. They gave me the names of their colleagues in Moscow, suggesting that these would be useful people to help me get started on the new job in what we all knew was a difficult country to cover.

One of the first things I did after arriving in Moscow was to call up a certain East European journalist and invite him to lunch. He was, of course, a member of his country's Communist party, and a fairly high-ranking one at that.

We were still waiting for the first course to be served when he suddenly asked me, "Why did you invite me?" Before I could stutter a reply to that question, he answered it himself, saying, "Because you think that I, as a Communist and having been here for a number of years, can be a good source of information for you." I mumbled something like, "Well, if you want to put it that directly . . ." He was already going on and said: "You're wrong. I am a Communist, I do speak Russian fluently, and I have been here for quite a while. But I still don't know any more about what's really going on here than you do. I work under the same restrictions you do. This place is so undemocratic, so dictatorial, and so close-mouthed that I can get no information. I have to do the same thing you'll be doing—read *between* the lines of *Pravda* in the morning to figure out what's going on. In that I probably do have an advantage. Being a Communist reporter and knowing how those things are done, I can make out the invisible ink a little faster than you."

When I met him again a few years ago in his own country, he reminded *me* of that conversation and said, "Now here maybe I could help you, but you won't need my help because compared to the Soviet Union this is an open society." He is right.

But if so, why are people's democracies like his likened to straitjackets?

One reason is that the ground rules of democracy have all been broken at one time or another in all of the countries and the democratic guarantees have been violated and ignored. Since the guarantees haven't changed, it follows that they can be got around in the future. Everything depends on the people in charge, not the law.

Another factor is that there is no legal opposition in any of the countries and practically no choice of candidates for elective office, the number of candidates being almost the same as the number of posts to be filled.

Unlike the Soviet Union where there is only one political party—the Communist—most of the East European countries *do* permit other parties, but most of them have become puppets. At election time their candidates appear along with those of the Communist parties on a single "National" or "United Front" ticket. Since there is no other ticket of candidates, it always gets somewhere between 99.1 and 99.9 percent of the total vote. About the only way to show opposition is not to vote at all, which is hard to do. The Communist parties' control at the grass-roots level—in neighborhoods, apartment houses, and villages—is so great and well organized that people who refuse to go to the polls can be immediately spotted. They are forced. And if they still refuse, they soon suffer—at work, for example, or through their children at school.

Finally, real control and government powers are not exercised by the elected members of the parliament, and not even by the prime ministers and their cabinets, but by the Communist parties, which maintain elaborate structures that serve as parallels to the governments. At every level, the party exercises a watchdog function over the government.

Conditions vary greatly from country to country, but most of the parliaments meet for only a few days or weeks each year to rubber-stamp what the prime ministers and their cabinets have already done. What they do, in turn, is largely dictated to them by the ruling bodies of the Communist parties—their "central committees," which are something like party parliaments; their "politburos" and "secretariats," which are the real power centers and can be compared to party cabinets; above all by the "first" secretaries of each party who are the real rulers of each country.

Usually the top members of the government cabinets, and always the prime ministers, are also members of the politburos, and the most powerful politburo members are those who are also party secretaries. The secretariats are like invisible cabinets. They have departments responsible, for example, for foreign affairs, defense, police, industry, agriculture, education, and culture just like the various ministries of the cabinets.

In three of the countries—Bulgaria, Czechoslovakia, and Romania—the Communist "first" secretaries—Todor Zhivkov, Gustav Husak, and Nicolae Ceausescu—are also the heads of state or presidents. In the other two—Hungary and Poland—the party chiefs, Janos Kadar and Edward Gierek, have *no* high-ranking government or state posts at all.

Yet Kadar and Gierek are the men who actually run their countries and they are treated like heads of government or state by the prime ministers and presidents of all Western countries, including the United States. They get the same

*The Hungarian Parliament in session; Party leader
Janos Kadar is in the second row, far right.*

twenty-one-gun salutes, honor guards, and banquets that a visiting monarch, president, or prime minister would receive.

Does that mean they are dictators? No, and the fact is that of all five Communist bosses in Eastern Europe, Kadar and Gierek are the least dictatorial and the most genuinely popular.

Knowing Hungary and many people there well, I am convinced that Kadar is so popular he could win any office for which he chose to run by a solid majority if there were really free elections. Yet he became Hungary's Communist party chief and ruler without having to stand election by the people. They had no choice, and they will have no choice as to who succeeds Kadar. If the successor turns out to be highly unpopular, he still stays in office and in charge. The decision is up to that small circle of powerful men who are in the politburo and secretariat—fifteen including Kadar. He could be overthrown by a majority of the others, though that is not likely to be the case in Hungary. Were he to die suddenly, the fourteen other politburo members and secretaries would have to choose a successor among themselves—probably the man Kadar had picked as "second" secretary and as his "crown prince," although a hefty power struggle lasting months, even years, can never be ruled out.

Not even the Hungarian Party's central committee would have much say because it, too, is largely a rubber-stamp parliament which merely approves decisions already made at the top, though, according to the Party's by-laws, the central committee is supposed to be above the politburo and secretariat and elects their members.

The example of Hungary shows why "people's" democracies are not real democracies as we know them. On the other hand, they are not entirely the undemocratic, totalitarian states they are made out to be. Pressure from below—from the people or sometimes from within the Party—can bring about changes at the very top, in fact even get the government to change its policies. It happened on several occasions in Poland, once in Czechoslovakia, and once over a minor local issue in Bulgaria.

Poland's leadership has been changed twice since the Communist takeover—in 1956 and in 1970—by what can only be called popular demand. Wladyslaw Gomulka was swept back into power in the fall of 1956 following months of demonstrations and unrest by Polish workers, students, and lower-level Party people who were rebelling against the previous Stalinist regime. Gomulka was popular for a long time, but held back Poland's modernization and industrial development. In 1970 bloody workers' strikes and demonstrations in a number of key cities swept him out of office. The members of the politburo and secretariat deposed him in response to public pressure.

Gierek, who succeeded Gomulka, also had to bow to public pressure in June 1976 when unpopular price increases were announced and again touched off strikes and riots. The price hikes were repealed overnight. Later, when some of the strike and riot leaders were arrested by the police, leading Polish intellectuals, many of them Party members, formed an illegal Committee for the Defense of the Workers (KOR). By appealing to public opinion at home and abroad it exerted so much pressure that nearly all the strike leaders were released. Then when the government arrested some of KOR's leaders, there was just as loud an outcry and they were sprung from jail.

Antonin Novotny's fall in Czechoslovakia in 1968, and his replacement by Alexander Dubcek, also came through grassroots pressures. Among them were student demonstrations and growing unrest in the Communist party over restrictions on cultural freedom and the way Novotny's policies had brought the economy to a halt. It took weeks to get rid of him and it was done in as democratic a way as in any Western country. I was in Prague covering the story from October 1967 to early January 1968.

However, it was a change of rule within the Party over which the public at large—the governed, as Jefferson called them—had no say. After all, the ruling Communist party in whose central committee all this took place had only 1.3 million members—less than ten percent of Czechoslovakia's population. And the fact that Dubcek turned out to be such a democratic, genuinely popular reformer was accidental. He could just as well have been a tyrant.

That citizens of Communist countries can force their governments to repeal unpopular laws, at any rate on local issues, was shown in Bulgaria in the fall of 1977. The triumph of the governed over the governors was on the question of banning private cars from the center of Sofia, Bulgaria's capital.

During a large international athletic tournament, held in Sofia in August 1977, the city council banned private automobiles from almost the whole downtown area in order to move spectators and athletes to and from stadiums more easily. Exceptions to the rule were government and official cars, taxis, foreigners' vehicles, and those belonging to residents of the "off-limits area." Most Sofians accepted the regulation, but revolted when the city council decided to make the "temporary" ban permanent.

The debate, which lasted for two months, brought editors and nationally honored poets, environmental engineers and veteran Communist party members, politicians and ordinary citizens to the front—virtually all against their city leaders. Bozhidar Bozhilov, a well-known poet who also happens to be a leader of the Bulgarian Automobile Club, called the ban "undemocratic and un-Communist" because it didn't apply to all cars. Letters to the editors of Bulgaria's government and Party-controlled newspapers charged "discrimination against hundreds of thousands of people . . . and special privileges for 'the bosses.' " The editors of *Starshel,* the humor magazine, called the ban "anti-Bulgarian" because it did not apply to foreigners. Another paper said it was actually discriminatory and harmful to people living outside the downtown area because air pollution and noise in their neighborhoods had become worse.

After weeks of this the Sofia city council backed down, repealed the ban, and promised that in the future "traffic problems will be studied more carefully and public opinion will be requested."

People Power? What else could one call it, despite the fact that there are only 300,000 cars in that country of eight million people.

The existence of or rule by only one political party is often cited as major proof that the Communist countries are not democratic. To be sure, it is a factor even in those of the countries where other parties are allowed to continue, although as puppetlike organizations. But even a single-party system need not be undemocratic if the party itself is democratic. By and large, the Communist parties are not.

They practice what Lenin termed "democratic centralism." Although it calls for indirect election of the parties' top leaderships by a fairly broad grass-roots base of members, it allows those leaderships, once elected, to impose their will and decisions without question or challenge on all those below. The leaderships thus become self-perpetuating. They have the power to dictate to the rank and file who should be nominated and elected as leaders in all subsequent elections. The system operates at all levels, to the point where even the delegates to Party congresses are, in practice, not elected by the rank and file but are selected by the top—on the basis of loyalty to the leaders. The parties, in other words, are all centralized and not democratic at all, and they have made "democratic centralism" a doctrine that all members must accept.

In addition, the East European Communist parties, like the Soviet Union's, adhere to the principle of "dictatorship of the majority." There may be fairly free discussion of proposals, ideas, and plans before a vote is taken. But once a ballot has been cast, the minority must bow to the will of the majority and carry out its orders. No further discussion of the issues is permitted and would, in fact, be considered "anti-Party activity," a serious crime.

Each Communist party also considers itself to be the "party of the working class," that is the class that represents the majority. Moreover, according to Marxist theory, that class is "historically" destined and entitled to rule. Each party therefore regards itself as "the leading force" in society.

Thus, by its own interpretation, it has the moral and historic right—Communists even call it a duty—to impose its will on everyone and to "guide and control" all aspects of public life. That is why the Communist parties actually run the governments, and also why they do not permit real opposition parties. Their doctrine, moreover, forbids their being voted out of power once in, because that would be like "turning back the clock of history" and bowing to the will of the "minority."

Finally, the parties consider Communism to be "scientific" and therefore infallible. Each party regards itself as always right and all those who disagree with it, its leaders, and their policies to be "incorrect."

These doctrines were all more or less laid down by Lenin at the beginning of this century and were among the things that led to the split between Bolsheviks and Mensheviks in the Russian Social Democratic party. They were extended and adapted to current needs by Stalin, Khrushchev, Brezhnev, and other Soviet Party leaders and theorists, and turned over to the East European Communists, especially the Moscow-trained ones, like laws or commandments given from on high. To be sure, they are not obeyed or enforced quite as rigidly in the East European countries, and there are differences of interpretation and practice among them. But the only time that an East European party seriously challenged these doctrines—Czechoslovakia's in 1968—the Soviet Party intervened with tanks.

Dubcek and the reformers who had gathered around him— many of them the "home" Communists who had helped put the party in power in 1948—wanted to change quite a number of the old ground rules of Communism in order to make the Czechoslovak Party more democratic and more popular.

For example, they announced that they would allow real opposition parties to organize and campaign in future elections. At one point in the summer of 1968 Dubcek even said that if any one or a coalition of opposition parties were to win such an election, the Communists would turn the powers of government over to them.

The Czechoslovak Party was also planning to hold a special congress in September 1968 by which its by-laws were to be changed. The draft of the new by-laws, published early in August, called for abolishing the principle of "democratic centralism." All Party elections were to be by secret ballot instead of the usual public show of hands, meaning that delegates and central committee members would no longer be afraid to vote against the leadership. The minority would be given the right to keep on presenting its case publicly and to try to gain support for its views even after final votes had been taken.

In Moscow's eyes all this was heresy. Even worse, if it caught on and spread to the other countries, especially the Soviet Union, it would threaten the powers and privileges of the Kremlin leaders themselves. That is why Czechoslovakia was invaded, and why the invasion came when it did—in August, so as to prevent that special congress, planned for September, from being held.

Although the East European Communist parties are patterned closely on the Soviet Union's and there are definite limits to how far the Kremlin will permit them to stray from the line, nowadays they are not mere puppets or subdivisions of the Moscow Party.

Their freedom of action and independence depends on a number of things: the personalities of their leaders, the geographical location of the country, the strength of its economy, the degree to which it must rely on the Soviet Union for vital supplies such as oil and gas or other raw materials, and the alliances it forms with other countries.

And it also depends on whether the greater freedoms the East European parties give to people in their countries pose a threat to the Soviet leadership or not.

Hungary's Kadar, for example, is such a strong and respected leader in the Communist world that he has been able to open up Hungary in a manner unlike any other Communist country. But he is also careful. He never embarrasses Moscow publicly, and the freedoms he has given Hungarians do not threaten the powers and privileges of the Soviet leadership. He has never tried to set them down constitutionally or by changing the by-laws of his party. That does mean, of course, that they can be taken away again more easily.

Ceausescu has made Romania more independent (though not freer at home) by developing close ties with China, with which Russia is at swords' points, and building up trade with Western Europe and the United States.

Though patterned on the Soviet Union, the East European countries' governmental forms are also different and take local traditions and customs into account.

Poland's parliament is called, as it has been for centuries, the Sejm. Czechoslovakia's President Gustav Husak lives in and governs from the Bohemian kings' ancient Hradcany Castle, high above Prague, the way Eduard Beneš and Tomas Masaryk did.

What they do have in common with the Soviet Union is that their government cabinets are all much larger than those of Western countries. They include ministries responsible for matters that are not even government business elsewhere. This is because under Communism industry has been nationalized and the governments own and operate nearly all the means of production. Granted, none of the cabinets, or councils of ministers as they are usually called in Communist countries, are as large as the Soviet Union's, which has eighty-five members, each heading a government department called either a ministry or state committee. But by our standards they are huge. Poland's prime minister, who is called the chairman of the council of ministers, has a cabinet of thirty-six; Hungary's twenty-three; Romania's forty-two; Bulgaria's thirty-three, and Czechoslovakia's twenty-six.

Some of these departments—foreign affairs, justice, finance, interior, defense, education, agriculture, transportation—are found in virtually every country. But others are exclusive products of the Communist system: heavy engineering, general engineering, metallurgy, mining, machine building, chemical industry, construction, food industry, light industry, electric power, and more.

Obviously, these "cabinets" are too large for the chairmen of the councils of ministers, or prime ministers, to meet with regularly. They all have "inner cabinets," made up of vice-chairmen and deputy prime ministers and the most important department heads, which meet at least once a week.

These cabinets and the prime ministers are appointed by and are responsible to the parliaments.

Bulgaria's is called the People's Assembly and has 400 members. Only 272 are members of the Bulgarian Communist party. There are 28 independents, and 100 deputies who belong to the Bulgarian Peasants' Union. But all were elected on a single Fatherland Front ticket, to which there were no opposition candidates, and which got 99.6 percent of the total vote in the last election.

Hungary's National Assembly, with 340 deputies, meets in the Gothic-style parliament building on the banks of the Danube in central Budapest, and it meets more often than most Communist legislatures. All the deputies were elected on the Patriotic People's Front ticket, which got 99.6 percent of the votes in the last election. The majority were members of the (Communist) Socialist Workers' party, though there are independents and those who represent "mass" organizations such as the trade unions, women's association, and others. Although there are no opposition candidates, the process of nomination to the single ticket is fairly local and democratic.

Poland's Sejm, with its 460 deputies, is probably the most democratic and independent-minded parliament in Eastern Europe. To be sure, the 460 are elected on a single "Front of National Unity" ticket which, the last time around, got 99.4 percent. However, the ticket and the Sejm's composition are rather unusual. The Communist Polish United Workers' party has 255 seats. But there are two other parties represented, the United Peasant party with 117 and the Democratic party with 39 seats. In addition there are 36 independent deputies and 13 who belong to the Catholic Pax and Znak movements. It is a parliament that meets fairly often and in which there can be rather lively debate and disagreement. And it is a parliament responsive to public pressure. Widespread opposition to certain constitutional amendments that had been proposed by the government resulted in their modification when the Sejm was called into session to ratify them in the spring of 1976.

Romania's Grand National Assembly meets only once every six months and rubber-stamps the laws enacted by the State Council and the government in the meantime. There is only one party—the Communist—though mass organizations and ethnic minorities are elected to parliament on a single unity ticket which got 99.1 percent approval the last time around. Members of parliament include bishops of the Orthodox Church whose attendance in their robes at least makes sessions colorful and solemn, though not more meaningful. Parliament's decisions are so automatic that Western observers were taken aback when, during a 1969 session, one or two representatives rose from the floor to question the sponsors of one bill. It was later reported, however, that they had been asked to do this by the Party in order to create an impression of democracy.

Czechoslovakia's system is complex because of that country's formal division into two autonomous states—Slovak and Czech. The two states, each with its own legislature, prime minister, and cabinet, now have considerable control over their own affairs, including justice, education, police, and certain aspects of the economy, whereas foreign and defense policy matters are decided by the federal government. Parliament, called the Federal Assembly, consists of two houses—the People's Chamber, whose 200 deputies are elected at large, and the Land Chamber, with 150 members, 75 appointed by the Czech and 75 by the Slovak state assembly. The Land Chamber has a veto power over bills passed by the People's Chamber. The Federal Assembly elects the president of Czechoslovakia, who appoints the prime minister and cabinet with Federal Assembly approval. Although other political parties exist in name, they, the mass organizations, and the Communist party stand election together on a single "National Front" ticket which got 99.9 percent of the vote in the last election held.

Four of the countries—Bulgaria, Hungary, Poland, and Romania—have so-called state councils elected from and by the parliaments. Smaller bodies, they are in session more frequently and enact the laws which are then ratified by parliament. The chairmen of these councils are the presidents, or heads of state. In Romania the system is slightly different because there is also a "president of the republic," but since Nicolae Ceauşescu is both President of the Republic and Chairman of the State Council in addition to being head of the Communist party, it hardly matters. He is the boss in every way.

Czechoslovakia has never had such a "mini-parliament," and except for its reorganization into a federal union in 1970 in order to give the Slovaks a greater say, its governmental structure has remained unchanged since 1918.

The structures of the Communist parties, which have the real power, are almost identical to that of the Soviet Union. However, their membership in the East European countries is proportionately greater than it is in the USSR. The Soviet Party, for example, has 15 million members in a country with around 260 million population—about six percent. Czechoslovakia, on the other hand, with only 15 million inhabitants, has almost 1.4 million Communist party members—nine percent. Bulgaria's Party membership is almost ten percent of the population, Hungary's and Poland's around eight percent, and in Romania the party membership equals almost thirteen percent of the total population.

Party members are considered, and regard themselves, as the leading and guiding force in East European societies. They represent an elite and are expected to set examples of honesty, clean living, morality, duty, patriotism, and public service. Immediately after World War II the ranks of the

East European Communist parties swelled with members. Hungary's, for example, grew from 2,000 members at the end of the war to 1.5 million by 1948, Romania's even more dramatically from 1,000 to 900,000. Not all those new members believed in Communism or even Socialism. There were many opportunists among them who knew which way the political winds were blowing and wanted to get in on the ground floor. There were even quite a number of local fascists who figured changing political colors was good camouflage.

Throughout Eastern Europe there have been numerous purges to clean out opportunists from the parties—and also to do away with the political rivals of whatever leaders were in power—so that memberships today are actually smaller than in the early days of the Communist takeovers. Membership also goes up and down with a particular party's popularity. The ranks of Czechoslovakia's Party swelled during the eight months of Dubcek's "Prague Spring." After the Soviet invasion tens of thousands of Party members quit in anger and disgust and an equal number were purged by the new pro-Soviet leadership in 1969.

Joining the parties is no longer easy. No one really applies to get into these clubs and it is an honor, always accompanied by at least a year's trial period as a "candidate" member, to be chosen. Many people, no doubt the majority, join because they believe in the system and in Communism. But many also know that membership is essential to their careers. Though it is possible to succeed in life, to get to the top, without being a Communist in Eastern Europe these days, it certainly helps and makes it easier. More and more, however, it is performance that counts.

On a long trip through Poland in 1977 I happened to visit the opera house in Bytom to do a story. I interviewed the general manager and chief conductor, and the Party secretary. I didn't pay much attention to him until someone mentioned that he was also the opera's leading lyric tenor. My first reaction—silently, of course—was to ask, "But can he sing?" Long experience in Eastern Europe had taught me to suspect that his top musical position probably depended on his top Party position. I was wrong. In fact, it was almost the other way around. He had sung at some of Western Europe's best opera houses and after joining the company in his native Bytom got the lead spot because of his voice. Only after that did someone say to him: "We need a Party secretary. You're our best singer, so be a good friend and do it."

Being a Party organizer or secretary at that level is largely a labor of love. It is volunteer work and the privileges hardly compensate for the time and effort spent. But starting at the village or district level in a city party work becomes a profession. The Russian word for these Party workers—used all over Eastern Europe as well—is *apparatchiki* because they are members of the Party apparatus, that is the Party machine.

Stalin once compared this machine to an army. He called the members of the junior Party professional organization "our noncoms," the middle-rank officials "our Party officers," and the leading *apparatchiki*—of which there are no more than a few hundred in each of the East European countries— "the Party's generals." Over them all is the "generalissimo"— the first secretary.

In all the East European countries this "army" of professional Party workers represents about ten percent of the total Party membership.

Theoretically, the privates—the rank and file members and volunteer organizers—are supposed to elect the noncoms, the noncoms the officers, the officers the generals, and the generals the generalissimo. It doesn't work in a real army, and it doesn't work in the Communist one because of the principle of "democratic centralism."

The only level in the Soviet and East European Communist parties where there is something close to real democracy is at the very top—among the generalissimos and generals in the politburos and secretariats. There votes are taken, discussion is frank, majorities are necessary, alliances shift, and "generalissimos" can actually be voted out of office. However, no politburo anywhere in Eastern Europe has more than twenty-two members—the men and women who decide the fates of their countries. And the democracy they practice is always behind closed doors. Their arguments, debates, and power struggles are like a free-for-all wrestling match under a blanket. You can hear the groans and grunts and it is obvious that something is going on, but nobody outside can tell who has a hold on whom, or why.

To most people in Western countries, the power that the Communist parties have over the governments is hard to understand.

One explanation is that the Party's power is everywhere. Most government officials, senior civil servants, factory directors, collective farm chairmen, university professors, school principals, judges, prosecutors, ranking police and military officers, newspaper editors, and radio and television programmers, are also Communist party members.

But another important point is that the parties themselves are "invisible" governments paralleling and controlling the visible ones. The central committees, for example, have enormous professional staffs of experts and administrators, divided into departments, that supervise virtually every activity of government and economic administration. This system filters down to industrial plants, collective farms, large offices, shops, and even opera houses, where each manager has a "twin" at his or her side: the Party secretary who often thinks he knows, but rarely does know, more about running the place than the boss.

I recall that at a Polish coal mine a couple of years ago the Party secretary sat in on my day-long visit. Every time I asked the manager of this huge operation with six thousand employees a question, the Party secretary would give the answer. My interpreter, himself a Communist, told him several times to stop interfering, but it was no use.

But there are signs that control is easing up and that even the more restrictive East European countries are becoming freer.

Over the years, for example, both the governments and the parties have built up vast administrations which often compete with each other for power and implementation of whichever course of action the one or the other considers better. The closest example of this in the West is the traditional rivalry and jockeying for budget allocations between the Army, Navy, and Air Force in the United States. The government experts responsible for getting the job done prefer to see real experts in charge; the Party administrators would rather see one of their own *apparatchiki*, whether skilled or not, running things in order to keep control.

As the need for ever more skilled technicians and administrators has grown in every country, this contest has become more intense, with the parties the losers.

There are other signs, too. Local governments have begun flexing their muscles and have become more responsive to the needs of their citizens, in part because those citizens no longer accept mismanagement silently. And the closer one operates to the grass-roots mass of the people—in villages, neighborhoods, towns, counties, or provinces—the more direct, grass-roots democracy there is going to be.

Over the years, too, various interest groups have arisen. One might even call them lobbies. They have become rivals for power and influence and have certain ideas about what should be done and how their countries should be run.

There are the trade union councils, for example. True, they are arms of both the governments and the Communist parties with no power to strike or bargain for higher wages. Indeed, to strike is a crime all over Eastern Europe. Moreover, according to official ideology, there is no need to strike when the workers—through the parties and governments—actually own the means of production. Actually, the unions' role is to get workers to produce more and better. But they do look out for better working conditions and play an important part in setting production plans and targets, making sure they are not unrealistically high. That function puts them into opposition to factory managers, who are appointed by and responsible to the government ministries, and whose future careers and personal comforts depend on producing as much as possible.

There are also competing interests between industry and agriculture. There are women's organizations which want more rights. There are writers' and artists' unions that demand more cultural freedom and less censorship. And throughout Eastern Europe—especially in Poland, Czechoslovakia, and Hungary—there are the churches that have not been suppressed and have become a kind of legalized opposition.

In all the East European countries—some more, some less—different opinions are finding expression in the press. Sometimes views are cloaked in Communist-propagandistic, gobbledegook-sounding kind of "code language" which means little to Westerners who are not trained in deciphering it. But most East Europeans can.

But increasingly, the discussions are more open. Letters-to-the-editor columns are filled with complaints. The fight against social evils—crime, drunkenness, environmental pollution—is carried on in very frank language. Moreover, in some of the countries there is easy access these days to outside, Western information. All major Western newspapers and magazines can be bought by any Hungarian in hotel lobbies and at the bigger newsstands. Poles can read them—and also buy them—in special reading rooms and libraries. Czechoslovaks can watch West German and Austrian TV if they live close enough to the borders. And Romania does not even jam the broadcasts of Radio Free Europe, the United States government station in Munich.

Even the nonelections to the East European parliaments are becoming a little more democratic. Though they couldn't lose even if they tried to, candidates do campaign and do meet with voters, defend their past policies, and make promises for the future.

The fact that East Europeans tell the kind of political jokes they do is a sign that the jackets they wear are more like straitjackets. But on the other hand, the fact that they *can* tell them, without fear, in broad daylight, and quite publicly, is also a sign that their "people's" democracies are becoming more like ordinary democracies.

In Hungary in early 1978 a well-known sociologist even published a scientific study on the jokes he had "collected" over a period of thirty years. He had kept a careful record of when they were told, by whom, and under what social and political conditions. Of the 3,000 jokes in his collection, some 2,000 were political and 486 referred to the economy and standard of living in the East European countries.

The one that struck me as most representative for what is going on in Eastern Europe these days, starts, like many political jokes, with a question. "What kind of power rules Hungary?" The answer: "The power of the workers—to exercise self-control."

8

Five Leaders

Among Romanian rulers dating all the way back to the ancient Dacians, only three have made indelible marks on the country's history. They were Vlad the Impaler, alias Dracula, Stephen the Great, and Michael the Brave.

Nicolae Ceausescu, president of Romania, secretary-general of its Communist party, chairman of its State Council, commander-in-chief of its armed forces, chairman of its Defense Council, president of its National Unity Front, and chairman of its Economic Council—and otherwise known as the *conducator*, which may be translated as *duce, führer,* or "maximum leader"—seems determined to follow in their illustrious footsteps.

Not that Ceausescu aims for the bloodthirsty reputation of Vlad Dracul, or that he would massacre his creditors (of which most are in the capitalist world) the way Prince

Michael once did. But he has already ruled Romania longer than either of them, and since coming to power in 1965 he has created a personality cult unmatched anywhere in the Communist camp since the era of Stalin.

No Communist leader anywhere holds as many offices simultaneously, has collected as many titles, has his fingers in as many pies, has put as many rivals on ice, has given as many relatives cushy jobs, rules with such absolute might, or is praised with as many words and pictures in the newspapers and on television each day as Ceausescu.

"What will this clown do next," asks an embittered Romanian dissident who in 1977 was forced by Ceausescu's secret police to flee the country, "crown himself?"

Born in 1918 into a peasant family in a village some seventy-five miles northwest of Bucharest, he has had little formal education. The same dissident, the novelist Paul Goma, says of him: "Ceausescu is probably the only citizen of Communist Romania who did not take advantage of the campaign to end illiteracy—which is why he hardly knows how to write; why he reads his speeches as if he were cutting wood with a spade; and why those speeches, in his mother tongue, set dogs howling in the four corners of his beloved land."

In 1936 he entered the ranks of Romania's illegal Communist party by way of its youth organization and shortly before the outbreak of World War II spent some time in prison for "agitation." Following the Communist takeover in 1944 hè became head of the Romanian Communist Youth League, then was appointed a political commissar in the army with the rank of major general.

As one of the few prewar Romanian Communists, he rose quickly in the Party hierarchy. His career was solidly launched in 1952 when he hitched his star to Gheorghe Gheorghiu-Dej's wagon in the purge of the "Moscow" faction. By 1957 he was the Party's "second" secretary and Gheorghiu-Dej's heir apparent. When Gheorghiu-Dej died in 1965, Ceausescu moved into the top slot and has held it ever since, amassing more and more power and titles, by eliminating and clipping the wings of any and all rivals or opponents.

He runs the tightest ship in Eastern Europe, supported by a huge secret police organization that makes the Soviet KGB look like a bunch of bungling amateurs. He has compelled the Romanian people to make tremendous sacrifices in his drive—often fruitless—to modernize and industrialize the country. Under his rule Romania has become the most puritanical country in the Soviet bloc with one of the lowest standards of living. Nevertheless, he is surprisingly popular because of his appeal to Romanian patriotism and nationalism and his policy of steering an independent course from—and thumbing his nose at—the hated Russians.

For Romanians, up to now at least, that has made up for the shortage of consumer goods and the lack of freedom at home.

His style in dealing with the government-run economy is rather similar to that of Nikita Khrushchev—lots of motion in neutral gear and constant reorganization and disorganization. But in his style of rule he comes closer than any man has yet to that of Stalin. He views all subordinates not as administrators but as messengers who are there only to carry out his orders and instructions.

"Actually I don't give orders," he once told United States Secretary of State William Rogers. "I make suggestions. But my suggestions must be followed."

Whenever his name is mentioned in the official Party and government press, which is up to a hundred times each day, he is usually referred to as "the Helmsman of Our Nation" and "the warmly beloved son of the people." His name and face dominate that press—almost to the exclusion of all other news. His many travels—he has been all over the world twice within the past decade and to the United States three times—his activities, his statements, and his speeches are reported in banner headlines and seemingly endless detail.

In March 1977 when Romania was hit by a serious earthquake the *conducator* rushed back from a state visit to Nigeria to direct personally the rescue and emergency operations.

With a Romanian network TV crew recording his every word and gesture, and a platoon of top Party and government officials in his wake, he imparted advice and instructions wherever he went. The impression given in the papers was that Ceausescu alone was pulling the dead and injured from under the rubble, dousing the many fires, clearing the streets, and getting public transport rolling again.

One six-page issue of *Scinteia,* the official Communist party daily, reporting on the disaster and rescue operations, mentioned Ceausescu's name, preceded by *all* his titles each time, no less than ninety-four times. Of the thirteen photographs carried in that edition, six showed Ceausescu surveying the damage and giving "suggestions."

His trip to the United States and meeting with President Jimmy Carter in April 1978 got only passing notice in America. But at home *Scinteia*—not to even mention Romania's other government and Party newspapers—gave the visit three full pages of the six it prints each day—for four days running.

He makes speeches and pronouncements, issues decrees or engages in some "newsworthy" activity such as visiting a factory, collective farm, shop, or market at least once daily. And it is all banner-headline, front-page news that runs for column after column inside. When the University of Bucharest awarded him an honorary doctorate a few years ago, a photograph of the diploma covered one fourth of page 1 of *all* Romanian dailies.

His picture hangs everywhere—in government and Party offices, in factories, in hotel lobbies, restaurants, butcher shops, theaters, and every classroom of the land.

On his sixtieth birthday in January 1978 *Flacara,* Romania's leading cultural weekly, devoted its entire twenty-four-page issue to Ceausescu and all over Romania hack poets and writers dripped and gushed with praise to his greatness.

The cult has expanded to include his entire family, for all of whom he has found jobs. Several of his brothers hold high Party and government positions. A brother-in-law was Romania's prime minister. The death of his father in April 1972 was announced in a full-page, black-bordered box on *Scinteia*'s front page and the funeral—except for the religious part to which Ceausescu, as a good Communist and atheist, objected—was telecast live by Romanian network TV.

By far the biggest buildup, however, has been accorded his wife Elena, a chemist by training, who became a member of the Romanian Communist party's central committee in 1972 and its politburo a year later. She accompanies him wherever he goes—on his many trips abroad and on his countless appearances in the country—and her power and position in the top ranks of the Party are matched by no Communist leader's wife anywhere. Nasty tongues say she is just "keeping an eye on Nicki." Others suggest that it is she who really runs Romania. Certainly her power is great. She once managed to get a Romanian foreign minister fired because his wife wore too short a skirt at a reception.

For three consecutive days in January 1979 *her* sixtieth birthday, simultaneously ballyhooed as the "fortieth anniversary of her revolutionary activities," was not merely front-page but virtually the only news in *Scinteia.* Two full pages of pictures showed her kissing babies and children, giving comfort to the injured victims of the 1977 earthquake, receiving honorary doctorate degrees, dancing with folklore groups, inspecting factories and scientific laboratories, and being awarded the Star of the Socialist Republic of Romania, the country's highest honor.

Once asked by a Western journalist whether he might not be carrying his personality cult too far, Ceausescu replied without a blush of embarrassment: "A good orchestra is nothing without a good conductor, just as the best conductor is nothing without a good orchestra. It is the same at the highest level of political leadership."

To Poland's Edward Gierek, political leadership means something completely different—winning the respect and cooperation of his people by efficient management, by setting a good personal example, and by keeping a low profile.

He may not be the most powerful and influential leader in Communist Eastern Europe—his portrait is never seen in public, not even in Party offices—but he is in many respects the most unusual and successful.

Of Eastern Europe's five top leaders, Gierek is by far the most Western in outlook, having spent the better part of his youth—a total of twenty-two years—living in France and Belgium. And he has built the reputation of being a kind of political wizard, a man who can work miracles.

Since replacing Wladyslaw Gomulka, toppled in December 1970 in the wake of strikes and riots that took an estimated two hundred lives, Gierek has turned Poland into the world's eleventh largest industrial power. Completely reversing the policy of thrift, austerity, and economic standstill which Gomulka had practiced for fourteen years and which triggered those bloody demonstrations in 1970, Gierek launched

Poland on the road to the greatest prosperity in its history.

There have been problems and setbacks, such as the price-increase riots of June 1976, most of them due to Gierek's trying to do too much too fast. However, Gierek has enabled Poles to live better than ever before.

In addition, he has given them more freedom than they had under Gomulka, and he has won their intensely patriotic hearts with such spectacular prestige projects as the rebuilding of Warsaw's Royal Palace.

All these achievements really surprised no one in Poland, for Gierek has always done the impossible—quietly, efficiently, and without fanfare.

He was born in 1913 in the village of Porabka in the coal-mining basin of Upper Silesia, the son and grandson of miners. When he was four years old, his father was killed in a mining accident. For the next six years his mother tried to manage on a modest widow's pension. But in 1923, when there was runaway inflation, she left with young Gierek and his sister and settled with relatives in a coal-mining region in France.

Gierek himself began working as a miner only three years later, at age thirteen. He dug coal for the next eight years—until 1934, when he, his sister, and mother, along with a hundred other Polish families were expelled as unwanted aliens by the French government, following a miners' strike.

Back in Poland, he was drafted into the army for a two-year hitch.

After discharge, unable to find regular work, Gierek, along with many of his countrymen, went abroad again—this time to Belgium where he landed a job as a miner in 1937, met and married his wife, and settled. When war broke out in 1939 and the Germans invaded first his native Poland and then his adopted Belgium, Gierek continued to work in a coal mine, but soon founded a Communist-oriented League of Polish Patriots and joined the Belgian anti-Nazi resistance movement.

Following Belgium's liberation by the Allies, Gierek's ties to Polish Communists got him a menial job at the Polish embassy in Brussels. In 1948, at age thirty-five, he returned to Poland where he joined the (Communist) United Workers' party, just at the time of the great struggle between the "home" and the "Moscow" Communists. Gomulka, one of the Party's founders, was still its first secretary but soon to be ousted by Stalin's stooge, Boleslaw Bierut. Gierek, being neither a "Moscow" nor really a "home" man, was not involved. Only a year later he was named Party chief and political and administrative boss of the Voivodship of Katowice in his native Upper Silesia, the most populous and industrialized of Poland's then seventeen provinces.

He set out immediately to give the Party leadership in Warsaw a dazzling display of his remarkable organizational and managerial talents. During the next two decades he made the Katowice coal, iron, and steel center a model of what Communism can do when the right man happens to be in charge. Under his leadership Katowice became the most efficient, productive, and prosperous province in the country. It had the highest wages, the most modern cities and acquired the highest standard of living.

His performance eventually landed him a seat on the Party politburo, and by the late 1960's he was being talked about at home and abroad as "a man to watch." But he was no pusher like his only rival for power, General Mieczyslaw Moczar, the interior minister and chief of secret police in those years, who was spending most of his time nibbling at Gomulka's political heels.

Though a politburo member, Gierek continued to spend

Gustav Husak of Czechoslovakia (top left); Nicolae Ceausescu of Romania, and Edward Gierek of Poland (bottom)

most of his time in Katowice trying to stay clear of the intra-mural debates and power battles in Warsaw.

When the December 1970 riots brought Gomulka's regime down, Moczar had neither the Party backing nor the political courage to get into the hot seat and run a country on the edge of revolution. The Party turned to Gierek.

Once asked why he accepted the challenge and took the risk, he replied: "I recognized the danger of unrest spreading from the coastal cities across the country, and I also recognized my responsibilities. Someone had to act."

Gierek acted largely by applying the same commonsense principles of political and economic administration to the whole of Poland that had proved themselves valid for the preceding twenty years in Katowice.

Though never aiming to be a "Polish Alexander Dubček," over the years Gierek has nevertheless been forced to retract some of his promises of greater freedom. A colder political wind began blowing over Poland in the spring of 1974, aimed at bringing Warsaw's policies more closely in line with those of Moscow, and it hasn't really stopped blowing.

Moreover, some of his economic policies got him overextended. To finance his investment programs Gierek has had to borrow fifteen billion dollars in the West and at the time of writing was still borrowing.

But despite the problems, Gierek is still firmly in the saddle, Poland is still on the go, and it is stronger and more self-confident than at any time since the seventeenth century when it was one of Europe's big powers.

Though he has been in power a year longer, those are claims Czechoslovakia's President Gustav Husak cannot make.

No East European leader has been in or near the seat of power as long as he. He has been around for so many years—

or at least has bounced back to the scene so often—that he is almost a Communist fixture. Yet, he remains a puzzle. No one knows what makes him tick, what he really wants or believes, or how he plans to get his country out of the doldrums in which it has been since the 1968 invasion.

With one important exception: Husak has always been, first and foremost, a Slovak nationalist who has put the interests of his people above the Czechs and above Czechoslovakia as a whole.

When President Eduard Beneš and his foreign minister Tomas Masaryk flew to Moscow in 1944 to talk to the Russians about Soviet help and Czechoslovakia's future, Husak was in on the negotiations. When the "home" Communists were purged in 1952, Husak was one of the first to land in prison. When the rehabilitations started, he was one of the first to be released. When Antonín Novotny was to be ousted as Party chief in 1968, it was Husak who helped put his fellow Slovak, Alexander Dubcek, into power. And when the Russians wanted Dubcek out, they picked Husak as his replacement.

A classic survivor, his career is remarkable by any standard. He has spent more years in prison for his political views and activities than any Communist leader in the world today.

Born into a well-situated, middle-class Slovak family in Dubravaka near Bratislava in 1913, he studied law, wrote his doctoral thesis, and graduated from Bratislava's Comenius University in 1937. By then he had been a member of the Czechoslovak Communist party for three years. He practiced law privately for four years, from 1938 until 1942. During that time he continued working for the Party which had been banned by the German and Slovak puppet regime authorities.

Although arrested and imprisoned several times by the Gestapo, he continued to work underground and became one of the chief organizers and leaders of the Communist-inspired 1944 Slovak uprising against the Nazi occupation and the pro-German Slovak regime of Father Josef Tiso.

He rose quickly in the Party ranks after the war, becoming the Slovak section's deputy chairman and a member of the national politburo. He was also made Slovakia's commissioner of internal affairs and used his powers to wage a repressive police campaign against all fascists and collaborators with the Nazis, but also against the Catholic Church and all non-Slavs. At one point he was quoted as saying that because there were 400,000 Slovaks living in Hungary, he had the right to deport 400,000 ethnic Hungarians from Slovakia.

By 1950 he was clearly one of the most powerful Communist politicians in Slovakia. A year later he was arrested, tortured by his own comrades into signing a confession in which he admitted the "crime" of "bourgeois nationalism," and was sentenced to life imprisonment. Of the nearly ten years that he was in prison—until mid-1960—he spent six in an isolation cell. When he was released he did a three-year stint as a construction worker, and it was not until 1963 that he was "rehabilitated" and readmitted to the ranks of the Communist party.

However, his political comeback was slow. Though he was one of Dubcek's most enthusiastic supporters, it was not until May 1968, five months after Dubcek had come to power, that Husak returned to the inner circle: first as a deputy prime minister, then as a member of the central committee, then the politburo, and finally as head of the Slovak branch of the Party. Within a few days after the Soviet invasion, though Dubcek stayed on as Party chief for eight more months, it was obvious the Russians were grooming Husák as successor.

He became Party chief in April 1969 and six years later, in August 1975, was also elected president of Czechoslovakia.

He is not an inspiring leader and he is anything but popular. He has had no success in getting Czechoslovakia moving again and off dead center since the invasion.

Yet, for all his international image as an ogre and as Moscow's "enforcer," Husak is actually a moderate in the Czechoslovak Party hierarchy. Within the top leadership there is a group of hardliners who are far more tough-minded, especially when it comes to dealing with Dubcek-era reformers and dissidents.

Most prominent among them are Vasil Bilak and Alois Indra, top-ranking politburo members believed to have co-authored the fake "appeal for help" to "combat counter-revolution" which served as the pretense for the 1968 invasion.

While Husak and some of his supporters recommend a lenient policy toward the 1968 reformers, suggesting that some be allowed back into the Party and government, the Bilak group, with Moscow's backing, continues to block such efforts.

In fact, Bilak is known to have warned several years ago that if any of the Dubcek reformers were to be rehabilitated, "all of *us* would soon be hanging from the lamp posts." On the other hand, had either Bilak or Indra gotten their way, Dubcek and other reform leaders would have been put on trial and imprisoned long ago instead of merely being made to work as janitors, cabdrivers, miners, and in the case of Dubcek himself, as a motor-pool dispatcher. But under those circumstances, Czechoslovakia's economic troubles would be even worse. Recognizing this, Husak has thus far blocked the hardliners with the result that Czechoslovakia is in perpetual political stalemate.

The two groups, each with allies in the Kremlin, are constantly jockeying for power. In early January 1978 the hardliners apparently tried to topple Husak, taking advantage of the fact that Soviet Party chief Leonid Brezhnev was ill and gone from the Kremlin. Husak put in a hurried call to Brezhnev on his sickbed. Brezhnev backed him up by sending the commander of Soviet forces in Czechoslovakia to Husak's sixty-fifth birthday party and having him hand Husak the USSR's Order of the October Revolution.

Husak was safe—for a while. But Czechoslovakia was still no better off. Ten years after the Soviet invasion it was a much sadder country than Hungary was five years after its revolution had been crushed by the Russians.

One reason is that Gustav Husak is not Janos Kadar.

They call him Mr. Tolerance, and among Eastern Europe's leaders, Hungary's Janos Kadar is unique. Though he keeps a lower profile, is quieter and more modest, he is more genuinely popular and has survived in power unchallenged longer than any of them.

He has been imprisoned and cruelly tortured three times— twice during the pro-German Horthy regime between the two world wars, once by his own political comrades—and has spent one tenth of his life behind bars.

He has been both the chief and the victim of his nation's once-dreaded secret police. He has risen to positions of power several times, only to fall again. He has betrayed his friends and been betrayed by them.

In November 1956 he took over a shattered land and a wrecked Party machine in the wake of the revolution that had been crushed by Soviet tanks. For that he was called a traitor to the cause of Hungarian freedom and a stooge of Moscow.

But he gradually gained the confidence of his fellow Hungarians by pushing for a program of national unity and by relaxing the rigid pressures that had triggered the rebellion in the first place.

His live-and-let-live policy in those dark years after the revolution was based on the slogan, "He who is not against us must be treated as being for us". He took pains never to anger the Russians unnecessarily or embarrass them publicly. He followed Moscow's foreign policy line; when he disagreed with it, he did so in private meetings. That gave him the freedom at home to put into action economic and cultural policies that have turned Hungary into a showcase, the most liberal and visibly affluent country in Eastern Europe today.

If anything worries Hungarians—Communist or not—about Kadar today, it is what will happen when he leaves the stage. They see no successors in the wings—at least none they would trust to fill his shoes or to continue his policies.

"Their concern is justified," a veteran United States diplomat in Budapest once confided to me. "There just isn't another Kadar around. He's the best man this Party has."

He was born in 1912, when Hungary was much larger than it is today, in the Adriatic coastal city of Rijeka, now part of Yugoslavia. Almost nothing is known about his father. While still a small boy, he moved with his mother to Budapest. At age fourteen, after finishing eight years of elementary school, he became a toolmaker's apprentice, and at seventeen got his journeyman's papers. He worked in various factories and became active in trade union activities as well as the Young Communist Workers' League. He got into trouble with the authorities for the first time at a mass demonstration in November 1931 during which he was arrested and held briefly.

In 1932 he joined the illegal Hungarian Communist party which led to his arrest a year later and a seventeen-month jail term. In 1937 he was again arrested and imprisoned for almost three years. After his release he played a key role in the antifascist, anti-German wartime resistance movement and in the underground Party, rising quickly in its ranks. In

1944 he was captured once more as he was trying to cross the border into Yugoslavia to establish contact with Tito's partisan forces. But he managed to escape, went to Budapest, and joined the Soviet forces that were already on Hungarian territory. His mentor and close friend throughout this time was Laszlo Rajk, the illegal Party's first secretary.

When the Hungarian fascist regime fled and the provisional government signed an armistice with the Russians in January 1945, Kadar was assigned to organizing the Budapest police and became Party chief of the city. By October 1946 he was deputy first secretary of the Party under Matyas Rakosi, the "Moscow" Communist who had come back with the Russians to take charge of the Hungarian Party. Kadar's friend Rajk was minister of interior and head of the secret police. In 1948, when Rajk was named Hungary's foreign minister, Kadar succeeded him as interior minister and chief of secret police. The Party, having swallowed up the Socialists, had been renamed the Hungarian Workers' party and he was one of its three deputy first secretaries as well as member of the politburo.

It was a period of Stalinist and police terror in which Kadar played a sinister role.

It was Kadar who ordered the arrest of Cardinal Josef Mindszenty, the primate of the Hungarian Catholic Church, who was drugged into confessing treason charges and subsequently sentenced to life imprisonment at a sensational show trial. And it was also Kadar who ordered the arrest of his close friend Rajk, who was accused of conspiring "against Stalin" and of trying to overthrow the Party's Moscow-trained leadership. Kadar visited Rajk in prison and persuaded him to make a false confession. Rajk was tried and executed in 1949 and it was not until 1956, when Kadar himself had become head of the Party, that the Rajk trial was declared an "error."

Put bluntly, Kadar, the "home" Communist, had become a stooge of the Stalinists and the "Moscow" team led by Rakosi, Erno Gero, and others. His "reward" was that he was soon to become their victim. Though he ranked virtually behind Rakosi and Gero in the Party leadership, he was arrested in April 1951 and accused of espionage, treason, and "Titoism." After cruel and humiliating torture—among other things, his finger nails were torn out—he was brought to trial in December 1951 and sentenced to prison where he spent the next three years.

The world he found on being released in 1954 was a different one. Stalin was dead. A "new course" had been proclaimed by Nikita Khrushchev in the Kremlin, and although the "Moscow" men and Stalinists were still in power in Hungary, their days were numbered. For the next two years they put Kadar into middle-ranking Party jobs at the Budapest county level. But in July 1956, four months after Khrushchev had given his "secret speech" at the Soviet Party's twentieth Congress exposing Stalin's many crimes, Kadar made his comeback.

That Khrushchev speech had turned Eastern Europe and the world Communist movement topsy-turvy. Hungary, like Poland, was in turmoil with Communist intellectuals, students, and writers demanding more freedom and an end to rule by the Stalinists and "Moscow" men. Khrushchev had dispatched his most trusted lieutenant, Anastas Mikoyan, to Budapest to clean house. He reorganized the Hungarian leadership. Rakosi was deposed and Kadar was reelected to the politburo and secretariat. The new team had one great flaw, however. Its first secretary was Erno Gero, as narrow-minded a Stalinist and as much a "Moscow" man as Rakosi had been.

Had Mikoyan installed Kadar as boss in July 1956, history would have taken a different course. There would have been no Hungarian Revolution and no need for the Soviets to send their tanks to crush it. By the time Mikoyan realized his mistake and did make Kadar first secretary—on October 25—it was already too late. Three months of Geros policy of repression had turned Hungary into a pressure cooker which exploded in revolution and virtual civil war two days before Kadar replaced him.

Kadar himself made many mistakes during the ten days between becoming first secretary and November 4 when Soviet troops and tanks moved in, turning Hungary into a bloodbath that left thousands dead. The biggest was to go on the air and broadcast a stirring support for a "Communist" uprising against Stalinist tyranny at a time when his own Communist party, discredited by eleven years of Stalinist rule and mismanagement, no longer had that revolution under control.

But others made mistakes, too. Mikoyan, "to preserve the impression of Party unity," at first did not let Kadar announce that he was the new boss, leaving Hungarians to think that the man they hated most—Gero—was still in charge. It fanned the flames of revolt. The Communist prime minister Imre Nagy, trusted and respected by most Hungarians, made the huge mistake of announcing that he intended to take Hungary out of the Soviet bloc and the Warsaw Pact. And the American CIA committed the unforgivable sin of letting its Munich-based station, Radio Free Europe, broadcast lies about the new Communist leadership and incite Hungarians to new violence with vague promises that American military help was coming, though no help was even planned.

When it was all over, Kadar, who had got the Soviets to crush the revolution, was called a traitor and a turncoat, but he was in the driver's seat and has been ever since. The amazing thing about him is that within five years after the revolution, which he allegedly betrayed, he already had Hungary on the road to more democracy, more freedom, and a better life—the aims of the revolution in the first place.

No East European leader is as faceless or as much a creature of Moscow as Bulgaria's president and Communist party chief Todor Zhivkov. Perhaps that is why he has been in power longer than any of them—since 1954.

Although a "home" Communist who came to power by purging "Moscow" men, he has made Bulgaria the Soviet Union's most reliable and willing ally. It is an alliance that goes well beyond the tradition of "Slav brotherhood" which has characterized Bulgarian-Russian relations for centuries. When the Kremlin wants to send up trial balloons in world affairs it gets Zhivkov to launch them. The relationship goes so far that in 1970, when Soviet Party chief Leonid Brezhnev also wanted to be recognized as an author and Communist thinker by publishing the first volume of his collected speeches and notes with the stirring title *Following Lenin's Path*, it was issued in Bulgaria—to test the market—before being released in the Soviet Union.

Throughout Eastern Europe, even among Communist officials whose loyalty to Moscow is beyond question, Zhivkov is referred to disrespectfully as His Master's Voice.

But it would be oversimplifying to attribute his long-livedness only to Kremlin support. True, he could hardly have survived without it. But the Kremlin does not back what it considers losers—at least not for a quarter century. Under Zhivkov's leadership, conservative and uninspiring as it may be, Bulgaria has entered a new age of unprecedented prosperity—and the modern world.

Zhivkov is a talented *apparatchik* who knows all the ins and outs of Communist power politics, a man who senses instinctively which levers to pull and which not to pull at just the right time in order to keep his machine humming, even when all others around him have ground to a halt or are clanking loudly with broken parts.

Looking back over the past two decades or so, there is

no country in Eastern Europe with as many top-level Party and government reshuffles, where ministers and Communist chieftains have been fired and replaced so often as Bulgaria. Keeping track of those who have come and gone through the corridors of power is like watching a passing parade. But the chief himself has remained firmly in the saddle.

As a result, Moscow has given him massive political and economic support, for which he pays with unswerving loyalty. He has convinced the Kremlin that in a country so vital to the Soviet Union's interests and so exposed to two non-Communist, NATO states—Greece and Turkey—he alone can maintain stability.

He lacks charisma and personality. His intellect is limited. But he certainly knows how to maneuver and manipulate. He is a dictator who rules not with the heavy hand of the secret police, but rather with the plodding machinery of the Party apparatus.

Born into a poor peasant family of Eastern Orthodox faith in 1911, Zhivkov comes from a village just north of Sofia. He completed the eight-year elementary school there, then attended a graphic arts vocational school in the capital.

In 1930, while working as a printer, he joined the Communist Youth League, and two years later, the Party. Throughout the 1930's and early 1940's he had a number of minor Party posts in various Sofia neighborhoods. His star did not begin to rise until he helped organize partisan fighters in his native Botevgard County in 1943 and then played an important role in the Communist takeover of Bulgaria in September 1944. From then he rose steadily through the upper ranks.

He survived all the intramural power struggles and purges of "home" Communists and in March 1954 was named first secretary, replacing Vulko Chervenkov, a "Moscow" man, who was then also—and remained for two more years—

Bulgaria's prime minister. At that time the Party leadership was less powerful than the prime ministership and Chervenkov was planning to use Zhivkov as a kind of puppet. But Zhivkov soon turned the tables and by 1961 had not only gained complete control but got Chervenkov kicked out of the Party. It was virtually a perfect replay of what Khrushchev had done to Georgi Malenkov in the Kremlin. In the years since then he has been both prime minister and president of Bulgaria, and now has the latter position.

His leadership has been threatened several times, but only once seriously. In 1965 a group of Bulgarian army officers—all Communists, of course—conspired to topple Zhivkov, apparently with the aim of making Bulgaria more independent in its relations with the Soviet Union. They were executed.

Zhivkov is a great traveler. Since coming to power he has made more than 120 trips abroad, including a number to the United States, yet at no time has he ever given the impression of being any kind of world statesman.

Perhaps because his country is such a small and little-known one, but perhaps also because he is so much his master's voice, Zhivkov stands a notch shorter than his four East European partners—Ceausescu, Gierek, Husak, and Kadar.

Someday There Will Be

Czechs were told in January 1978, that the "pin crisis" would "surely" be solved by the end of that year. The government, a high-ranking official of the ministry of trade announced on Czech network television, had issued a decree authorizing the ministry to increase production of pins by five hundred tons during 1978.

On the other hand, the official admitted, meeting the demand for hinges, nails, thumbtacks, pliers, bedroom furniture, and approximately 140 other categories of goods "currently in demand" might take a little longer. Perhaps 1979, more likely 1980, but "hopefully not beyond that date."

The trouble, I should explain, is that those other products "currently in demand" had not gotten quite as much attention from investigative reporters on Czech TV as had pins.

Pins came into the limelight when the network sent out a

woman reporter to try and buy some. Her search proved harder than the proverbial one for a needle in a haystack. She traveled from Pilsen to Prague, from Ostrava to Brno, and couldn't find a single shop or department store that had them in stock. Moreover, as she discovered, that's the way things had been for at least three or four years. No pins. Why?

Well, it seems that a state-owned, Prague factory called the Ko-hi-Noor plant has a Czechoslovak-wide monopoly on pin (and sewing needle) production. In 1967, when the plant underwent its "third reorganization and enlargement," the planners apparently forgot about the pin manufacturing department. Pins, after all, are pretty small.

Of course, this "unfortunate" oversight was later corrected—around 1969 or 1970. But then a "number of other problems" cropped up. One of them, the Ko-hi-Noor factory's deputy commercial director, a very efficient-sounding man, admitted to the reporter, "is that we have had several production breakdowns." These were caused, he said, almost whispering, "by machinery that is too old."

Besides, most of the factory's output of notions items such as needles, pins, snaps, zippers, and eye hooks is earmarked for export to foreign countries.

"And as you know, comrade," said the deputy commercial director, "the Party's central committee has issued a resolution, and the state planning commission has issued a decree, that production for export must be given priority.

"Besides, pins aren't our only problem. We actually make hundreds of items and give priority to those which dovetail with others. That's modern efficiency, I'm sure you'll agree."

However, he did assure televiewers that, considering the "intense public interest," the Czech pin shortage would "certainly be over by the end of 1978" even if it requires "improvising, more overtime work, unscheduled imports and reduced exports."

The Czech pin crisis tells a lot about the economies of all the East European countries and what is wrong with them.

With the notable exceptions of Hungary and Poland, virtually all industry, business, commerce, and trade in those countries are owned and operated by the governments—everything from mines, factories, and department stores to newspaper stands, shoe shops, and beauty parlors. Everyone, from the butcher and the baker to the candlestick maker, either directly or indirectly works for the state.

In each of the countries, in order to operate its vast business enterprise, the state has created a huge bureaucracy of government ministries and committees, subdivided into departments, agencies, and local administrations, that is responsible for everything—from supplying the raw materials with which to produce the goods on down to distribution of the goods to consumers.

This system has been in operation more or less since the East European countries became Communist after World War II. It is called a "centralized command economy" and was brought to them by the Soviet Union where it has existed for almost sixty years. On the one hand, there can be no question that it has benefited them a great deal.

The five countries, according to Western estimates, now have *per capita* annual gross national products (GNP) ranging from around $2,500 in Romania—the lowest—to almost $4,000 in Czechoslovakia—the highest. This puts the more productive and affluent of the countries into the same league as such West European capitalist nations as Spain and Italy, whereas the poorer ones—Bulgaria and Romania—are certainly not worse off than Greece, Turkey, or Ireland.

Except for Czechoslovakia, all of the countries are much better off today in terms of standard of living and industrialization than they were before World War II.

Poland's state-owned steel company is now bigger than

Great Britain's which is also state owned. In fact Zjednoczenie Hutnictwa Zelasa i Stali, as the company is called, ranks one notch behind America's United States Steel and one ahead of Bethlehem Steel Corporation in the world output listing. Poland has become a major copper producer and exporter. It is not only the fourth largest coal producer—behind the United States, Russia, and China—but the Polish mining industry is so modern that it sells its machinery and know-how to America.

One of the first things the Poles did when they gained access to more than four hundred additional miles of Baltic coastline after World War II was to turn their long-landlocked country into a sea power. Poland's merchant marine is one of the largest in Europe today. Szczecin and Gdańsk—both minor, unimportant harbors before the war—are now the two largest ports on the Baltic. And with an annual output of nearly a hundred vessels, including supertankers, Poland today ranks as the world's ninth largest shipbuilding country.

The pace in Poland is dizzying. Poland today has the world's youngest machinery park and, among industrialized nations, the highest annual growth rates. New industries are literally being carved out of its soil; entire new cities are mushrooming out of the ground.

Hungary has become Europe's largest manufacturer of city and cross-country buses. The Ikarus factory which makes them has begun exporting them to the United States where they are now being used by municipal transit systems in Los Angeles and Portland, Oregon. Hungary is also a leading producer of chemicals and medicines. And in Budapest there is now a state-owned company called Videoton, started in 1969, which is planning an assault on the electronics and data processing market in the 1980's that is beginning to look

Gdynia, one of Poland's busy new shipbuilding ports

like a replay of the Japanese game of the 1960's. It already does more than $300 million worth of business a year and soon expects to corner the West European market for small and medium-size computers by offering a high-quality product at rock-bottom prices.

Bulgaria has completely industrialized its agriculture with 170 so-called agro-industrial complexes which provide the markets of all Europe with fresh fruits and vegetables, high-quality canned goods, and preserves. One of its government-owned and -run companies also operates the largest international trucking fleet in Europe. Wherever one drives on the continent these days, one sees huge semitrailers, marked with the word "Bulgariya" in Cyrillic lettering on the sides. They are carrying Black Sea grapes to Holland and French fashions to Iran, tomatoes from Sofia to Denmark and West German machine tools to Turkey.

Romania, thanks to its own oil and that which it imports, has become one of Europe's largest refiners and processors of petroleum products.

Moreover, all the countries are better off than the Soviet Union itself in standard of living, in per capita production, and in the quality of their goods.

To be sure, all the East Europeans still work harder and longer than the Russians. While the average work week in the Soviet Union is now 40 hours spread over five days, in the East European countries it ranges from 42.5 hours in Bulgaria and Czechoslovakia to a high of 48 in Romania. But they all have to work fewer minutes, hours, days, or weeks than the Russians to buy such things as an average weekly family food-basket, furniture, appliances, clothing, and that most important status symbol of all, a car.

By comparison, they are all so much better off that they are starting to get choosy about what they buy from the Soviet Union, other than the raw materials they absolutely need. In 1977, for example, *Magyar Import,* a monthly magazine of Hungary's Chamber of Commerce, reported that twenty to thirty percent of the consumer durables imported from the Soviet Union have "quality and design deficiencies" which lead to their rejection by Hungary's national quality-control institute.

But the big question is still how much better off the East European countries would be had they not become Communist and—most important—had they not been forced to adopt the Stalinist style of centrally run and planned command economics.

The basic fault of this type of economy is that it ignores the laws of supply and demand and either does not provide enough incentives or provides the wrong ones. It also places the emphasis on production for the sake of production, on tons or sheer numbers of goods, not on their value to consumers, their prices, or the chances of selling them.

Just as in the Soviet Union itself, the East European countries work strictly according to five-year plans, and because they are all members of Comecon, the Communist-bloc version of the Common Market, the plans and plan-periods are now closely coordinated.

Each five-year plan is worked out by the experts in the country's state planning committee, a ministry whose head is a member of the prime minister's "inner cabinet." Once the plan has been approved by the country's central committee, whose staff experts also work on it, and the parliament, it assumes the force of law and determines how much of what is to be produced by whom and at what price each year during the five-year period.

In some of the countries the plan is more rigid, in others more flexible, but the principle is the same.

The plan sets out how much steel will be produced, how many cars will be manufactured, how much coal will be mined, how many ships will be built, how much electricity will be generated, or how much oil will be imported. But it also determines how many shoes, shirts, diapers, hairbrushes, teakettles, refrigerators, television sets, tubes of toothpaste, and, of course, how many pins will be made, or not made. It prescribes the number of apartments that will be built, how many kindergartens will be opened, or how much wheat is to be harvested. If the demand for pins is greater than what the plan calls for, then people are just out of luck until the next five-year period or a quick adjustment is made because that particular shortage got a lot of publicity.

But there are hundreds and thousands of shortages of one kind or another in Eastern Europe, some permanent, some temporary. And shortages always cause lines. There are lines wherever you go and look in Eastern Europe. People spend unnecessary hours each week standing in them. And it makes them angry.

"If there is ever a real revolution against Communism," a Polish acquaintance once said to me, "it will be started by someone who stood in line too long."

The plans, the quotas, and the production norms rule the lives of all working citizens. Steelworkers, coal miners, and machine operators all have targets to meet. So do bricklayers, painters, and carpenters. Scientists and doctors are expected to meet predetermined quotas. Collective and state farm workers must produce a specific amount of grain and fishermen must catch a certain amount of herring or cod. In Czechoslovakia—no kidding—I once saw a sign in the window of a funeral parlor proudly proclaiming; "We have overfulfilled our annual plan target for burials by seven percent."

The system really has nothing to do with socialism or communism. It is not what Marx or Lenin had in mind. It was invented by Stalin and his economic "thinkers" in the late

1920's and early 1930's. Like anything to which Stalin signed his name it became dogma. After all, he was supposed to be infallible. Stalin's "Moscow" Communists brought it with them to Eastern Europe, where it also became law. Like any system, it became a way of life and accumulated a huge bureaucracy with vested interests. And the Communist parties soon discovered that the system was an ideal one for maintaining total control over their societies. So, although Stalin has been dead more than twenty-five years, the system lives—in part because the men and women who have vested personal interests in it live: the economists, the managers, the bureaucrats, the Party *apparatchiki,* and the theorists. It justifies their existence and gives *them* privileges.

The system is not, as a prominent Soviet economist says, "the supreme advantage of Communism over capitalism." It is Communism's greatest disadvantage.

The name of this game at both the manager and worker level is "beating the quotas" because both collect bonuses and premiums when they do. All have shown ingenious ways of doing that, without, however, meeting the needs of the economy or of daily life. It's the *production,* not the *sales* plan, that counts.

The results are often hair-raising. Not long ago, somewhere in Hungary, an apartment house was built. But after the scaffolding was removed, it turned out there was no staircase in the building. The plan called for building it in a hurry. That's also why a hotel restaurant was built in a large Hungarian provincial town without a kitchen. A more frightening case of "beating the quotas" was recorded in the town of Nagykaniza where an entire high school for six hundred pupils was built without a foundation. No one noticed until huge cracks appeared in all its walls.

The system is also ideal for passing the buck, since one ministry's plan can also become another's downfall. Take the case of Czechoslovakia's Calex refrigerator company whose management was fired in the spring of 1978 because its products had become so bad. That is, the refrigerator's inner walls were cracking after only a few weeks' use. The reason? The Kaucuk Works, manufacturers of the lining material, had overfulfilled its production plan by reducing quality. The new management of the Calex company, installed by the ministry of general engineering, hasn't even bothered to renew the delivery contract with Kaucuk. Instead, it imports the lining material from abroad. The result is a refrigerator that lasts, but at an increased price. Incidentally, it now costs 3,130 Czechoslovak korunas (about $331 at the tourist exchange rate)—more than a month's salary, 2,490 korunas ($263.50), for the average Czechoslovak industrial worker.

Meanwhile, back in Bulgaria, the minister of internal trade and services promised that by 1980, "in accordance with the decisions of the July 1976 plenum of the Party's central committee," the shortage of "certain items which so far have been only occasionally obtainable," will have been alleviated. The items: baby foods, baby carriages, strollers, blankets, carpets, enameled saucepans, and men's woolen socks. But in the same breath he admitted that there are still "certain difficulties on the domestic market, of which we are well aware." They will not be solved by 1980.

Fortunately, East Europeans have a sense of humor and can still tell jokes about all this.

Asked by a member of the audience what the next five-year plan will actually accomplish—so goes one joke making the rounds in Poland—a Party propaganda lecturer in Crakow replies, "The first year, comrade, will bring you a pair of shoes, the second year a bicycle, the third a motorcycle, the fourth a car, and in the fifth you will have your own airplane."

Somewhat taken aback by all this, the man asks, "But what is an ordinary citizen like me supposed to do with a plane?"

"It will enable you to get to Warsaw faster and be at the head of the line if and when meat goes on sale."

Two of the East European countries—Hungary and Poland—have in recent years taken steps to move away from rigid state and government ownership in order to provide for a better supply of goods and services at the retail level. Both had always ranked as the two nations with the highest degree of private enterprise and trade, and since 1975 have introduced measures to help and encourage small private business.

In contrast to what happened in most other East European countries, private enterprise had managed to survive in Poland through the first postwar decade of Communist rule and when Wladyslaw Gomulka came back to power in 1956, it was officially recognized, though with limitations and restrictions. When Edward Gierek took over in 1970, he encouraged this sector.

Poland has some 200,000 artisan establishments and small manufacturing plants employing nearly 400,000 people. There are 8,000 private grocery outlets and 7,000 other retail shops. More than 100,000 Poles are employed in privately managed retail trade, including virtually all of the country's gasoline stations whose operators lease them from the government petroleum monopoly. Some 3,600 restaurants—almost a third of the country's total—are under private management of some form today. In 1970 there were less than 1,000.

Since these enterprises all operate for personal profit, their owners and managers have real incentives to do better. They know how to obtain the goods that the managers and clerks in state-owned stores are often too indifferent either to put on the shelves or order from state wholesalers. They provide better service. Poland is the only Communist country where gas station attendants actually wash my windshield.

In 1977 the Polish government enacted a number of laws to give these small private business people more support and incentives: tax reductions, social security benefits, and access to low-interest government loans. The number of people that private businesses are allowed to employ was also increased.

Private enterprise also plays a major role in making Hungary move. More than one fourth of all personal services, from hairstyling to shoemaking, and sixty percent of all semi-industrial services, such as building and automobile repairs, are performed by private craftspersons. And if Janos Kadar had his way, there would be even more.

Presently there are about 60,000 private artisans and craftspersons in Hungary—10,000 *less* than in 1970—and some 11,000 private retailers, though their numbers have been declining, too.

The problem is that too few young Hungarians want to go into private business, preferring instead the shorter and more regulated hours as well as the fringe benefits of jobs in state-owned enterprises. At last count there were 1,200 self-employed plumbers but only 32 apprentices learning the trade to replace them someday. The 3,000 shoemakers had only 6 apprentices in the "pipeline" and the 300 dry cleaners merely 5. To induce young people to go into these trades, and eventually into business for themselves, the government has introduced a number of support programs such as "scholarships" for apprentice training and low-interest loans to help retailers improve their shops and raise their earning potential.

These Polish and Hungarian efforts to encourage private enterprise naturally worry Moscow and other East European capitals because they look like moves in the direction of capitalism to conservative, dyed-in-the-wool Communist purists. On the other hand, since this little bit of capitalism has made Communism a lot more livable, has reduced public complaining and thus actually strengthened the positions of Gierek and Kadar, nothing has been said very loudly nor has anything been done about it thus far. In all likelihood, nothing will be done—*if* Kadar and Gierek do not go too far.

That something is basically wrong with the system of centralized and command planning has been obvious to more enlightened Communist economists, even in the Soviet Union, at least since Stalin's death in 1953.

Nikita Khrushchev started to tinker with it in 1957 by abolishing some twenty of the Soviet Union's technical ministries and creating 105 "economic councils" responsible for running industry on a regional basis instead of from the center in Moscow. During the first few years this measure yielded good results. But since it meant sending thousands of unhappy managers and bureaucrats to the boondocks, where amenities were few, and destroying the traditional power bases of both government technocrats and Party *apparatchiki,* resistance mounted. Modifications were introduced that, in practice, destroyed the experiment. After Khrushchev was replaced by Leonid Brezhnev in 1964, it was abandoned and the old system of many central ministries reintroduced.

A more promising—probably the only—road to improvement is something called "economic reform." It calls for introducing the forces of supply and demand, the principle of profit (though not private since the means of production remain in government or public hands), real cost accounting, and real incentives for both management and labor. The basic idea was originally worked out and suggested by a Polish economist, Professor Oskar Lange, in 1956.

Lange's ideas were adopted and enthusiastically propagated in the Soviet Union by Yevsei Liberman, a Kharkov University professor. He spelled them out in an article in *Pravda* in 1962. The principles have been known as "economic reform," Libermanism, or "new economic mechanisms" throughout the Communist world since then. The labels are interchangeable.

Libermanism contradicted the basis of existing Stalinist economics which recognized only one law—that of production expressed in physical units regardless of quality or cost—and only one method of running the economy—that of direct command and unquestioning obedience by lower echelons.

Under the Stalinist economic system, factory managers are little more than bureaucratic errand boys whose only job is to implement the production plan imposed from above.

Moreover, managers were not only told how many pieces or how many tons of a given product to make, but also how many component parts, how many workers to hire, what wages to pay, and how much in capital investment they were to put into making it.

"Economic reform"—and there are a number of variations on the basic theme—calls for a completely different approach.

In its ideal and most far-reaching form, it limits the number of plan targets to two: total output and delivery date. However, instead of output, an enterprise's performance is judged by its sales, efficiency, and the money it earns. These standards, in turn, determine the bonuses, premiums, and wage increases for management and labor. Reinvestment capital, instead of being allocated and budgeted by the state, must come out of profits or be borrowed from the state banks at interest. Market forces of a sort—that is the law of supply and demand—should prevail. These in turn would determine prices. Suppliers and manufacturers, manufacturers and wholesalers, wholesalers and retailers—all of course state-owned—should deal directly with one another instead of channeling deliveries and requisition orders through the bureaucratic ministerial maze.

In a sense, it is capitalism and the profit system without private capital or profit.

If carried to its logical conclusion, "economic reform" poses a serious challenge to various powerful vested interests in Communist societies: the Party, the government bureaucracy, and the managerial caste which has to learn new ways of doing things. The threat posed to the Party is fairly easy to recognize. If managers are given the authority to run their enterprises almost freely according to the laws of supply and demand, then they tend to become an independent force in society and to endanger the Party's self-proclaimed "leading role" in the economy. But managers, too, are threatened, because they must take the initiative and assume responsibilities for which they are unprepared after years of working in a centrally planned, command-type economy.

This is why "economic reform" has met with stiff opposition and has not got off the ground thus far in any of the Communist countries, with the exception of Hungary.

The first country to try, experimentally, was Czechoslovakia in 1963, only to drop its reform the same year. A "new economic mechanism" adopted in East Germany in 1963 proved very successful, but since 1972 exists in name only with detailed planning and decision-making back in the hands of central ministries and some big state-trusts. The Soviet Union introduced "economic reform" in 1965, but with so many built-in trip wires and hedges that in practice it was killed before it started and today operates on paper only. In 1968, under Dubcek, Czechoslovakia tried again and was well on the way to a workable, successful new system when the Russians invaded and ordered it stopped. In 1978

Romania's Nicolae Ceausescu announced a watered-down version of reform that was to take effect in 1979, and Czechoslovakia also made still another try: "economic reform" principles of management are to be tried in twelve big trust-like enterprises with 150 branch plants all over the country between 1978 and 1980. If it works well, the system will be adopted for the whole economy starting in 1981.

Thus far, only Hungary has introduced real Libermanism—in 1968—and has stuck with it ever since with the result that its economy is the most vibrant in Eastern Europe today. Government-owned companies compete against each other for shares of the market at home and abroad just the way privately owned firms do in capitalist countries.

Hungarian enterprises have incentives that those in the other countries can only dream about. For example, if they produce for export, they are allowed to keep most of the foreign exchange they earn, instead of having to turn it in to the central treasury. That way they have the dollars, West German marks, French francs, or Japanese yen with which to buy know-how and modern technology abroad to make their operations even more efficient.

What kind of life do the East European economies provide for the average citizen? The question is harder to answer than it might seem, for it depends by which standards one measures—theirs, ours, or the Soviet Union's.

By the standards of an overabundant and affluent America, or those of the wealthier West European countries, they are backward and poor, though it is important to remember that in none of them do you find the slums and abject poverty that are part of life in large American cities. For the average East European, life today is infinitely better than it was before World War II, and it is much better than it is for the average Soviet citizen.

Per capita annual incomes in 1974 (the most recent year

for which worldwide United Nations figures are available)
were $1,200 in Romania, $1,650 in Bulgaria, $2,000 in Poland,
$2,300 in Hungary, and $3,000 in Czechoslovakia. This compared at the time to $2,200 in Spain, $2,200 in Ireland, $2,700
in Italy, $3,600 in England, and $6,000 in West Germany.

But statistics like that tell only part of the story. Since
there are very few really rich or really poor people in the
Communist countries, "per capita annual income" is more like
real average income per person than it is in Western nations.
Moreover, the gap has narrowed since 1974.

Consumer durables such as cars, appliances, furniture,
clothing, and all but basic foods are comparatively much
more expensive. They take much longer to earn than in
Western countries and take a bigger chunk out of a family's
income. But other costs of living such as rent, which is never
much more than ten percent of any family's total income,
public transportation and utilities, recreation, and entertainment, cost far less. Both higher education and medical care
are practically free.

The comparison becomes less favorable when you take into
account the low quality of all products on the home markets,
the many shortages, and the fact that there is little choice of
brands, models, or designs. The dilemma usually facing
shoppers in all the East European countries is not the choice
among various kinds, colors, designs, or price ranges of a
given product, but whether it is stocked at all. And for the
two things most in demand—housing and automobiles—there
are long waiting lists.

Housing is the number one problem throughout Eastern
Europe.

Between 1960 and 1975 more than 1 million new apartments were built in Hungary, and another 430,000 are due for
completion by 1980 for which tenants have already been
earmarked. Some 460,000 additional families—about 1.5 mil-

lion people, or fifteen percent of the country's total population—remain on the waiting lists. In the meantime they are living with relatives or, as Hungarian papers reported in 1977, "in cellars, basements, attics, sheds, and even lean-tos."

The state-controlled rents are very low, but so are the standards of these accommodations. The rule of an average ten square yards of living space per person—meaning a tiny two-room apartment plus kitchen and bath for a family of three—is still the average. In fact, only nine percent of Hungarian families—regardless of size or number of children—have apartments with more than three rooms.

In Poland the woman vice-mayor of the city of Wroclaw told me proudly in 1977 that "ours is a city of love. We have the highest marriage and birth rate in the country." But housing them will be the chief problem for at least another ten, if not twenty, years.

"We are building six thousand new apartments every year," she said. "But that is not enough. Our population is growing at a rate of ten thousand annually. In addition, older housing, some built sloppily right after and some before the war, has to be replaced. We would like every young couple to be assured of an apartment when they get married, but that is a distant dream."

In fact, with an average of only eight to ten yards of living space per person, those couples are lucky to have even a bedroom of their own.

In Hungary thirty percent of all families now have an automobile. In Czechoslovakia it is close to forty percent. Poland, Bulgaria, and Romania are catching up.

I sometimes think cars are all East Europeans are interested in, and what has happened in Poland is typical.

Shortly after replacing Gomulka in 1970, Edward Gierek made Poles a promise: private cars for the masses. True to his word, he negotiated a contract with Italy's Fiat company for production of small and medium-size cars in Poland on franchise. In 1978 the two main factories, one in Warsaw, the other in Bielsko-Biala, reached full-capacity production and were turning out 300,000 automobiles a year: the Baby Fiat, a pint-size four-seater which costs 87,000 zlotys ($2,650), or about twenty months' take-home pay for the average industrial worker; and the larger, five-passenger Fiat 125 which sells for almost twice that.

The principle of purchase is the same as in all Communist countries: pay now, drive later. That is, the buyer must plunk down in cash at least half the price upon signing the contract and the balance on delivery.

But given the increase in individual income under Gierek, the lack of other consumer durables on which to spend it, and the widespread practice of moonlighting, there is no shortage of cash in Poland these days. As a result, waiting lists have gotten longer and longer and by the spring of 1978 a Pole with the money to pay for a car had to figure four years from the time of purchase until actual delivery.

Any shortage situation like this in Eastern Europe immediately produces a black market. In this case it was one in "used" cars.

A large family, for example one with four adults, would sign up for four cars simultaneously, and upon delivery immediately sell as "used" three they did not need for a handsome profit. A virtually new "used" Baby Fiat will easily sell for 130,000 zlotys ($3,965)—43,000 ($1,310) more than its list price. Even those which had been among the first to come off the assembly line, and were up to five years old in 1978, were still selling for more than what they had cost new. The car craze is so great, in fact, that almost any automobile brings a profit on the used car market. One Polish acquaintance, a journalist, sold his ten-year-old, plastic-body, two-cylinder, East German–made Trabant, a sort of motorized puddle-jumper with a roof, for exactly what he had to shell out for his new Fiat.

Who said capitalism is dead in Eastern Europe?

An even faster way to get a car—one month's delivery time instead of four years or buying it "used"—is to pay for it in "hard" foreign currency, notably American dollars or West German marks. Because of the large number of relatives that most Poles have abroad, there is no shortage of *valuta*, as foreign currency is called. It comes in thousands of envelopes from uncles, aunts, nephews, nieces, and cousins every month. And those so unfortunate as to have no kin in America or elsewhere can easily get it from tourists by offering black market exchange rates. Indeed, by mid-1978 there were some $250 million in private savings accounts in Poland and the amount grows by almost $10 million every month.

Up to the mid-1970's black market dealings in Western currencies were illegal in all five countries—both for the foreigners who sold, usually in order to make their vacations cheaper by getting exchange rates fantastically better than in their hotels or at the bank, and for the East Europeans who bought. There are many cases of Western tourists who got into trouble by selling their *valuta* in dark alleys to "dealers" who were agents of the secret police.

But along about 1977, as their trade deficits and debts with the West reached record heights, the East European regimes began taking a less stern view of black market transactions. The new attitude seemed to be that it made no difference how the *valuta* came into the countries—and eventually the national banks—just as long as it came in.

Although, technically, black market currency dealings are as illegal as they always were, mere *possession* of Western *valuta* has entered a new gray, no-questions-asked zone in some of the countries and is quite legal in others.

Along with the changed official attitude has come a flood

of government-run and -owned foreign-currency stores where highly desirable Western, as well as hard-to-get Communist-made goods are sold at surprisingly low prices to anyone who has the dollars, marks, yen, pounds, or francs to pay for them.

Such special stores have always existed in Eastern Europe and, in fact, trace their origins to the Torgsin chain started under the Stalin regime in the Soviet Union in the 1930's. But, like duty-free airport shops, they were intended primarily for Western tourists, diplomats, businessmen, foreign journalists and the privileged members of the Communist party elite.

Now they are for everybody and they are all over the place. Hungary has 86 Intertourist stores in principal cities; Czechoslovakia has 77 Tusex outlets, 24 of them in Prague alone; and in Poland there are no less than 427 Pewex shops around the country. They no longer stock merely American cigarettes, Scotch whiskies, French perfumes, and a few local handicrafts and souvenirs, but a wide array of merchandise either not available at all or at outrageous prices in regular stores. The inventory ranges from Western razor blades to cars available in a month. There are food and clothing departments, appliance sections, camera and optical goods counters, and housewares divisions.

Along with them, however, a two-currency and two-class system has started throughout the allegedly classless Communist world. East Europeans with friends and relatives abroad have become privileged citizens. So have those who are not afraid to sell their zlotys, korunas, or forints at inflated black market rates for dollars, marks, or francs to tourists in hotel lavatories or dark side streets. The underprivileged are those who obey the law or have no cousins in the West.

Meanwhile, it seems there is a practical parody on Karl Marx's favorite quotation: "From each according to his abilities, to each according to where his cousins and uncles live."

In many ways Eastern Europe is like an often-told joke about the difference between Capitalist and Communist fairy tales. The capitalist stories, so the joke goes, always start with the words, "Once upon a time . . ." Communist ones begin with the phrase "Someday there will be . . ."

But East Europeans—Communist and not—who know how little there used to be are keenly aware of how much there already is.

One of them is Zbigniew Malewski, a top executive of Poland's big steel trust—a man I have known for many years and interviewed on a number of occasions.

His rise to the top, as one of Poland's highest-paid managers, is as typically a Communist as it could be a capitalist success story. Born into a worker's family he was fourteen when the Germans invaded. He became a smithy's apprentice and during the war worked twelve hours daily in a foundry in addition to attending an underground school to get his high school diploma by 1946. He then worked his way through college and after getting his engineering degree in 1952, started the climb up the executive ladder of Poland's steel industry.

Of himself he says: "I am typical of those in my country and of my generation who were robbed of freedom, national identity, and our language during our youth. By the time the war ended, we were young adults with but a single goal—to show the world there was still a Poland which we wanted to make the best Poland in history.

"You cannot imagine what things were like then. Before the war Polish steel production had totaled only about one and a half million tons. More than eighty percent of our plants and installations were then destroyed. We were a backward country with no industrial tradition. Before the war we had only one college turning out metallurgical engineers, and in twenty years between 1919 and 1939 it had managed to graduate two hundred seventy of whom only seventy were left alive when the war ended. To get this industry started again we used foremen as technicians, technicians as engineers, and kept our fingers crossed.

"Even today half of our full-fledged engineers are village-born and peasant-raised—a first generation of people coming into contact with modern industry and technology. We have none of the inbred traditions of Western countries to fall back on. Yet my company today is one of the largest in the world and by 1980 will be producing twenty-two million tons of steel.

"With that kind of achievement to look back on," he said, "you tend not to ask many questions about the political or economic system."

Adolf Kasprzycowic tends to agree with him. He is a driller in a Polish coal mine where he has worked since getting out of the army in 1949.

"I was born and raised on a farm close to the Czechoslovak border," he told me when I met and visited him in the summer of 1977. "All I knew about coal was that city people used it to heat their stoves, but I decided to try mining."

It was the right choice. Miners are the highest-paid workers in Poland and earn more than three times the average.

Kasprzycowic, his wife and their little daughter live in a mine-owned, two-room, fifty-square-yard apartment which did not have central heating until 1975. But it is unbelievably cheap—324 zlotys ($9.80) a month, which barely puts a nick into his average monthly paycheck of almost 12,000 ($366). Moreover, it is crammed with all the glittering gadgets of the consumer society, including a fully automatic washing machine.

When I met him, he was just expecting delivery of his pint-size Polski Fiat 126 which, at his salary, had cost him less than a year's pay. When he retires in 1984, at age fifty-five, after thirty-five years in the mines, he intends to return to his native village and farm. He is a man who is proudly conscious of his achievements.

"I was ten when the Germans invaded," he said, "and not only was my family dirt poor, but I had no childhood or youth. I think I have a right to be proud now. I've worked for everything with my own hands."

To him the system has never mattered.

"It's what you do with it that counts," he said.

10

More Goulash

As recently as 1960 the major business of Eastern Europe was agriculture. Nearly sixty percent of the population was rural, living both on and off the land. Industry in such countries as Hungary, Poland, and Romania contributed less than forty percent to the national income and gross national product.

Today, less than half a generation later, the proportions are reversed. Nearly sixty percent of Eastern Europe's population is urban. In the same three countries agriculture accounts for less than sixteen percent of the GNP, in Czechoslovakia for a mere eight percent, and even in Bulgaria, which has industrialized it and made food its chief export item, farming accounts for only twenty-two percent.

This dramatic transformation in the social structure, outlook, life-styles, and working habits explains much about Eastern Europe today.

Nevertheless, more than a quarter of Eastern Europe's labor force—about 9 million adults—is engaged directly or indirectly in farming and in feeding the rest. By comparison, in the United States, with almost two and a half times the population of Eastern Europe, only 3.5 million are employed in farm work. But in the Soviet Union, a land almost three times as populous as the five East European countries, one third of those employed—about 30 million people—are in agriculture.

Those figures tell in statistical terms what is obvious to anyone who has traveled and lived in all three places: agriculture in Eastern Europe is far less efficient and productive than in the United States, but more so than in the USSR.

As in the Soviet Union itself, agriculture in Eastern Europe—with the important exception of Poland—is collectivized and state-run. That has been one of the problems.

When the Communists first took over after World War II, the big estates were taken from wealthy landowners, broken up, and the lands redistributed to the peasants whose poverty had been the cause of great misery and unrest for centuries. This policy did much to make the Communist parties popular in the early postwar years. But it wasn't long before the "little Stalins" who had come in with the Soviet forces—the "Moscow" Communists—started doing what Stalin himself had done in Russia in the late 1920's and 1930's: practically taking the new lands away from the newly independent small farmers and forcing them, often by the cruelest means, to join collectives.

It was a bitter period and there were strong objections not only from the peasants' and small farmers' political parties which were represented in the coalition governments, but also from the "home" Communists who knew the situation and attitudes much better than those who had spent the exile years in Moscow.

Poland's Wladyslaw Gomulka, then the Party chief, warned as early as May 1945 against collectivization of agriculture. "When the right conditions under which one can pursue collectivization exist in Poland," he said at a meeting of functionaries, "then our Party will not hesitate. But conditions in Poland are not ripe for it."

Ripe or not, collectivization was pushed by the harshest means and Poles paid dearly, for the results were terrible. By 1951 harvests were worse than at any time before World War II. Gomulka also paid for his opposition. He was purged and imprisoned.

One of his first moves after returning to power in 1956 was to reverse the policy. Farmers were allowed to contract out of the cooperatives and collectives they had been forced to join and within six months the number of such collectives had dropped from 10,500 to a mere 1,700. Today nearly eighty percent of Polish agriculture is privately owned.

Elsewhere in Eastern Europe, however, collectivization remained compulsory and, along with outright state ownership, has become the principal way of farming.

The system varies somewhat from country to country, and in each of them has been tinkered with from time to time. Large collective and state farms have been joined into even larger, more efficient associations with enormous pools of equipment, each specializing in some product. In Bulgaria they have been formed into "agro-industrial complexes" which combine farming with food processing and marketing. But whatever the form, it is strikingly different from farming in Western Europe or the United States.

The backbone of the system remains the collective farm, usually comprising one very large village or a number of smaller ones. Each farmer in them was forced to contribute his or her fields and livestock and theoretically each owns a share of the collective, its proceeds and profits, on the basis

One of Bulgaria's immense agro-industrial complexes

of the *kind* of work he or she does and the number of "labor days" he or she contributes each year. There are various basic types of work—administrative, mechanical, "horse and hand," animal raising, scientific-technical—which determine the *value* of each labor day, along with the profit the collective farm earns from selling its produce to the state, state-owned food-processing industries, or direct to consumers in big-city collective-farm markets.

In theory, to manage each farm, the members elect a chairman who in turn appoints various brigade leaders, each usually in charge of one village. The brigade leaders can hire outside help and experts such as tractor and combine drivers, agronomists, and various specialists.

The proportion of chairmen who are local and have worked their way up to gain the confidence of the members, and those who are graduates of agricultural colleges and are brought in from outside, usually by the local government or Communist party administration, varies from country to country.

In addition, each farm family is allowed to have a personal plot of land—about an acre or two—and "private" cows, pigs, sheep, goats, chickens, geese, and ducks. The yields from these private holdings can be sold in the markets.

In all the East European countries, the collective farms have been losing in importance to *state* farms which are not only larger and more industrialized, but are *owned* by the government. All the people working on them receive regular salaries, like factory workers. They have less independence and are further removed from traditional concepts of the East European peasant. But they work shorter hours for better pay. They have better housing, educational, recreational, and medical facilities, and life on state farms tends to be more like life in a city than life in a village.

Most state farms are huge, not unlike some agricultural

enterprises in the United States, particularly in the western states.

In all of Bulgaria, for example, there are only 170 agro-industrial complexes. Each has an average of 60,725 acres and 6,500 employees.

State farms throughout Eastern Europe are vast modern businesses. In Poland, a couple of years ago, I visited an association of them in Olsztyn, capital of what used to be East Prussia. It comprises twenty-three state farms, each with an average of 18,750 acres, a fish hatchery combine spread over 125,000 acres of lakes, and a fur ranch with thirty-five thousand foxes, mink, skunks, and weasels. The association—we would call it a big trust—does an annual gross business of $196 million.

Wladyslaw Ziajka, a farmer by upbringing and an agricultural engineer by education, is the man in charge. He presides over this huge enterprise from a suite of executive offices in a modern five-story building in downtown Olsztyn. Prim, efficient secretaries are at his beck and call, a bank of telephones and intercoms is at his finger tips. Computers help him keep track of the operation, and he is chauffeured about in a Soviet-made Volga sedan.

He drove me out to one of the farms. It comprises one large village and specializes in dairy products and cattle breeding. The herd numbers six thousand cows. Nearly a thousand people work on it. They and their families live in individual, farm-owned houses or apartment buildings with modern facilities of a kind that a generation ago would have seemed like a fairy tale promise in that backward region of Poland.

The administration center includes a whole complex of cultural, social, and recreational facilities. There is an auditorium seating two thousand, a library with several thousand volumes, a day-care center and preschool for farm workers' children, a café, large restaurant, and a discotheque. The center includes arts and crafts shops with full-time instructors. The farm has its own amateur theater group, orchestra, and dance ensemble, and the monthly entertainment schedule includes concerts, plays, and performances by professional artists from all over Poland.

The original intent behind the collectivization of East European agriculture—besides obeying and copying Stalin—was largely ideological. That is, being opposed to free enterprise and capitalism, the Communists believed that farming should be as socialistic as they were making industry and trade. Farmers and peasants are especially independent-minded people. The postwar land reform, after decades and centuries of oppression, had for the first time given them fields to till and livestock of their own to raise. They put up stiff resistance to collectivization, and the stiffer their resistance, the harsher the authorities became in forcing it. For a number of years the East European countryside was almost in a state of war—under siege from Party officials and security police who used blackmail, imprisonment, and physical violence to get what they wanted.

But since the late 1950's and early 1960's Communist ideology has had little to do with collectivization of agriculture.

The purpose, instead, has become simply modernization, mechanization, and industrialization of agriculture as well as raising the standard of living and improving the quality of life for those who work the land. Given the nature of the countryside and the traditions of farming in Eastern Europe, that has been a very sensible approach.

Except for the huge estates of the landed aristocracy and feudal barons, what private farms there were in Eastern Europe had always been tiny. Most of them never had more than a few acres, a couple of cows and pigs, some chickens and geese. When the big estates were broken up by the Communists and coalition governments after World War II, plots were handed out to landless farm laborers and tenants. While that raised the number of independent farmers, their farms were still tiny, so tiny that although they could support the families living on them, they did not leave much surplus for the growing city populations. Such farms were also too small to work profitably with expensive mechanical equipment which might raise the yield. The ox-drawn wagon or cart, the horse-drawn plow, the sixteen-hour day for the entire family, the cottage with no running water or electricity—those had been the characteristics of East European small farming before the war and well into the 1950's. In some areas they are still the characteristics. Eastern Europe, one must always remember, is a small chunk of real estate inhabited by a great many people who until quite recently were living under systems and according to traditions that had gone out of fashion in Western Europe several centuries earlier.

For all the suffering, misery, bitterness, and resentment they caused in the early years, collectivization and state ownership have changed the ways of Eastern Europe's agriculture and the face of its countryside for the better. They brought industrial means of farming: tractors, combines, and harvesting machines; irrigation programs; the use of chemical fertilizers; crop dusting; modern management and marketing; sharp drops in the agricultural labor force, and higher standards of living for those still in it.

And they brought more food for the growing urban and industrial populations. Since 1960 most of the five countries' actual production and per-acre yields of the most important grain crops have doubled. So has consumption of foods with higher nutritional values such as meat, milk, and other dairy products.

Moreover, some of the collectivization and state-ownership programs have actually become models for other countries.

Bulgaria's impressive agro-industrial complexes have created much interest in the less developed countries of Asia and Africa. Iran, India, and Algeria, for example, have signed "technical assistance" agreements that provide for Bulgarian help in setting up similar complexes there.

In Poland I once met the director of a state farm, Edmund Apolinarski, whose cattle- and sheep-breeding methods are so successful that even American agricultural students copy them.

Apolinarski, a man in his sixties, is a kind of Communist country squire. He is master over four hundred workers, ten thousand lush acres, fifteen hundred Holstein-Friesian cows which deliver an average of fifty-seven hundred quarts of milk annually, and thirty thousand sheep. He drives about in a flashy Mercedes car and lives in a two-hundred-year-old country mansion.

Apolinarski is living proof how well Communist agriculture can work when properly managed. On numerous trips to the United States he became interested in the high milk yields of American Holstein-Friesians, finally bought three hundred of them, and shipped them in three planeloads to Poland. Then he bred them and the best Polish cows with semen from prize American bulls. The results have been sensational and his breeding methods are now so respected that each year a dozen or so American students from colleges around the country come to spend the summer and watch his techniques at the state farm near Wschowa in western Poland.

Managing a big estate—not owning one—had always been his dream. He got his chance in 1945 accompanying the Soviet and Polish armies westward into former German territory. The farm he now runs is located on a huge estate that used to belong to a German landowner.

Communist agriculture has had its problems, of course,

and will continue to have them, especially in the less efficient and poorer countries.

There are periodic shortages of some products and persistent shortages of others, especially in Romania where investment in agriculture has been sadly neglected in favor of Ceausescu's efforts to industrialize the country. There are weaknesses in the systems similar to those one finds all over the Communist economies: bad management, lack of incentives, transportation snarls, equipment shortages. As a result natural calamities such as bad weather affect harvests more seriously than in Western Europe or America.

In Hungary the official press reports regularly that large state farms have too much office staff and not enough qualified specialists to do the actual work. In 1977 there were complaints that four thousand new wheat combines were needed on farms, but delivery of only two thousand could be expected. Allied Communist countries, notably East Germany, Czechoslovakia, and the Soviet Union, had failed to deliver the tractors and harvesting machines they had promised, and those they did deliver were obsolete or didn't work right. Substitutes had to be ordered from Western countries, which costs *valuta* currency.

At harvest time in some East European countries, city dwellers are sent to the countryside as "volunteers" to help bring in the crops because the collective and state farms are shorthanded or lack the necessary equipment. These "volunteers" usually work sloppily, often with the result that much of the crop is ruined. In Bulgaria a few years ago one state farm had a harvest of twenty-eight tons of tomatoes per acre, but only fifteen tons could be put on the market because the rest had been mishandled by "volunteer" workers.

It often seems that there is a chronic scarcity of all kinds of foodstuffs that are readily available on shelves in Western Europe, and Communist agricultural officials make no secret of the fact that things would be worse were it not for the products from collective farmers' personal plots of land and livestock that they sell privately in markets.

But no one goes hungry and all East Europeans not only eat better but eat more cheaply than people in the Soviet Union. Moreover, whereas the Soviet Union, despite its vast landmass and varieties of growing zones, must import grain and other foodstuffs, Hungary, Bulgaria, and even Poland are net exporters of food. In fact, their food exports account for an important part of their foreign currency earnings.

What surprises many people is that Communist-style agriculture works as well as it does and that the only country with primarily private farming—Poland—has so much trouble.

A joke told in Poland tells of a young suitor wooing his beautiful, prospective bride. "Marry me, my darling, and your every wish will be my command," he says. "You can have everything your heart desires—furs, diamonds, a Polski-Fiat sedan, a weekend cottage by the Baltic Sea, and all the finery you want. *Everything*. Except ham."

And it is not just the famous Polish ham that is scarce. All kinds of meat, sausage, poultry, sugar, and fresh vegetables and fruit were in short supply during the years 1975 through 1978. And it wasn't the first time it had happened.

In late 1976, lines up to three hours long could be seen in front of many food stores; occasionally they formed as early as five o'clock in the morning.

Special containers for collecting stale and hard bread to be used as animal fodder were set up next to the garbage and trash cans at most large apartment houses in Warsaw and other major cities.

Sugar rationing, with stamps reminding people of wartime days, was introduced early in 1977. Meat was so scarce that all butcher shops were ordered to close on Mondays.

How can this happen in a relatively rich and fertile country where nearly eighty percent of agriculture is in private hands? There are several answers and they are all complicated.

First of all, Poland exports roughly seventeen percent of all its gross agricultural product—high quality hams, geese, lamb, and beef—to help finance the import of modern technology and the ambitious industrialization program.

Second, private agriculture was for many years—until quite recently—hopelessly old-fashioned. The majority of Polish farmers had no mechanized equipment at all—not even tractors. Output depended largely on ox, horse, and human labor, and with the population shift to the cities, human labor has simply disappeared. Moreover, the state and collectivized sector of agriculture was sadly neglected for years—from 1956, when Gomulka came back to power, until after Gierek replaced him in 1970. In deciding to back private farming, without having any idea how outmoded it really was, Gomulka also ignored the collective and state-owned farms that were not disbanded. Throughout his fourteen years in office there was almost no investment in either private or Communist agriculture so that the things that are necessary on the farm these days—machinery, chemical fertilizers, insecticides, irrigation—were just not available.

It was not until the mid-1970's, well after Gierek took over, that the policy began changing.

As Wladyslaw Ziajka of Olsztyn's state farm association told me: "Agriculture got a new lease on life. Both state and private growers were given a new status as feeders of the nation. But before then, many mistakes were made for which we will be paying for a long time."

Third, sixty percent of Poland's private farmers are over fifty years of age and of this group seventeen percent have no heirs, or at least heirs willing to farm.

Two thirds of private farms have less than twelve acres and are too small to be profitable. Also, because of the inheritance practices of past centuries, these small holdings are usually divided into postage-stamp-size individual parcels, badly laid out and often located miles from each other at the far corners of townships. In countless cases fields are many miles long but only a few feet wide and bordered by stone fences. They are too narrow to farm mechanically even if the equipment were available at prices farmers could afford.

According to official Polish sources, in 1977 the mechanization of Polish agriculture was fifteen years behind that of neighboring Czechoslovakia and East Germany, ten years behind that of the Soviet Union, and twenty years behind such West European agricultural countries as France and Italy.

Of course there are private farmers who do quite well and some who are wealthy by Polish standards. One I met is Stanislaw Baginski, a trim, wiry, leather-faced man with thick, work-worn hands who owns thirty-seven acres of good land and breeds cattle not far from Wroclaw in western Poland. He has a large house filled with all modern conveniences. He does not own a car, however, because he is investing his money in another house where he intends to retire when his teen-age son takes over the farm after graduating from an agricultural school. He has a Polish tractor and a shed full of mechanical equipment and in 1977 netted 200,000 zlotys ($6,100)—50,000 ($1,525) more than a well-paid coal miner and almost four times what the average industrial worker earns. But he is more the exception than the rule.

Gierek's new agricultural policy, so Poles were hoping, would lead to more farmers like Baginski. It calls for giving farmers more incentives by making more mechanical equipment and chemicals available at prices they can afford and for higher purchase prices by the state-owned food-processing monopolies. Private farmers have been given better tax breaks and subsidies, and have been included in the governmental old-age pension and social security program. Finally, restrictions on buying more land—from neighbors who want to move to cities or retire—have been lifted.

What results these measures will have will not really be known until the 1980's. But it is ironic that up to now the last big preserve of capitalism in an otherwise Communist world has performed so poorly.

11

A Reporter's Notebook

"We have two official churches—Catholic and Communist," a highly placed Pole said to me. "That's why we have both meatless Fridays and meatless Mondays."

Jokes about the meat shortage and the endless lines of desperate customers at butcher shops are many in this unusual country.

The official explanation for the meat shortage is that Poland has suffered three consecutive bad harvests that led to emergency slaughtering, a reduction in livestock population, and increases in fodder prices. Farmers have no incentive to raise more beef and pork.

Moreover, say government officials, Poland has to export much of its quality meat, especially ham, to pay for the import of modern technology. Yet, a prosperous private farmer near Olsztyn disagrees with the official explanations.

"There is only one cause for the so-called meat shortage," he said. "People are just too well off and have too much money to spend on food."

There is some truth in what he said.

For despite the meat shortage, Poland is booming and Poles have literally never had it so good. Seven straight years of ten percent annual growth in the GNP, twenty percent yearly increases in investment, and more than a doubling of personal take-home pay—with stable prices—have changed the face of Poland beyond recognition.

Private motorcar ownership has more than tripled since Gierek replaced Gomulka as Party chief. To be sure, there is still a waiting period of more than four years for a car, but parking spaces in downtown Warsaw and other major cities are already hard to find. Rush hour traffic jams have become part of the Polish way of life. And the country is getting a network of well-paved two- and four-lane highways.

In the countryside the horse-drawn cart, almost a symbol of Poland before 1970, is giving way to the tractor. There are now more than half a million of them.

Compared to a few years ago, and compared to some other Communist countries, the assortment of consumer goods— most of them well made, attractively designed, and within the average Pole's means—is surprising.

At least in the big cities the appearance of Poles is becoming harder to distinguish from that of Western visitors, though, as one Pole points out, that is because so many Poles have emigrated in decades and centuries past.

"What you see people wearing," he said, "is what their relatives abroad have sent them or what they have bought in the hard-currency shops with the dollars their overseas kin have stuffed into the letters."

Next to ham, the housing shortage is issue number one and openly admitted as such by the Gierek regime. Poland has the youngest population and one of the highest birthrates in Europe—East or West—and what Poles want most these days is proper housing for their growing families.

So, the discontent is mostly over the little daily troubles that are part of life in all Communist countries. Or, as one Warsaw acquaintance put it: "What good are all the cars, automatic washers, new coal mines, copper smelters, and shipyards if I cannot find a pair of shoelaces or have to stand in three one-hour lines to buy a roll of toilet paper?"

The supply problem is not the only contradiction in this land of strange contrasts.

The Catholic Church claims ninety-five percent of the adult population as practicing believers, the Communist party almost ten percent of all Poles as members, with the result that there are hundreds of thousands who belong to both the Church and the Party.

It is a Communist country where one sees neither portraits of Lenin nor the Party and government leaders in public offices—only the white Polish eagle on a red shield. Moreover, Poland is the only Communist country where regimes have twice been toppled by popular uprisings and where the government has had to revoke unpopular measures under public pressure.

All these factors make the Polish ball game a different one in the East European league.

According to an old Polish saying, "A hungry Pole is an angry Pole." Though Poles today are far from hungry, they are angry.

Their discontent, as one high-ranking Party official told me, may be because "we made too many promises we couldn't keep, raised expectations too high, and failed to tell the truth in a convincing manner. No doubt we have lost confidence, but we are learning—the hard way."

Bucharest

Long lines in and outside stores in Romania are the rule, not the exception.

But the lines that formed at barber shops on Bucharest's busy Victoria Street one Saturday in September were unusual even by Romanian standards. Those waiting were nearly all long-haired teen-age boys who needed haircuts in order to be readmitted to schools and colleges the following Monday after summer vacation.

There is no written law requiring male students to shear their locks, and no one can say for sure just how short a boy's hair is supposed to be. But it is quietly understood that teachers, principals, and deans expect to be able to tell the difference between the sexes at first glance and will give students trouble if they can't.

The nationwide trimming of a summer's growth was but one symptom among many of the straitlaced drive of puritanism in Romania these days.

The regime of Nicolae Ceausescu has also launched an antialcohol campaign. Some two thousand bars and taverns around the country have been closed and turned into quick-lunch places, bakery shops, and pancake houses.

There is a chronic shortage of food and consumer products. The regime blames it on floods in the Danube basin and the earthquake that rocked the country in March 1977, but Romanians in the know grumble that the supply was never good. To me the consumer goods situation looked worse than on previous visits in the late 1960's and early 1970's.

Moreover, the available merchandise is shoddily made by any East European standard and outrageously priced in relation to the average industrial worker's monthly take-home pay of 1,700 lei ($141 at the tourist, $380 at the official, exchange rate).

By day, Bucharest—often described as the "Paris of the East"—gives the impression of a bustling, affluent metropolis. If one does not look too closely.

Its wide streets such as the Boulevard Magheru and Boulevard Gheorghiu-Dej vibrate with traffic. Romanian women are by far the most strikingly beautiful, the men the most handsome, in the Communist world. Both men and women have a remarkable ability to put their natural attributes to the most advantageous and tasteful display with a minimum of fashionable clothing—most of it bought illegally and on the black market from Western tourists.

But at night Bucharest is blacked out as if expecting an air raid. Neither store windows nor neon signs are illuminated and the only lights on the streets are dim, flickering yellow lamps.

The brownout was imposed after the 1974 world energy crisis, but has remained in force ever since. Officially it is explained as an economy measure, but Romanians suspect there may be other motives. The darkness, they hint, keeps these night-life loving people at home and gets them to bed early.

That not only assures their reporting to work punctually in the mornings to keep the wheels of industry rolling, but probably stimulates the birthrate which the government has been trying to raise ever since it outlawed abortion in 1967—then as now practically the only means of birth control.

"We export electric power to places as far away as Austria for hard currency and the Party keeps telling us how successful we are," said one woman, "but here things just get darker and darker."

Restaurants, such as they are, are crowded to the point of bursting—a sign, so Romanians point out, of the constant food shortage in grocery stores as well as the lack and inadequate selection of consumer goods on which to spend what excess cash there is.

But even by the rather modest standards of other Communist capitals, restaurant food is bad and service worse. Except for a half dozen that cater largely to foreign visitors, all restaurants close with a frightening suddenness at 11:00 P.M.

Nowhere in Eastern Europe is the power and the presence of the state quite as evident as in Romania—in the form of an endless parade of uniformed police as well as less obvious, though no less watchful, guardians of law and order.

As one acquaintance said sarcastically: "Ten percent of the population is made up of officials and bosses. Forty percent are policemen. The remaining fifty percent supports the other half. No wonder we aren't making any economic progress."

Yet despite all the cops, nowhere in Eastern Europe have I been stopped so often and openly on the street by black marketeers offering lucrative exchange rates for dollars or determined, literally, to buy the shirt off my back. Although penalties for such transactions are high, the dealers swarm like locusts.

"It's the only way to make ends meet and live in reasonable comfort," explained one when asked why he persists in the face of the high risks. "And after all, you live but once."

What also disturbs Romanians are the restrictions on travel abroad, explained officially by a shortage of hard currency in the national bank, but due, according to Romanians in the know and Western diplomats, to a sudden rise in the defection rate.

A two months' wait for an exit visa and passport is standard, regardless of whether the destination is West or East, and then it is often like playing a lottery. If a passport is refused, there is never an explanation and no way to appeal.

To make up for its trade deficit and foreign exchange shortage, the government requires all tourists visiting Romania to exchange a minimum of ten dollars daily and has banned them from renting rooms in private homes or living with relatives and friends.

The measure is counterproductive. It has put a damper on tourism, especially on the many Italians who used to come and who cannot afford expensive government-operated hotels.

The method behind all this seeming madness remains Nicolae Ceausescu's efforts to stake out Romania's independence from the Soviet Union. That policy appeals to the deep-seated national pride and patriotism of Romanians. Despite more criticism about his airs and activities, the *conducator* and "beloved son of the people" remains surprisingly popular.

The question both Western observers and thinking Romanians are asking these days is how much more sacrifice Ceausescu can demand?

"Of course we want to preserve our independence from Russia," said one Romanian acquaintance. "And we are proud that our country is regarded as an important partner by other world powers. We also understand that this requires a lot of effort and self-denial. But there comes a time when we should also ask whether the price is not too steep or the effort perhaps self-defeating."

No one, it seems, ever asks whether a different approach with less wasted motion might not reduce the price.

Budapest

"You cannot imagine how glad I am to be back in Budapest and how fortunate I now consider myself to live in Hungary."

The young Hungarian who made that remark in a Budapest café is not a propagandist for the regime of Janos Kadar but a graduate student who had just returned from a year of Russian language studies in Moscow.

He was comparing life in his hometown and native country with what he had seen and experienced in the Motherland of Communism.

The comparison is striking.

If Moscow is a constant reminder of the oppressiveness and deficiencies of Communism, then Budapest presents an elegant, carefree, and affluent argument for "Communism without pain."

Hungarians themselves often call their country "the merriest barracks in Eastern Europe." Those who visit it from the West, remembering how the Hungarians staged a bloody revolution that was crushed mercilessly by Soviet tanks, will find it hard to completely ignore the feeling that it is a barracks. But seen from the perspective of Eastern Europe, the merriment seems a fantasia of free and easy living.

According to a popular Hungarian saying, a Hungarian is someone who enters a revolving door second but comes out first. There is evidence all over the country that the saying is true.

Hungary's door has revolved three times since those tragic weeks in the fall of 1956 when Eastern Europe's first attempt to liberalize Communism was crushed by Nikita Khrushchev's armor.

The initial turn came in December 1961 when Kadar called a halt to the repression practiced after the revolution and coined his famous slogan, "He who is not against us, is for us."

Two years later, in March 1964, on an official state visit, Khrushchev himself gave the door another spin. Departing from his prepared text during a speech at a Budapest lightbulb factory, he said:

"There are some people who call themselves Communists and Marxist-Leninists and claim they are working for a better world. But they do not consider it important to strive for higher living standards. They only call for revolution, revolution, revolution. But revolutionary passion alone is not enough. We also need a good plate of goulash—better clothes, good housing, schools for the children . . ."

Although Khrushchev's off-the-cuff remarks were directed against Red China and Mao Tse-tung, in Hungary, where goulash is like daily bread, they were taken at face value.

Finally, in 1968, in order to implement "goulash communism," the Hungarian Party launched the "new economic mechanism"—the only real system of "economic reform" in the Soviet bloc. It encouraged Hungarians to work harder for more money and provided the goods to buy so as to make their efforts worthwhile.

One mark of its success is the ease with which meat prices were raised in the summer of 1976 without causing so much as a ripple, let alone the sort of uprising that rocked Poland a few weeks earlier when its regime tried to do the same thing.

As an influential Communist editor once put it when asked what political effect a summer drought might have: "None except that vegetables may become more expensive. Isn't that just what happens in your country?"

Budapest is still—or perhaps again—one of the great cities of Europe, although the stucco facades of its gingerbread, Victorian-style buildings are crumbling, its creaky yellow streetcars all need a coat of paint, and there is a general scruffiness which tends to leave a Parisian or a Roman unimpressed.

The country swarms with tourists—sixteen million in 1978, more than Hungary's population. One fourth of them are from the West.

Every third family now owns a car—all imported since Hungary makes none of its own. Parking spaces in the capital are at a premium any time and during rush hours the jams reach New York-like proportions—something to which chok-

One of Budapest's finest old buildings is
the ornate State Opera House.

ing and coughing Hungarians still point with pride rather than alarm.

As in Poland, the housing shortage remains the number one problem. But Hungarians are solving it in their own way. More than sixty percent of new accommodations are being built for sale, not rental, and the chief complaint is the high cost of credit.

More than forty percent of both urban and rural families (although only thirty-two percent in Budapest itself) now *own* their houses or apartments. And along the banks of the Danube as well as the shores of Lake Balaton, private weekend cottages are shooting up faster than the mushrooms that are so important to Hungarian cooking.

Store windows and shelves bulge with merchandise of every kind and origin. There is so much that a baffled Russian visitor, accustomed to nothing but empty shelves and bare counters at home, recently asked a Hungarian friend: "Your shops are so full of merchandise. Are people so poor they can't buy anything?"

The words "line" and "shortage" seem to have disappeared from the language.

Most striking, however, is the relaxed way of Hungarian-style Communism. Budapest boasts two thousand seven hundred restaurants, cafés, bars, taverns, and night clubs—more than in all of Russia—and they vibrate with the sounds and smells of Hungarians living the good life.

The country's four hundred rock and pop ensembles seem to disturb only the older generation, not the guardians of Communist morals.

Western newspapers and books are available to everyone, everywhere.

There are no red banners calling on the masses to work harder, almost no statues of Lenin. But there are open churches and wayside crucifixes and shrines.

The best-known dissidents, of which there are few, belong to the New Left which does not complain of a lack of human rights and freedom but that the regime is not Communist enough.

Above all, Hungarians can travel. Every three years they can draw up to $250 a person for a trip to capitalist countries, and if relatives or friends abroad are willing to pay, they can go as often as they like.

It is only at the borders, on leaving, that one is reminded that this is a Communist country. The search for refugees believed hidden under the hoods or seats of cars is long and careful. But the guards are not looking for Hungarians. The searches are a favor to East Germany, Czechoslovakia, and Romania, whose less fortunate citizens try to use Hungary as an escape hatch.

Prague

"We've already taken care of other little countries, so why not yours, too? And as for the intellectuals, don't worry. In fifty years there'll be a new generation, healthier than this one."

These cold remarks, according to reliable sources, were made by Soviet Party chief Leonid Brezhnev to Czechoslovakia's Alexander Dubcek in the week after the 1968 invasion.

More than ten years have passed since then with nearly forty left to go. So there's still time.

But if the mood in Prague these days is any indication, Brezhnev's timetable for "normalization" is running behind schedule.

Outwardly, of course, everything looks normal enough.

Personal incomes have risen and the stores have enough consumer goods on which to spend the money.

Butcher shops are well stocked. So well, in fact, that Poles come from across the border on long weekend shopping sprees to buy the meat they cannot find at home.

Delicatessens brim with smoked hams, sausages of many varieties, plump roasted chickens revolving on spits, tins of Chinese pork, Mexican prawns, Scotch whiskies, and even Coca-Cola, which is made on license.

According to the official press the supply of automobiles exceeds demand, making Czechoslovakia the first Communist country to reach this degree of consumer bliss. To persuade more people to buy them, cars several years ago were made available on the installment plan with thirty percent down and three years to pay at five percent interest.

Prague is proud of its new subway. The streets teem with traffic. People seem busy.

But visitors who can penetrate this facade of well-being soon find a different picture—of apathy, disillusionment, passive resistance, and pent-up hatred.

There are the little signs, the hints between the lines of the tightly controlled press, the chance remarks, the carefully worded viewpoints which form a picture of a sad country and people.

Take the movie houses which have been showing some very excellent Russian films. They are nearly empty. But those where the trashiest movies from the West play are packed and crowded.

Then there's the man who recently bought a Soviet-made Fiat-Zhiguli car and who says defensively, "Well, it *is* a good automobile, but I prefer to think of it as Fiat first and then, maybe, a Zhiguli."

Or there's the fellow who says that the only political issue to arouse any interest is an increase in the price of beer.

A taxi driver—until the purges after the invasion he was a Party member and prominent researcher at a scientific institute—is seen reading a book while waiting for fares. He keeps it wrapped in newspaper. "I just think it's better not to show everyone what I read," he explains. "Besides, it has not been published here. I got it from a German tourist." The book was a novel by West German Nobel prize winner Heinrich Böll.

A prominent but purged and discredited writer tells an Italian Communist correspondent: "Things were better even under Antonín Novotný. At least there were discussions in the Party, different viewpoints and opinions. Now there is nothing but intellectual hibernation."

The official press admits that Communist party membership is down more than 500,000 from its spring 1968 high and probably at its lowest point in more than thirty years of Communist rule.

A foreign ministry official concedes that despite an amnesty aimed at persuading sixty thousand émigré Czechoslovaks to return home, the number who have come back "is not too great . . . perhaps several thousand."

In the fall of 1977 a group of former university professors— all fired and purged after the invasion—formed a small organization known as the Association of Stokers with Higher Degrees. Stoking coal is the dirtiest, most poorly paid work in Czechoslovakia. It is what large numbers of the old elite have been doing since falling from grace a decade or so ago.

There are research scientists working as night watchmen in their old institutes. Department heads have become clerks in their old ministries. One Western ambassador's chauffeur holds a doctor of laws degree from Prague University.

These are fleeting impressions of the mood and situation in Czechoslovakia today.

But the most unforgettable sign is the grave of Jan Palach, the student who set himself afire in Prague's Wenceslaus Square in January 1969 in protest against the Soviet occupation. It is covered with fresh wreaths and new flowers every day.

The conflicting picture between the "outer" and the "inner" Czechoslovakia results from Party chief Gustav Husak's attempt to conduct a two-faced policy. He is offering the "carrot" of beer-and-dumplings Communism in order to offset the intellectual and political repression which he still wields.

Most observers in Prague doubt that it will work. Dissent is becoming stronger and louder, especially the human rights movement, which has as its leaders some of the most prominent Dubcek-era politicians and thinkers. And the economy is practically at a standstill.

An estimated forty percent of the country's industrial managers were removed during the post-invasion purge of the reform movement. Some 100,000 of the most able intellectuals, politicians, teachers, professors, scientists, engineers, and technicians were fired. That drain on the country is beginning to show.

A decade after the invasion, the men whose reform ideas triggered it are forced into silence and kept from view. The new kind of Communism they hoped to create remains a shattered dream.

12

The New East Europeans

"But you're a nobody if you don't have them," a sixteen-year-old Budapest girl complained.

"Them" is a pair of genuine, imported blue jeans for which she was willing to pay more than 1,500 forints on the black market. That is about $80 at the tourist exchange, or about ten days' average pay in Hungary.

Jeans, like numerous other items of Western clothing, have become status symbols in Eastern Europe, and officialdom does not like what they symbolize—a fascination for things alien, especially American.

There is, of course, no formal ban on having them.

In fact, state-owned clothing factories in all the countries actually make them, and in 1978 Hungary even signed an agreement with Levi Strauss and Company to manufacture jeans on license according to the original American designs and patterns.

But only foreign jeans have status value. Domestic ones, hard to tell from the imported except by label, don't. And it is status that counts among East European youth.

"Our country's population," a Hungarian newspaper commented in the fall of 1977, "can be divided into two categories: those who are wearing foreign-made jeans—old, new, or tattered—and those who are not but would like to."

Long hair and beards also give status. So do American military insignia and slogans sewn on clothes; T-shirts with the names of American colleges and universities on them; black market rock and pop records; chewing gum; and motorbikes. It's also popular to lace conversation with foreign words, especially American slang expressions. "Status" is anything that sets young people off from the Communist norm.

And that irritates the Communist regimes.

"Too many young people," a Czechoslovak magazine said not long ago, "have the wrong priorities—free time, money, an apartment, a cabin in the country, travel. Of course, these values are not to be condemned. But for many they have become the ultimate aims in life. They do not realize that other values should rate higher: their attitudes to work, for example, toward their Communist homeland, and to the struggle for peace and Communism in the world."

In Bulgaria there is deep concern about such "alarming" things as "disfiguring beards, side whiskers, and disgraceful clothes . . . which are expressions of anti-Communist behavior that lead to political nihilism."

"It is high time," Bulgaria's prosecutor-general Ivan Vachkov said a few years ago, "to initiate restrictive measures that will prevent such abnormal ways among youth." He recommended that schools, plants, offices, and local town councils impose penalties and use the police to control them. "And if those measures prove inadequate," he said menacingly, "there are other ways to prevent and eradicate such displays of anti-Communist attitudes and behavior."

What Eastern Europe's Party leaderships—some more, some less—hope for in the young generation is a propaganda cliché: millions of youths marching diligently and in unison toward a bright Communist future with portraits of Lenin held high. They would like to think of them as all studying hard, all obeying their parents and surrendering their seats to grandmothers on the streetcars and subway trains, all ready to ask what they can do for their countries, all grateful for what the governments have already done for them, all highly disciplined, and all total believers in Communism.

But Eastern Europe's youth is not like that. In fact, the young people of the Communist world are in many respects like young people everywhere.

They want to travel—and not just to other Communist countries. Poles and Hungarians can. Young Czechoslovaks, Bulgarians, and Romanians cannot.

They want their own idols, not those of their parents, much less those put on pedestals by the Communist parties.

They resent restrictions and being disciplined. But by the very nature of the political system under which they live, they face more restrictions and more discipline than youth in Western democracies.

They object to being told what to do and how to do it, but it is in the nature of Communism to tell them both. They dislike being regimented and having even free time and social activities organized for them, but regimentation and organization of life are essential to the system under which they live.

Like youth everywhere, young East Europeans are concerned about their futures. But more than young people else-where, they are extremely cynical about their prospects—because of the credibility gap between Communist promise and reality.

They are critical and they question. But the system tries to deny them this universal right of youth because it claims to be perfect, infallible, and to have all the answers.

The result is that the East European countries are faced with enormous "generation gaps."

A survey of attitudes and free-time preferences among teen-agers completely baffled older Czechoslovaks in 1977. Asked about their greatest interests and how they would like to use their spare time, the majority listed going to the movies, watching TV, playing sports, dancing, listening to records or tapes, meeting boys or girls, "not doing anything," riding or working on motorbikes and in cars, going to a café, and playing musical instruments.

"Obviously," said the Party paper which published the survey results, "we must do more to inspire educational and cultural activities among youth by organizing better facilities. Just watching movies, TV, sitting around, or playing with cars and motorbikes is not very constructive."

Hungary, for example, has an extensive program to pro-vide organized summer work for high school and college students. Most of the jobs are on construction sites and in factories, and those young Hungarians who participate—the program is voluntary—live in camps. The official aims are "to give youngsters an opportunity to appreciate and learn to love work, which is part of Communist education" and to supply labor for the economy during the summer "mainly in seasonal jobs and to replace workers on vacation." To the 250,000 young Hungarians who participate, however, the main purpose is "to get some forints into my pockets."

What they do learn seems to be the exact opposite of what the Communist Youth League and the Party, which organize the summer programs, would like them to learn.

"I worked in a cannery," said one high school junior. "They said the foreman would show me what to do, but he only came around for a few minutes in the mornings. Most of the time we fought great tomato battles. The red juice splattered everywhere. It was just like a crime movie."

"They pushed me off into a corner of one of the offices and the grown-ups never noticed me," said another. "They only worked when the boss was in the room. The moment he left they started saying all sorts of bad things about him and stopped working. Sometimes I was left alone in the room. No one would have noticed if I had gone to the movies."

What also worries the official adult world in Eastern Europe is the spread of a "consumerist mentality" among youth. Bulgarian authorities, for example, expressed "grave concern" about the answers Sofia high school students gave when asked in a survey several years ago where they would most like to live. The majority replied "America" and a number were even quite specific about where: "Florida."

"There's nothing for me to do here, no future," one youngster replied. "The only thing that's important to me is how to get to America." His reasons were the higher standard of living he expected to find there.

To the Communist party leadership such attitudes result from "capitalist, Western subversion and infiltration." They rarely stop to think and question their own failings.

One exception was Elena Panova, an assistant professor of philosophy and lecturer on Marxism at Sofia University who asks: "What has prompted these youngsters to think that living in the U.S. is so much better? Is it just the illusions they get from Western magazines and movies, or are we, perhaps, too clumsy in our own propaganda? Our comparisons with the capitalist world are so bad that critically minded young people find it hard to grasp the real and sometimes unsolvable problems facing the young generation in capitalist America."

The Party would have been wise to heed her words. Instead it launched a campaign for more of the usual indoctrination and began cracking down on young people "not engaged in socially useful work." A government decree was issued requiring all high school students to apply either for jobs, college admission, or military service within one month after graduation. They must accept jobs assigned them within fifteen days or face fines of up to 200 leva ($222).

The "pro-Western, consumerist mentality" also disturbs officialdom in Czechoslovakia. In the early years after the Communist takeover, Prague's weekly *Tvorba* complained not long ago, "the young were enthusiastic and showed initiative. Today their interests focus mainly on modern music and their desire to own a tape recorder."

The Party attributes this change in attitude to "enemy ideology and propaganda." To combat it, there are the usual recommendations for a change in educational programs that will assure "a deeper identification with the ideals of Communism." It should begin even in preschools and kindergartens by stressing "collective thinking" among the very young and combatting "egoism and individualism."

The antimilitaristic and pacifistic mood among the young also concerns East European authorities.

Czechoslovakia's armed services, for example, are having difficulty recruiting volunteers and face strong antiauthoritarian and antimilitaristic attitudes among draftees.

"Pacifistic views and moods among youths who have experienced neither capitalism nor war are especially dangerous," *Rudé Právo,* the Party daily, warned a few years ago. "We must strengthen the socialist military awareness of young people."

In Bulgaria the Communist Youth League leadership was reshuffled in 1975 only to imbue young Bulgarians with a "more positive and patriotic view" of military service.

But these efforts seem to be having little effect.

Young Czechoslovaks, for example, refuse to accept the idea that large standing armies are even necessary in an age of nuclear standoff. Moreover, such armies strike them as harmful in a period of improving East-West relations.

"Why do they bother us with this?" remarked one young Czech when called up for a military exercise as a reservist. "After all, talks about disarmament are going on everywhere."

"If I had the money this show costs, you can bet I'd know what to do with it," said another, summing up a civil defense display in a town just north of Prague.

Throughout the world—capitalist and Communist—the generation gap is probably greatest when the discussion between old and young turns to the question of rock and pop music. But to the older generation in Eastern Europe—and the Soviet Union—it seems to be less the sound of the music that bothers them than its alleged "anti-Communist ideological content." The music, accompanied by the trend to long hair, beards, and "outlandish clothing," struck most of the high priests of Communist orthodoxy as a huge capitalist conspiracy to undermine their systems and subvert their youths. But it spread like wildfire—underground, on the black markets in the form of smuggled records and tapes rerecorded from Western radio transmissions, or bought illegally at sky-high prices from foreign tourists.

Unable to fight the trend, officialdom decided to join it. The strains of rock and pop were given grudging approval—

*Party officials frown on the continuing
popularity of rock music.*

provided the texts accompanying the electronic sound met the requirements of ideological purity. Marx and Moog, not to mention the electric guitar and organ, entered a period of shaky "peaceful coexistence." The results were sometimes puzzling, if not amusing, to the Western ear.

Thus Romanian teen-agers rocked to the sounds of a pop group called Red Guitars playing such lively numbers as "Glory to Our President," "Communist Years," "Comrade, Hurry Up," and "The Party, Ceausescu, Romania."

About the mid-1970's, however, both the young generation and Party theorists began having second thoughts about the odd marriage between capitalist sound and Communist words. The kids began complaining, as one Hungarian youth put it, that "the words are just plain stupid." Many of the pop groups started writing their own. The guardians of Communist morals reacted by cracking down on the groups and spread of the music.

The most drastic crackdown was in Czechoslovakia, where in the spring of 1976 police arrested twenty-two members of what were once Prague's most popular rock groups: The Plastic People of the Universe and DG-307. They were charged, among other things, with "long-haired rowdyism," "illegal public performances," and "damage to public property."

Public performances by both groups had been outlawed since shortly after the Soviet-led invasion in 1968 and virtually all the clubs, bars, theaters, and discotheques in which they used to play were closed down. But the Plastic People and DG-307 continued to do their thing—in private homes and, when those were not available, outdoors in forests and fields. Their illegal performances were recorded and filmed amateurishly. Copies existed by the thousands, sold faster than Czechoslovak dumplings, and became the main attraction of the youth subculture.

The immediate causes for the arrests were performances by the Plastic People at a private party in a Pilsen youth club, December 1975, and at the wedding of Ivan Jirouš, one of the members of the group, in Prague, February 1976. More than a dozen of those arrested were tried and sentenced to terms of up to three years in prison.

Rock, jeans, pacifism, skepticism, and the "consumerist mentality" are all expressions of youthful rebellion against the rules and regulations of Communist society and the way the Communist parties attempt to regulate and regiment the young through the official Communist Youth leagues.

But another form of rebellion is juvenile delinquency. In Czechoslovakia juvenile crime has more than tripled in the decade since the invasion.

In 1968, the year of Alexander Dubcek's "Communism with a human face," nearly five thousand youths aged fifteen to eighteen were sentenced for criminal offenses. Nowadays the number is more than seventeen thousand and according to official Czechoslovak statistics the increase has been steady since 1968. Publicly, of course, Czechoslovak officials would never dare mention a link, but the timing of this dramatic increase seems more than just a coincidence. Moreover, the message is clearly legible between the lines. As a government spokesman once put it, "The rise is due to the crisis of society and the destruction of social conscience and morality."

Juvenile delinquency in Czechoslovakia takes many forms: vandalism, rowdyism, and drunkenness head the list, but more serious crimes such as larceny, robbery, rape, and murder are not too far behind.

Among the causes mentioned are those also familiar to Western authorities: poor housing, lowered values of life as a result of industrialization and urbanization, and other features of alienation that are part of modern society. But those factors were just as strong under Dubcek as they are today and do not explain the sharp increase since 1968.

Juvenile crime worries officials all over Eastern Europe more than any kind, because it does not jibe with the Marxist textbooks. Since crime is supposed to be a product of capitalism, the young generation, born since the Communist takeovers thirty years ago, is supposed to be the least criminally inclined.

Despite the signs and symptoms of Eastern Europe's youth rebellion, the young generation is not basically anti-Communist, nor is it really disloyal.

"I don't see what wearing blue jeans or a Harvard sweat shirt has to do with politics or ideology," a young Hungarian once said to me. "It's just fashionable. As for beards and long hair, well, Karl Marx wasn't exactly bald or clean-shaven."

Unlike their parents, the new East Europeans have not suffered the backwardness of their countries, fascist dictatorships, Nazi occupation, war, or Stalinism. By the standards of their elders, they are privileged, pampered, and perhaps even spoiled or too demanding. But at the same time they are refreshingly critical, well-informed about the world outside, and surprisingly outspoken. I have yet to meet a young Pole, Hungarian, Czech, Slovak, Romanian, or Bulgarian who was afraid to voice an opinion.

Those who can travel abroad also want to return to their homelands.

"Of course I know life is better and easier in the West," said one young Pole. "But for people my age, the future is at home. I am not a Communist, but neither am I anti-Communist or in favor of a return to capitalism. I want more freedom and a better life, and I want it for Poland. And I think we can get it by being a little less narrow-minded, more flexible and more tolerant than the generation of Communists who brought us the system after World War II."

As in the Soviet Union, East European youth activities are closely regulated by the Communist Youth leagues or similar Party-controlled organizations. Membership age ranges from fourteen to twenty-nine. Some twenty-five million East Europeans are in that age group, but only around twelve million belong. Membership, though not mandatory, is an important stepping stone to Party and government careers and to getting ahead in life.

To get ahead in Eastern Europe, as everywhere, one needs an education. And there is no denying that the Communist regimes have done much to educate their people. This has historical origins. All the parties have roots in the nineteenth-century German "workers' education societies" which, influenced by Marx, gave birth to both modern Socialism and Communism. Dedicated to the principle that "knowledge is power," education has always been as much a part of the Communist platform as revolution. Thus, illiteracy, once widespread, has been virtually eliminated. Schooling is universal and free.

The educational systems vary considerably from country to country, however, being patterned after the Soviet ten-year model in some, such as Bulgaria, and the twelve- to thirteen-year programs of Germany and Austria in other countries such as Hungary. But no matter what the system, the programs are tough and demanding.

Traditions—some dating back to the eighteenth and nineteenth centuries—play an important part in East European education.

In the Polish city of Nysa, for example, local officials proudly showed me the Karolinum, a seventeenth-century *gymnasium,* or high school whose best-known graduate was King John Sobieski. It was famed then as now for being one of the toughest but finest secondary schools in the country.

In Romania pupils are still required to wear school uniforms, a tradition that goes back more than a hundred years. In fact, in 1972 the ministry of education ordered that young-sters must wear the uniforms after school hours as well. This caused a howl from teen-agers who complained that the drab, gray clothing "standardizes" and "makes us ugly."

Throughout Eastern Europe there has been a virtual ex-plosion of higher education since before World War II and the Communist takeovers—in numbers of students as well as the number of college- and university-level institutions. The most striking example is Poland, where the number of higher schools has more than tripled from twenty-eight in 1939 to the present eighty-nine, and the number of students has mush-roomed more than ten times, from 14 per 1,000 population to 145 per 1,000 in 1977. The Polish educational explosion was greatest in those territories of western and northern Poland that were German until 1945. In those regions there were only four universities and colleges with a combined enrollment of about 6,000. Today there are twenty-nine with more than 110,000 students.

This educational boom has done much to change attitudes and life-styles in Eastern Europe.

Take the case of the Polish city of Gliwice, called Gleiwitz when it was German. It was there on August 31, 1939, that the German SS staged the fake attack on the radio station that served as Hitler's pretext for invading Poland the next morning. In those days it was a sleepy provincial town. To-day it is a bustling, energetic city of 200,000 inhabitants, more than ten percent of whom are students and academics, for Gliwice is now the home of the Silesian Polytechnical Uni-versity. It was started by Poles from the eastern part of the country which Poland lost to Russia.

"We literally built this school from scratch," Dr. Woiciech Sitko, one of the deans, told me. Sitko himself was one of the first graduates, having enrolled shortly after the war. "All that was here was an abandoned elementary school and most of the students in the early years were as busy actually building the school as they were studying."

With a student body of nineteen thousand and a faculty of more than two thousand, it ranks as the second largest polytechnical institute in Poland, and it has completely changed the character and life-style of Gliwice.

The city has one of the highest proportions of academics and intellectuals in Poland. A town of professors and scientists, of dozens of special research institutes, it is literally the "brains of the Silesian coal and steel basin." It bustles with student- and faculty-run cultural activities, art galleries, satirical theaters, and political cabarets, all open to and regularly attended by the general public.

Most students in all five countries receive some form of assistance covering tuition, books, and room and board, though these scholarship programs vary from country to country as do the percentages of students receiving aid. In Poland it is nearly three fourths, in Czechoslovakia over half. In Romania tuition itself is free and sixty percent of the students are accommodated without cost in dormitories and receive free cafeteria meals. Scholarships and aid are based on both family incomes and academic performance in all the countries.

Under the Communist regimes there has also been a pronounced shift in the social and class makeup of the student body. In Poland, for example, children of peasant and worker families represented a scant twenty percent of the total enrollment in 1938, compared to almost fifty percent today.

East European education is good in terms of quantity. Quality is a different matter. How you judge it depends on what you expect from an educational system in the first place. If it is supposed to dispense only knowledge, then the East European systems do very well indeed, probably better than America's. But if the aim is to teach people to think, question, and challenge, then Eastern Europe's, though much better than the Soviet Union's, do not match up.

There are various reasons for this. These are *European* systems in which traditionally the emphasis has been, and remains, on discipline, rote learning, and the accumulation of a large number of facts. In science classes, for example, the teachers do the experiments, the students merely copy the results while memorizing formulas and equations. In literature courses they devote more time to memorizing the works than learning to interpret. To an extent this is true for education throughout Europe, Eastern and Western. But in Eastern Europe one must add the Communist effort to instill political orthodoxy in the young, to raise them as willing, obedient, patriotic, unquestioning supporters of the regime.

Thus, education requiring real thought and questioning as part of the course is frowned upon. History and social studies courses are generally loaded with political propaganda which teachers are required to drill into their students. In both high schools and universities ideological and political indoctrination, dispensed through such courses as "Marxist-Leninist Theory," "Scientific Socialism," and "Dialectical Materialism," is mandatory. And the course materials are taught by drill, rote, and recitation.

But the young in Eastern Europe are no easier to fool than anywhere. They are cynical about all this, because they have eyes and ears with which to match promise against reality. They are not above snickering about their teachers and professors—behind their backs. But they go through the motions because they know they must in order to keep up their grade averages, the scholarship money coming in, and to get their diplomas and degrees.

Those degrees are an open sesame to a better life in Eastern Europe, and if anything troubles the Communist regimes these days then it is the Pandora's box of degree mania which their policy of education-for-all has opened. Eastern Europe is haunted by the spectre of having too many chiefs and not enough Indians. In societies that pride themselves on being "workers and peasants" and where monuments to heroic steelworkers and tractor drivers dot public parks and squares, most young people no longer want to smelt steel or plow; they want to become doctors, teachers, engineers, scientists, and researchers.

"If the trend is not reversed," one worried East European economist once remarked to me, "we face the danger of becoming an economically stagnant, impoverished nation made up entirely of professors and intellectuals."

Of 128,000 Czechoslovak pupils questioned a few years ago, forty-two percent wanted to go to college after high school graduation, although the state plan—not to mention university facilities—foresaw that only thirty-two would do so.

On the other hand, only forty-seven percent wanted to become apprentices and train for trades, though the plan had spelled out a need for sixty percent. Too many of these, moreover, wanted more prestigious jobs such as aircraft technicians, electrical-engineers, mechanics, automobile body makers, and agricultural-machinery technicians. Too few expressed interest in becoming chimney sweeps, plumbers, miners, bakers, forgers, or lathe operators.

Youngsters, said a Czech ministry of labor official, should be "counseled to make sure that differences between their wishes and society's requirements are as small as possible."

The differences between those wishes seem to be even greater in Romania where a similar survey revealed huge gaps between pupil aims and the needs of society. Some eighty-seven percent of high school students said they wanted to go to college after graduation; five percent wanted to take post-high school vocational or technical training courses. Only one percent wanted to become workers for life.

In 1975 the Romanian government introduced a measure that requires all college-level graduates to spend three years at production jobs before starting in their chosen professions. No physicians, teachers, engineers, or scientists are allowed to go into their career fields without first working in factories or on farms.

"That may not solve the problem," a Romanian official admitted, "but at least it reduces it."

Competition to get into colleges and universities is stiff because there aren't enough places to accommodate applicants. Obviously excellent high school grades and high marks on entrance exams play a role. But preferential placement is given to those who have worked in industry and agriculture for a few years before applying. And "loyalty" to the Communist regimes is also a factor.

Indeed, a Czech ministry of education official said as much not long ago.

"The selection of applicants must be clearly political in character," he said. "We make no secret of the fact that we want to guarantee that future graduates will support Communism and place their knowledge at the service of Communist society. Where this is not the case, we have no reason to accept an applicant."

Do such policies make loyal citizens of young East Europeans?

Perhaps.

As one young Hungarian put it, "My homeland lies where the money is."

13

The Next Revolution

"Our country has scored historic achievements in the emancipation of women and in changing their role in society," a female vice-mayor in Poland once told me. "For example, during International Woman's Year in 1975 the United Nations adopted a number of resolutions and conventions dealing with the status and rights of women around the world. In our country those had all been enacted long before."

It is a line of argument you can hear throughout Eastern Europe.

Yet, when one talks to ordinary women—the vast majority, not the vice-mayors and those in official positions—one hears the almost universal complaint that "in practice, in daily life, nothing has really changed."

The truth lies somewhere in between.

On the one hand, women in Eastern Europe have reached

a degree of equality and enjoy rights matched in only a few Western countries. The role they play in society is one of which their own mothers, not to mention their grandmothers, would never have dreamed.

On the other hand, this new role is not without complications. Women may feel much freer, but they work just as hard, if not harder, than before World War II or the Communist takeovers of their countries. In Romania, for example, eighty percent of all women were peasants and farm laborers before 1941, six percent were in industry and trade, two percent were engaged in menial work, and twelve percent were full-time housewives. Today more than half of all adult Romanian women work outside the home and the proportion of those employed in industry and trade is much greater. But who can say whether mind-dulling work at an assembly line in a noisy factory is any easier than the back-breaking labor of Romania's primitive prewar agriculture?

Certainly women in Eastern Europe have scored some significant breakthroughs. Some sixty to ninety percent are employed, and their share of the total labor force ranges from a thirty-six-percent low in Romania to a forty-eight-percent high in Czechoslovakia.

In Hungary they account for thirty percent of the physicians, in Bulgaria for as many as fifty percent.

In Hungary eleven percent of all engineers are women, in Romania forty-three percent. In Poland seventy percent of the biologists, half of the geographers, forty percent of the geologists and mathematicians, forty-seven percent of the chemists, thirty-two percent of the physicists, and twenty percent of university lecturers and professors are women. There are even three hundred women in the Polish merchant marine. Anywhere from twenty to twenty-five percent of the judges, prosecutors, and lawyers in Eastern Europe are female.

And across the board it seems that women are better educated than men. Their percentage of the total college enrollment ranges from forty percent in Czechoslovakia to almost fifty-eight percent in Bulgaria. While in prewar Romania, for example, women accounted for seventy-five percent of all adult illiterates, today they comprise forty-three percent of the total number of engineers, technicians, and highly skilled workers.

On the other hand, East European women also perform the most menial tasks. They lay bricks, dig ditches, shovel manure, sweep streets, and collect garbage.

Certainly East European women play key roles in helping to *make* their countries run, but they have almost no *say* in running them.

To be sure, they are better represented at the local government level than women in most Western countries. And their share of seats in the national parliaments ranges from a fifteen-percent low in Romania to a high of nearly thirty percent in Czechoslovakia and Hungary.

But those parliaments, as we have seen, are largely rubber-stamp legislatures, and local administrations in Eastern Europe have virtually no authority.

In the power centers that really count—the Communist parties and their top-echelon ruling bodies; in the central committees, politburos, and secretariats; in the government ministries—women are very much underrepresented and play a minor role if they play one at all.

Nowhere does female membership in the Communist parties exceed the twenty-eight percent claimed in Hungary, and it is as low as twenty-three percent in Poland. Representation in the parties' central committees is less than ten percent throughout Eastern Europe, and at the very top of the power structure you can literally count on two hands the number of women. There are exactly 7 women among the 120

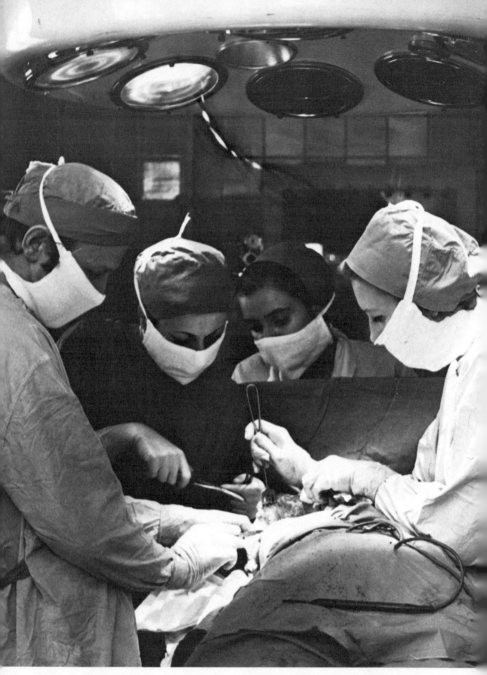

Large numbers of women are trained in the medical professions in all the Eastern European countries.

politburo and secretariat members and 169 governmental cabinet members of the five East European countries. Of the 7, I venture to say, 2 have gotten to the top, not because of a breakthrough for female power or even tokenism but merely because of their family connections. One is Romania's Elena Ceausescu, and the other Bulgarian president Todor Zhivkov's daughter Lyudmilla, who heads that country's cabinet-level committee on art and culture.

Throughout Eastern Europe, as a rule, it is also the men who have the more responsible and attractive jobs.

Large numbers of women may be physicians, but male doctors run the hospitals and give the orders.

In Romania, for example, only 5 of the country's 2,684 collective farms are headed by women.

In Czechoslovakia, nineteen percent of female specialists with secondary educations are not in jobs that would correspond with the education and skills they have acquired. In industry, twice as many men as women are in managerial and executive positions, in commerce three times as many, and in education nine times as many. Nearly every second man with a full secondary education, but only every tenth woman with the same education, is in a managerial post. One man in four with a college degree, but only one woman in thirty with the same degree, is an executive.

Women remain the victims of discriminatory employment practices, both in pay and placement, although equal pay is prescribed by law in every East European country. The laws are not obeyed. In Czechoslovakia, for example, women earn about thirty percent less than men in thirteen key categories of the economy. In Hungary, where women account for forty-four percent of the total labor force, men outnumber women in skilled jobs four to one.

There are a number of reasons for this.

One, no doubt, is the traditional and popular male view,

often shared by women themselves or dictated by economic pressures, of what work suits them.

Another, as Marta Záhorská, a Slovak labor expert, has pointed out, may be the safety and health regulations that have been enacted to protect women on the job. Designed to help women, they actually work against them. Many of these rules require expensive outlays. Rather than spend the money to install them, managers will just hire men.

"Men also work more overtime hours," she said, "and are employed on the night shifts from which many women are barred by law for health and safety reasons."

Yet another factor is that despite legal equality, the women still bear and rear the children. This biological fact influences hiring and payment practices in a number of ways.

All the East European countries have enacted very progressive and admirable laws to protect pregnant women and mothers of infants and small children. They are entitled to paid maternity leave which ranges from a minimum sixteen weeks in Poland to as long as thirty-two weeks in Bulgaria. There are strict regulations on the number of hours and the type of work pregnant women are allowed to perform, though they are entitled to their full prepregnancy pay. All the countries have laws allowing women up to three years' unpaid leave after giving birth, with no loss of seniority or accumulated social security benefits during this period.

In a number of the countries working mothers also have the right to thirty days off a year, at full pay, to care for young children who are ill. Factories and offices are generally required to contribute to the upkeep of day-care centers, nurseries, and preschools as well as to the cash allowances mothers receive with the birth of each child.

All these rules and regulations cost state-owned companies money in premiums and bonuses and disrupt their production plans. Personnel managers thus have built-in prejudices against hiring women, especially for responsible and highly paid jobs.

An equally important explanation for what appears to be discrimination is that many married women in Eastern Europe view their jobs as sources of supplementary family income, either to compensate for the husband's low earnings or to acquire the "extras" of life which his salary does not cover.

They tend to choose jobs that are close to home, school, or kindergarten. They fulfill their production quotas, but rarely trouble to improve their skills and qualifications. Lacking either time or interest, they cannot keep pace with technological progress or acquire new skills. They are thus relegated to the less attractive jobs.

Things might be different if the majority of East European women worked outside the home by choice. But they don't. The economies, with the exception of Romania's, are all short of labor and need them. There are strong societal pressures to take jobs, and there are also strong personal and family pressures. Those consumer goods that are now making Communism more livable—appliances, better furniture and clothes, weekend cottages, and cars—are virtually unattainable with only one wage earner in the average family.

But not only do East European women face discrimination at work, they must deal with it at home. Three decades of Communism have done little to change the average East European man's belief that woman's role is to keep house and do the cooking, washing, sewing, and cleaning, even if she is holding down a full-time outside job.

"All our efforts at emancipation have failed to free us from the 'cult of males,'" says Irena Falska, an announcer for Polish television. "When the men come home, they sit down to read the papers while we rush into the kitchen to make their tea and cook their supper."

In fact, this "traditional" female role seems to have official support in the male-dominated East European societies. In 1977 a Czechoslovak weekly newspaper published a series of articles giving statistics on how the supply of household appliances and housekeeping aides had improved and increased in Eastern Europe in recent years. It also explained that the number of supermarkets, laundromats, and self-service grocery stores, the supply of prepacked and easy-to-fix foods as well as other service aids was increasing. The assumption was that such consumer goods and services were for the benefit of women only.

Statistics vary from country to country, but the pattern is always the same: The man has one job, the woman two—at the office or factory, and then at home. Whether highly skilled or menial laborers, women in the Communist countries do nearly all the housework, raise the children, and also do the shopping which can be a daily ordeal.

Throughout Eastern Europe one can hear and read the same sad story: women have anywhere from twenty-five to fifty percent less leisure time than men.

No American woman could begin to appreciate the conditions under which her East European counterparts must live, or understand how few modern conveniences they have.

In Czechoslovakia, the country with the highest standard of living in Eastern Europe, only eighty percent of the households had washing machines (not necessarily automatic), seventy-five percent had refrigerators, and sixty-six percent had vacuum cleaners in the mid-1970's. And the percentage goes down accordingly in Hungary, Poland, Bulgaria, and Romania.

Shopping remains a test of will and stamina, thanks to the shortage of goods and stores. Common household items may be missing from the shelves for months, if not years.

Nor are attitudes toward women changing very quickly

or dramatically. That is evident from a survey among first-grade pupils in one of the countries. They were asked to describe the daily activities of their mothers and fathers. Mother, according to most of the kids, "cooks the meals, does the shopping, mops the floor, washes the clothes, and sews on buttons." Father "reads books and newspapers, watches television, drinks beer, and smokes cigarettes."

Much has been said and written in the West about the Communist countries' nursery, day-care, and preschool programs that are supposed to free women from the daily drudgeries of infant and child care. Undeniably, the system is better than in most Western countries, but it still falls far short of the goals the East European countries themselves have set.

In Hungary, for example, there are day-nursery facilities for only ten percent of the one- to three-year-old children and preschool places for only seventy-six percent of those whose parents have applied.

Yet, all of the countries, with the exception of Poland, want more children. In fact, while most Western countries are trying to curb population growth, Eastern Europe's are anxiously looking toward more babies. Declining birthrates in the past have left their population balances dangerously overaged and threaten their relatively inefficient economies with possibly crippling labor shortages in decades ahead.

To encourage population growth, Bulgaria, Hungary, Czechoslovakia, and Romania have in recent years all imposed sharp restrictions on their previously liberal abortion policies. Some have also curbed the sale and distribution of contraceptives. Moreover, various incentives such as cash payments, longer and better-paid maternity benefits, monthly subsidies, and low-interest loans for acquiring apartments and furniture have been introduced.

The restrictions on abortion, in particular, have caused

widespread resentment in Eastern Europe. Coming at a time when other countries are liberalizing their policies, the East European limitations contradict Communist claims to have achieved complete emancipation of women. In fact, what the East European regimes seem to be saying is that a woman's body is not her own but property of the state.

Moral and religious considerations, such as those behind the American "right to life" movements, have nothing to do with what has been happening in Eastern Europe. The governments simply decided they needed more children.

Romania set the current trend in 1966. Faced with a steadily declining birthrate that had dropped to an all-time low of 14.3 live births per 1,000 population—250,000 babies per year —Ceausescu's government banned abortions, except under very special circumstances, and sharply curtailed the sale of all kinds of contraceptives. Previously any Romanian woman had been able to get an abortion at a state clinic for less than $1.50. In the absence of any other kind of birth control, trips to the gynecologists for some were almost as frequent as visits to the hairdresser.

"Some of my patients were only twenty-five years old but had already had twenty abortions," a Bucharest physician explained to me at the time.

About nine months after the ban was imposed, Romania's hospitals became jammed with mothers-to-be, often two to a bed. There was a run on store shelves for baby foods, diapers, cribs, prams, maternity dresses, and infant wear.

But the government's population planners had every reason to be pleased. Births in 1967 came to 527,000—more than double the 1966 rate. Since then, however, despite the continuing ban, the birthrate has declined steadily again.

The reasons: a flourishing black market in contraceptives, bought from foreign tourists, and illegal abortions which cost from $70 to $360—a considerable sum in a country where the average monthly wage is only around $150.

Warning of "the danger of our aging society," President Ceausescu continues to call for stricter enforcement of the abortion ban and intensified measures to stimulate the birthrate. Doctors who perform illegal abortions face up to fifteen years in prison.

Apparently encouraged by the Romanian experience, and facing similar birthrate problems, Bulgaria, Czechoslovakia, and Hungary followed suit by repealing their liberal abortion laws in 1973. But unlike Romania, they linked their bans to wider distribution of contraceptives and a variety of monetary incentives to encourage more children.

In Czechoslovakia the incentives brought immediate results. Among them were cash grants for each new child, extension of paid maternity leave to six months, an increase in the monthly allowances for couples with two or more children, and low-interest loans of up to one year's salary with which to acquire apartments and furnishings for newlyweds. Upon the birth of each child, the couples can deduct ten percent from the principal of the loan.

Hungary, besides restricting its abortion policy, also introduced a variety of monetary and material incentives to stimulate the birthrate, which had dropped to 14.7 per 1,000 in 1972; it is now above 18. However, Hungary also took steps to improve sex education and to introduce methods of birth control other than abortion. It began manufacturing, importing and distributing antiovulation pills to all women over eighteen at greatly reduced prices. But the basic aim of the Hungarian measures is the same as that in the other countries: to raise the birthrate.

That is a disturbing thought. For the meaning of all the changed laws in Eastern Europe is that the practice of birth control, whether by contraceptives or abortion, is not an individual right but a privilege which the government can withdraw whenever it desires in order to satisfy what it considers the nation's economic and population needs.

This implied attitude toward women shows that they are far from being as free and emancipated as the East European regimes claim they are. How long East European women will put up with their present status remains to be seen. But when they rebel, then Eastern Europe will be hit by its next revolution. And contrary to what the Communist parties say about their postwar takeovers, that will be Eastern Europe's first real revolution.

One sign of it, though an unpleasant one, is already on the horizon—the rising divorce rate. But then, revolutions are never peaceful or pretty.

"It's horrifying," said a judge in Bulgaria. "The way things are going, in ten years there won't be a single family left in this country."

Compared to the United States and a number of West European countries, East European marriages and families are actually very stable. The highest East European divorce rate, Hungary's, is less than half that of the United States. But what is worrisome is that in all the countries, with the exception of Hungary, the rate has more than doubled within the past twenty years. In Romania, in fact, the increase has been more than fourfold since 1968.

The most common cause listed in divorce proceedings, the majority of which are started by women under thirty-five, are physical and mental cruelty, alcoholism, and violations of marital obligations. But increasingly East European sociologists believe that the causes listed in courts are superficial and that the real explanation is to be found in the changing roles between men and women.

There is weighty evidence to support this theory.

First of all, the majority of East European divorces are initiated by women. Given the traditions of the East European patriarchal societies in which men used to have all rights and women almost none, this would have been unthinkable two or three decades—barely a generation—ago.

Women just feel freer and more independent these days and are less fearful of striking out on their own.

Bulgarian studies of the divorce pattern tend to agree. The lowest proportion of divorces is among couples whose wives have only primary or secondary educations, the highest among those with college-level training or degrees.

"Women's liberation," says one East European sociologist, "is making today's marriage less stable. Young couples are in a transitional period between the patriarchal family, in which the husband's supremacy was complete and unchallenged, to a 'biarchal' one in which husband and wife enjoy equality.

"This transition is difficult, since men do not want to yield their positions, and women refuse to go back to their former inequality. The women are rebelling, so to speak, and quite rightly so. But so are the men who express their rebellion in drink and physical and mental cruelty, also adultery, which then appear a 'cause' on divorce petitions.

"The whole family relationship is changing. Both husbands and wives are now breadwinners, and in many families the women's pay is equal to that of the men. Often young women today are better educated than their husbands and place higher intellectual and moral demands on them. But all too often they marry into families where husbands and in-laws expect them to fall into traditional roles of doing all the housework and performing servant duties. When they balk, you get the conflicts that end up in the courts.

"What we need is premarital counseling to help young people understand themselves and their changing relationships," he said.

One country—Hungary—made such counseling obligatory in 1974. That may be one reason why Hungary's divorce rate, though the highest among the five countries, has barely risen in the past fifteen years.

To get married in Hungary these days, anyone under thirty-five must go through a thirty-day "cooling off" period before actually going to the altar. During that month couples must attend obligatory "marriage advisory schools" where they are not only taught "the facts of life," but hopefully, so Hungarian sociologists say, "how to get along with each other as equals."

14

Imperfections

"Their fathers' liquor cabinets are stocked with the choicest foreign brands. These teen-agers do not even know the taste of water. Nor does anyone else in their circles. They prefer expensive French wines. The spoiled darlings walk dogs of exclusive breed; their pockets are filled with money. I bet they do not even know the price of a loaf of bread. Seeing the antics of these pampered brats fills me with rage."

A description of "upper class" life in Eastern Europe before the Communist takeovers?

No. It comes from a Hungarian labor union newspaper in 1975 and is part of an article about that country's Communist elite, the "upper classless," as they are sometimes called.

If one were to believe the official propaganda, the East European countries ought to be on the threshold of utopia. They are described as near-perfect societies in which class distinctions and the glaring inequalities between rich and poor already have been, or are being, erased. Crime, corruption, abuse of power, greed, vice, drunkenness, and drug addiction are alleged to be the ugly ways of capitalist societies that have already withered away, or soon will, under Communism.

It would be grand if it were true. But the fact is that life with all its imperfections continues pretty much the way it always has. Not only do classes and class distinctions still exist, but the more privileged are constantly looking for status symbols that will set them off from the masses.

In Poland, for example, tennis has now become the latest stepping stone for young people—and their parents—who aspire to be middle and upper class in a theoretically classless society. With tennis rackets under their arms, in clubs of their own, the privileged young Poles feel themselves above the soccer masses and the bicycling crowd.

Everybody must learn Russian in school, and the majority also study English. But among the offspring of Poland's "new class," the so-called golden- and red-spoon-fed youth—children of high-ranking Communist party and government officials; industrial managers; establishment writers, artists, performers, and intellectuals; former aristocrats; rich farmers and shop owners; professional people; and military officers— the "in" language to learn is French.

It is the beginning of a kind of minor Communist nobility, and it exists in every East European country, though the status symbols vary.

For Hungarians one of them is a summer cottage on the shores of Lake Balaton; another is flaunting one's academic titles. Radio Budapest once complained that some officials sign documents and letters stressing their titles and degrees in such a way that their actual names can barely be read.

For Romanians it may be a small place in the mountains,

*New department stores in Hungary satisfy
the need for consumer goods.*

for Czechoslovaks a house in the country. With this goes at least one car in the family—or two if the father is high enough in the rankings to have an official one with chauffeur for his personal use—Western hi-fi equipment, trendy imported clothes for the kids, and a pedigreed dog.

Money counts less than style and connections. With "connections" and rank you don't have to stand in queues for hours and you don't have to wait years for cars, apartments, refrigerators, washing machines, or other amenities.

For girls in the top social rungs, having a job is mostly a form of social camouflage so as not to embarrass their parents. To not work is considered "un-Communist." For boys it is having the "right" job—a slot in a central committee or government department, a budding career in the diplomatic service, or an assistantship in a university that will eventually lead to a tenured professorship.

"Most of my students," a Polish professor once explained, "are the sons and daughters of government ministers, ambassadors, and high-ranking Party and government officials. The girls want a good marriage, the boys a good time and an easy, cultured job. Politics mean nothing to them. They consider the Party an irritation.

"Women's lib? No, the girls have no time for that. For them it would mean equal work and equal pay with men, when all they want is to be comfortably settled without working."

Little is said or done about this new Communist elite—unless one of its members goes too far or runs afoul of his or her own comrades.

Such was the case a few years ago with Dezsö Illés, a former member of the Hungarian parliament and high-ranking Party *apparatchik* who, until his arrest, was managing director of the Somogy County Forest and Timber Processing Farm. Decorated three times with the Order of Labor, a holder of the Medal of Merit of the People's Republic, and one of the key figures in the collectivization of Hungarian agriculture in the late 1950's Illés was known to those who worked for him as the Red Baron. To judge from his lavish way of living, it was a fitting description.

When arrested, he was accused of, among other things, having his Lake Balaton summer home repaired and renovated by the state farm workers at government expense.

He had also bought an orchard in which he built a two-story villa with material and labor from the farm to the tune of 300,000 forints ($16,670), or the equivalent of six years' salary for the average Hungarian worker. As he had no use for this second summer home, he rented it out for the season at 50,000 forints ($2,780).

Illés also built hunting lodges—equipped with all modern conveniences—in the various forests under his control at state farm expense. The cost ran into millions. He had promised that the government would be reimbursed by renting these lodges to foreign tourists, but they were rarely rented. One, built at a cost of 3 million forints ($166,700), was used exclusively by Illés and his political friends.

Those who criticized the Red Baron were either fired or subjected to so much harassment by him that they left on their own. He replaced them with ex-convicts.

When an investigation of his activities started, Illés tried to intimidate his subordinates into testifying for him. One of his friends made the rounds of the farm's foresters, identified himself as an officer of the "secret military service," and ordered them to write letters to the authorities in Illés's defense.

The Red Baron was subsequently sentenced to a long prison term, but the question that has intrigued Hungarians ever since is how many more there are like him.

The rise of an elite and of large-scale corruption are not the only signs that Communist societies are not what they pretend to be.

258 / Eastern Europe

A huge black market—based on bribes, favors, and hard foreign currency—exists in all of them.

A couple of packages of American cigarettes will get anyone a free tank of gasoline in Romania. Prague's taxi service is free to the customer willing to change soft Czechoslovak korunas for hard American dollars. The long time spent waiting to see a doctor can be drastically reduced anywhere by presenting the receptionist or the physician with a carton of cigarettes. Services taken for granted in Western countries are only available by under-the-table payments or huge tips. Bribes make life easier at every level.

Although the official press often reports with finger wagging and tongue clucking about such "immorality" and "misdeeds," no one, it seems, is really willing to do anything about them.

"Let's be honest," a Polish economist once said. "The black market could be closed overnight, but then what would we have? It may be immoral and inconsistent with Communist theory, but it is real and it is a market where people can get things not ordinarily available elsewhere. It also soaks up excess spending power. Is that so bad?"

"Besides," a Czechoslovak expert added, "it gives the authorities, who let it exist, a hammer to hold over the heads of anyone who has a guilty conscience about other things. The state also receives hard currency, and the rest of us have a better life than really puritan Communism would give us. So everybody benefits."

There is prostitution in Eastern Europe. The country where it is most rampant is Hungary, though Poland and Czechoslovakia don't rank far behind.

Hungary closed its brothels in 1950, but that accomplished little toward controlling or decreasing sex for pay. Each year, to judge from the Hungarian press, the number of women charged and tried for prostitution increases. The crimes connected with prostitution—especially procuring—are on the increase too, and so are venereal diseases, especially among teen-agers. According to Hungarian medical statistics, eighteen percent of the males and thirty-seven percent of the females treated each year are between the ages of fifteen and nineteen.

There is also legal gambling in the form of horse betting, lotteries, and soccer pools.

In Poland, in fact, thanks to the national lottery and football pools, there are some sixty new zloty millionaires every year.

To be sure, eyebrows and questions are sometimes raised as to whether gambling is compatible with Communist scruples and morality, but as the head of Totalisator, the Polish government lottery and soccer fund, puts it: "How could it be immoral? It is a state enterprise and therefore, by its very nature, moral." In fact, the state encourages it and has even issued a booklet entitled *How to Win—All There Is to Know About the Numbers Game.*

The biggest winner is always the government itself. It rakes in almost 3 billion zlotys ($100 million) from the two games called Toto and Loto each year. Almost all that money is earmarked for building sports stadiums, gymnasiums, and to subsidize athletes.

The reaction of winners is one indication that capitalism remains a strong human force in that Communist country. Although Totalisator offers payment by check, money order, or bank transfer, most big winners prefer to come in to the organization's downtown Warsaw office to collect in cash. Nearly all of them also insist on counting the piles of crisp, new 1,000-zloty ($30) bills. For the convenience of "customers" who may be reluctant to go out on the street with a large sum of money, Totalisator has installed a back door which leads straight to a branch of the government savings bank where the loot can be deposited. The winnings are tax free.

The winners are usually workers and farmers and once they've become rich—by Polish standards—they want to remain that way. Charity is furthest from their minds.

"I recall one man who immediately set aside an amount for a wheelchair for an invalid friend," says a fund official, "but the majority contribute only twenty-five zlotys to one of the orphanages we sponsor, then carry the remaining nine hundred ninety-nine thousand, nine hundred seventy-five zlotys to the bank."

Item number one on nearly every winner's purchase list is a car, though the amount of ready cash will not always speed up delivery. After that, if they're not afraid to let friends and relatives know how much they've collected, it's usually a private house with a garden, starting prices for which are 400,000 zlotys ($12,200). And then, of course, the winners go after consumer durables.

Many, however, prefer to keep their new wealth secret.

"There's a stigma to having money in our society," one anonymous Toto-millionaire told the Polish weekly *Polityka* a few years ago.

Perhaps the saddest case of all was a young couple in their mid-twenties who, despite a million in the bank, continued to live in a shabby Warsaw apartment and to dream of owning a car, a color TV set, a tape recorder, and a vacation abroad. They could have none of that, nor tell anyone about winning.

The husband, a mechanic in an automobile plant, was also an official of the Young Communist League. He was afraid that admitting to wealth would ruin his political future.

What good did all the money do him then?

"Oh, a lot, a lot," the young *apparatchik* insisted. "It gives me a sense of security. As long as I have that money I know that some day, should I feel like it, I can stand up at a Party meeting and express my own views, even if they run counter to the Party line."

There is also crime in Eastern Europe, despite Lenin's claim that crime is a "disease of capitalism." Not only is it increasing but it is becoming more violent.

In Hungary, in 1977, there were more than 129,000 individual felonies—an increase of seven percent over the preceding year. More than half the offenses were crimes against property—both public and private. Theft and damage of public property cost the Hungarian state an average of more than 260 million forints ($13.8 million) annually.

Poland has been ravaged in recent years by razor-wielding, mugging punks who call themselves *Git*—"Goodies." They number only a few hundred, but periodically terrorize sections of Warsaw and other large cities. What makes them especially frightening is their eerie resemblance to the "droogs" of *A Clockwork Orange,* though the book was never published, and the movie based on it never shown, in Poland.

Many of the Goodies acts of terror are against their more straitlaced fellow students, whom they call "suckers." One father complained that his son used to come home regularly with cigarette burns on his lips, welts on his temples, and once with his scalp slit open. The boy finally admitted that the Goodies had ordered him to steal and when he refused had tortured him.

Romania was hit by a huge crime wave in 1977 and 1978 after Ceausescu amnestied thirty thousand convicted criminals all at once. The aim behind the amnesty was both noble and practical. Practical in the sense that the regime needed the manpower, noble in that Ceausescu believed Romania had reached a "new stage" in its development that called for doing away with prisons and letting inmates play their role constructively in society. Those released were serving terms of five years or less. They were trained and offered jobs in factories, on construction sites, and on farms. Thousands did go straight, but thousands also did not.

There were suddenly scores of muggings, purse snatchings, armed robberies, burglaries, and supermarket heists. There were countless rapes and assaults. Romanian life changed within days. People began locking and bolting their doors; women did not dare go out on Bucharest's dark, unlighted streets at night.

Although no figures were ever released by the government, by the spring of 1978 the police were back to making wholesale arrests of those who had been amnestied and released from prisons just a few months earlier.

Drugs became an officially recognized problem in Eastern Europe in October 1971 when senior customs and law enforcement officers from all the Communist countries met in Sofia to coordinate their drives against smuggling and trafficking. The meeting was prompted by the realization that Eastern Europe, especially the Balkan countries, had become a principal overland route between the drug-producing areas of the Middle East and Asia and the profitable West European and North American markets.

At first the authorities tried to treat the problem largely as one of smuggling, and primarily by non-Communist foreigners. Bulgaria announced the arrest of a twenty-three-year-old English woman driving from Afghanistan to Western Europe with a camping wagon in which she had hidden nearly two thousand pounds of hashish with a street value of twenty-four million dollars. In Prague five Afghans bound for West Germany were caught with hashish. Hungary announced the arrest of thirteen foreigners smuggling heroin.

But it didn't take the Communist countries long to realize

that their drug problem was more than merely one of transit and smuggling. "Why this capitalist evil should have found its way to our world has not been explained," said a Prague magazine in 1973. "But whatever the reason, to close our eyes to the problem would be not only foolish but very dangerous. Many people in this country are already addicted."

Since then the problem has gotten steadily worse.

Use of barbiturates has doubled within a decade in Czechoslovakia. So has the demand for a Czech asthma remedy, easily available without prescription from pharmacies. Taken with beer it has an effect similar to LSD.

Both Bulgaria and Hungary have reported increased drug usage and addiction.

But the country with the greatest problem is Poland.

More than eight percent of Polish teen-agers, according to one survey, have experimented at least once with drugs and narcotics.

"No one knows the number of our drug addicts," one Warsaw daily reported, "but the facts are alarming. We are having an epidemic."

"Hippies" or other long-haired, blue-jean wearing youths get most of the blame for the drug scene in Eastern Europe.

In Czechoslovakia the "high standard of living" is also considered at fault. "The young," according to *Večernik*, a Prague daily, "have had things too easy and have become soft. They want to make themselves noticed by their appearance, but at the very first setback in life they swallow pills."

Poland, on the other hand, sees a connection between increased drug addiction and peddling and the Goodies.

No one really knows whom to blame for alcoholism and drunkenness, but it is definitely the number one social problem in Eastern Europe. "Drinking," Marx's friend Friedrich Engels once wrote, "is a disease of capitalism." In Eastern Europe, where capitalism has more or less been banned officially for more than three decades, that old Marxist claim is now being questioned, for the statistics show that alcohol abuse is becoming worse by the year.

Poland, for example, with a population of thirty-four million, now has two million known alcoholics. Alcohol consumption has more than doubled within a decade and at fifteen quarts per capita each year among males aged eighteen to sixty is now among the highest in the world. More than 85 percent of industrial accidents, half of all crimes, and nearly 70 percent of violent crimes are caused by or linked to drinking. Polish industry loses anywhere from 19 billion to 28 billion zlotys ($575 million to $848 million) a year due to absenteeism, accidents, and sloppy workmanship caused by alcohol abuse.

The government's approach to the problem, similar to that in the other countries, has been to raise the price of liquor, particularly vodka, the Polish favorite, and reduce both places and hours of sale. But this seems to have had no effect. Despite tripling the price of vodka since 1960, consumption has more than doubled.

Drinking at all hours of the day, and even at work, is the rule, not the exception, in Poland. Whenever I have visited Polish officials and industrial executives in their offices, toasts of vodka or brandy—often as early as 9:00 A.M.—were the custom and to refuse was considered an insult.

"Our drinking habits," says the Polish magazine *Czas*, "seem not to have changed since the fifteenth century. We drink too much and too fast and often without eating. And it seems the aim of drinking is always to get drunk."

Hungarian sources place that country at the top of the world listing for consumption of hard liquor, in third place for wine, and fifth for beer.

Official statistics show 150,000 alcoholics—about 1.5 percent of the population—though what really worries the authorities is a sharp increase of drinking among the young. According to a 1978 survey, 80 percent of all Hungarian high school students drink "from time to time," 41 percent do so "frequently," and nearly 1 percent consume alcohol "regularly."

Numerous regulations have been enacted to limit both the places and the hours during which alcoholic beverages by the bottle and glass may be sold. A total ban on driving after drinking is sharply enforced. When Hungarians go out in the evening to dine, knowing they will also drink, they insist on going by taxi or public transport. In 1975 the government enacted a law calling for *compulsory* treatment of alcoholics. They can be committed for periods of two years to special work-treatment hospitals being established all over the country. But these measures thus far have had little effect in curing what Hungarians themselves describe as "a rapidly spreading national disease."

Alcoholism, drug addiction, crime, vice, corruption, and the rise of a new class are all developments that orthodox Communists believed were impossible under their system.

What they hoped for—I believe them when they tell me that—were societies based on total justice and equality, without crime, without social ills, without greed, poverty, or classes. Their mistake, perhaps, was to ascribe the causes for such things to capitalism and the governments that came before. What their thirty years in power have shown is that governments and political and social systems can be changed quickly—by force. To change human nature, if at all, will obviously take a little longer.

15

God Is Not Dead

Karl Marx called religion "the opiate of the masses," and officially the Communist parties of Eastern Europe all profess atheism.

But whatever one may have read and heard about the suppression of the churches, I can report that God is not dead in Eastern Europe and that religion there is thriving today.

Take the case of Poland. To think of its thousand-year history without also thinking of the Catholic Church is not to think of it at all. The two are inseparable, and Communism has not changed that. In fact, the Church and the Party are two equally powerful forces in society. That has never been more apparent than since 1978 when a Polish bishop and cardinal, Karol Wojtyla of Cracow, was elected as Pope John Paul II.

It has long been somewhat of a standing joke in Warsaw that, although Party chiefs may come and go, Cardinal Stefan Wyszynski, the primate and head of the Polish Church since 1948, stays and stays. Considering that he has survived Bierut and Gomulka thus far, and is still primate with Gierek in charge of the Party, it is hardly a joke. Cardinal Wyszynski is so powerful, influential, and respected in Poland, that when he celebrated his seventy-fifth birthday in 1976, the Party and government press gave front-page headlines to the event and Gierek sent the cardinal a telegram of congratulations and a huge bouquet of flowers. The two men have met to discuss the country's problems periodically and among those who know them both it is said they genuinely like and respect each other "because regardless of the differences of political and religious belief between them, both are first and foremost patriots and Poles."

The Vatican and Poland were close to establishing diplomatic relations at the time of writing, and that ties between Church and State would improve with Wojtyla's election as pope was to be expected. His visit to Poland in June 1979 was the first ever by a pope to a Communist country.

Poland, moreover, is a Communist country in which all Catholic holidays, of which there are many, are legal holidays observed by Communists and Catholics alike.

One of them is Corpus Christi, celebrated on the Thursday after Trinity Sunday. It is not a national holiday in the United States, not one even in the Protestant areas of West Germany, where it is celebrated only in mainly Catholic regions such as Bavaria and the Rhineland. But Communist Poland is locked up tight on Corpus Christi.

I once arrived in Warsaw for a number of article assignments a few days before Corpus Christi. After settling into my hotel, I began making telephone calls to line up appointments: with, among other people, the minister of finance, the

Pope John Paul in Warsaw, 1979

president of the foreign-trade bank, and a government press and information agency official.

"Thursday?" asked the finance minister's press spokesman, somewhat unbelieving. "Oh no, that's Corpus Christi. All government offices are closed. Perhaps we can fit you in on Friday."

"We don't work on Thursday," said the bank president's secretary. "That's a Polish holiday."

"What are you, a heathen?" asked the information agency official.

I was beginning to get the message, so I called an old friend—a Polish journalist who is a veteran Communist and a member of the Party's central committee. I just couldn't imagine a high-ranking Communist taking a religious holiday off. Maybe he'd be free for lunch. Oh, no. Both his paper and the Party central committee would be closed and he was going into the country for the day. But he'd be delighted to have supper with me. Late, please, as traffic back into Warsaw might be heavy.

Polish Communists—today at any rate—also make no secret of the fact that they could not have rebuilt and developed the country without the help of the Church.

"Settling and integrating the western and northern territories that we got from Germany after the war," a high-ranking official once told me, "would have been impossible without the moral, patriotic, and unifying role that the Church played there."

It is a tribute that the Reverend Jerzy Stroba, bishop of Szczecin, the former German Stettin, has come to accept with dignified pride.

"Yes," he told me, "we returned to this originally Polish region as Catholics and as Poles. The Church helped the people who were settled here from eastern Poland, which was ceded to Russia to overcome the shocks of war, occupation, and migration. Many were the villages and towns where new settlers first refused to stay until there was a priest.

"Moreover," he said, "people came from so many different regions. Not just the east, but central Poland and the West European countries of Polish emigration, such as Belgium and France. They brought with them different customs, outlooks, cultural levels, and dialects. But what they all had in common was their Polish Catholic faith. Often we acted as mediator between the people and the new state."

Poland is by no means the only East European country where people mix their Communism with Christianity.

Christmas is so important in Czechoslovakia that even top Party leaders celebrate it. The main reason, for example, why Alexander Dubcek wasn't named to replace Antonin Novotny as Party chief until early in January 1968 was because the central committee, which had been debating and deliberating Novotny's fate in December, called a Christmas recess. With nearly disastrous results, I might add. While most central committee members were busy with their traditional Christmas goose and New Year's carp, Novotny, knowing his days were numbered, almost succeeded in mobilizing the army and secret police to arrest them all.

In Romania six bishops of the Orthodox Church serve as members of parliament and attend its sessions in the full regalia of their religious office. The patriarch's official residence and office is right next door to the parliament building on Government Hill in Bucharest.

Visitors to Hungary are taken to churches as part of their regular sightseeing tours by official guides who tell them quite openly that although the government professes atheism, two thirds of the people are practicing Catholics and twenty-four percent Protestant. The government tourist agency offers excursions to important sites of Hungarian Christian tradition, such as Esztergom Cathedral, the seat of the primate of Hungary. Countless streets, squares, and boulevards in Budapest are named for Catholic saints and Protestant leaders.

As a general rule, the more nationalistic a country's Communist government, the more tolerant and friendly it is toward its established church because that church played a key role in history, unified and defended the country, and is a fountain of national identity and patriotic pride.

Minority religions, however, tend to have a hard time.

In Orthodox Romania, Roman Catholics worship under very difficult conditions. The Uniate Church—it uses Eastern Orthodox rites but has been loyal to the pope and the Vatican for four hundred years,—was banned completely by the Communist regime in 1948 and had all its property confiscated. It has not been allowed to reorganize itself since then.

Bulgaria's Muslims, who represent eleven percent of the population, are suppressed and discriminated against, because as Turks they are both a religious and an ethnic minority.

All the East European countries, with the exception of Czechoslovakia, have long histories of anti-Semitism and Jews have never had an easy time there. Most of the Jews of Eastern Europe were either murdered by the Nazis during the war or emigrated shortly after. Large Jewish communities today exist only in Hungary and Romania.

But on the whole, especially compared to the terrible persecution they suffered in the late ninteenth and early twentieth centuries, Romania's eighty-four thousand Jews have fared relatively well under the Communist regime. Romania was also the only East European country not to break diplomatic relations with Israel after the 1967 Six Day War. It has a fairly liberal policy toward Jews who want to emigrate and go to Israel.

Hungary has gone furthest in protecting the rights of Jews.

It has the largest Jewish community in Eastern Europe—approximately 100,000—and the only Jewish seminary in the entire Communist world.

Hungary is also the country that is most tolerant of its non-Catholic minorities. The Calvinists and Lutherans have long had good relations with the government and the Party. In 1977 it even opened its doors to a tour by American evangelist Billy Graham.

It is important to remember, however, that although religion thrives in Eastern Europe today, this has not always been the case. In fact, the present "peaceful coexistence" between the Communist states and their various churches does not date back much more than a decade, and even today there are problems and the relationship can become tense.

The worst period, especially for Catholics, was from the time the Communists came to power until a few years after Stalin's death—the era when the "little Stalins" and the "Moscow" men of Eastern Europe were in power.

For all the stature and respect that he enjoys today, it is important to remember that Cardinal Wyszynski was imprisoned in Poland under the Bierut regime from 1953 to 1956. Indeed, it was not until Gomulka came to power in 1956 that he was rehabilitated, though the relationship between those two tough and determined men was itself not very good. And it was not until the 1970's, after Edward Gierek had become Party chief, that the Church and Party began an era of peaceful coexistence.

Both realized that they need each other and that Poland needs them both.

"We finally learned," a senior Party official told me, "that Catholicism in this country is absorbed by every baby with its mother's milk. Poland and the Church are one."

Today, when one hears them speak and preach, it sometimes seems as if Gierek and the cardinal use the same speech writer. Both are concerned with the morale and the morals of the country, with its economic well-being and its future.

In Hungary, one should recall, it was none other than Janos Kadar, as minister of interior and head of secret police, who in 1948 ordered the arrest of Cardinal Josef Mindszenty, the primate of the Hungarian Church. The cardinal was sentenced to life imprisonment on trumped-up treason charges. He was freed during the 1956 Hungarian Revolution but, when the revolution was crushed, escaped to the American Embassy in Budapest, where he lived a kind of voluntary imprisonment and involuntary isolation for fifteen years.

During that time relations between the Communist government and the Church were very strained. Budapest and the Vatican were in a standoff over what to do. By the mid-1960's, after the cardinal had been living in the embassy for a decade, Kadar and the pope began moving toward better ties, but Mindszenty—a proud, strong-willed man—objected.

I know, from covering the story as a correspondent in those years, that relations between the Communists and Catholics could have improved much earlier had it not been for him. Numerous times in the late 1960's there were high-level contacts between Rome and Budapest aimed at giving the Church more rights and status in Hungary. The condition was that Cardinal Mindszenty leave the American Embassy—which was guarded night and day by Hungarian secret police—and the country. Kadar promised that nothing would happen to him. That suited the Vatican also, but not the cardinal, who insisted he was the primate and archbishop of the country. Pope Paul VI sent many high-ranking Church emissaries to persuade him, but Cardinal Mindszenty refused to budge. Finally he agreed but under conditions that the Kadar government could not accept. Among other things he demanded to hold one more mass and deliver a sermon at

Esztergom Cathedral. In 1971 the pope finally forced him to leave by retiring him.

Subsequently, relations between the Vatican and Hungary improved quickly, as did conditions for Hungarian Catholics. The Church was allowed to appoint ten new bishops to dioceses that had been vacant for years. Following Cardinal Mindszenty's death in 1975—he was living in Vienna—a new archbishop and primate was appointed and recognized by the Communist regime. Budapest and Rome have established relations just a step below the formal diplomatic level, and in 1977 Kadar become the first East European Communist leader to be received by the pope.

In Czechoslovakia the Catholic Church was cruelly persecuted and suppressed within a year after the Communists had gained power in 1948. The most prominent victim was the archbishop, Cardinal Josef Beran—a far more liberal and democratic man than Hungary's Cardinal Mindszenty—who had spent three wartime years in Nazi concentration camps. Along with other bishops he was tried on false treason and spying charges and sentenced to fourteen years' imprisonment. Meanwhile the Communist government removed hundreds of priests, monks, and nuns from their posts in an attempt to destroy the Church and weaken its influence in Czechoslovakia.

Cardinal Beran was not exonerated until 1963, after having served his full term in prison. But even then he was not allowed to preside over the Church. Instead, the Party demanded that he be exiled. He went to live in the Vatican where he died in 1969 at age eighty.

Relations between the Czechoslovak Party and the Church, and with them conditions for Catholics, did not really begin to improve until the spring of 1978, when Cardinal Frantisek Tomasek was approved and installed as archbishop of Prague and head of the Church in Czechoslovakia. His appointment—to fill Cardinal Beran's position—came only after long drawn-out negotiations between the Czechoslovak government and the Vatican.

Czechoslovak Catholics have protested often that the government discriminated against them, limited religious education, prevented the training of priests, and punished those who did not knuckle under to Party and government orders. Cardinal Tomasek, in fact, was not allowed to leave Czechoslovakia and go to Poland when Pope John Paul II visited there.

Though religion is surprisingly alive in Eastern Europe, is it also well?

There is no easy answer to that, for antireligious policies of the Communist parties and governments vary not only from country to country but often from week to week.

In Hungary, the Party, while hardly discriminatory, worries about its own members who practice Christian customs and express religious beliefs. One campaign in the mid-1970's was directed against baptisms, confirmations, church weddings, and religious funerals.

Some eighty percent of all newborn Hungarian children are baptized, and according to the horrified Party leadership, many of them are the babies of Party members.

More than half the weddings are Church weddings, and once again it is obvious that either brides or grooms—and sometimes both—are card-carrying Communists.

How can one be a member of a party that believes in atheism and still do that?

One Party ideologist, Jenö Faragó, has an explanation. The children of Party members, he says, are frequently baptized, enrolled in religious classes, and confirmed at the insistence of grandparents. "The Party member," says Faragó, "should not be held responsible, but he is guilty of negligence if he fails to report to his Party organization about these acts and if he has not done everything in his power to counteract religious education in his family."

One of the most difficult questions for a "good" Communist is what to do about religious funerals.

"No one," says Faragó, "can be faulted for attending the religious funeral of a close friend or relative. However, it is a Communist's duty to persuade family members not to have a religious ceremony. Failing at that, it is proper for him to attend. Indeed, he would hurt the family's feelings, insult the memory of the dead, and give the Party a bad reputation if he didn't."

As in the other countries, Hungary has various nonreligious rites and ceremonies to compensate for the pomp and circumstances of religious ones. There are Communist weddings, funerals, and versions of baptism and confirmation.

In fact, each city and county magistrate's office has a "master of ceremonies" on its staff.

Budapest's is Dr. Géza Katona, who complains that his hardest task is to compete with religious funerals, "though our prices for burials are lower than those of the Church."

"The priests," he says, "have an advantage. They can tell the next of kin and mourners that the deceased has passed into the hereafter, into eternal life. All we can say is 'Goodbye.' For many of the bereaved that is not enough."

Not even for many Party members, Katona admits. "You'd be surprised how many insist on being buried by the Church." Perhaps because in the hereafter their Party careers can no longer be hurt. Or are they just playing it safe?

On the other hand, the Hungarian Party often warns its officials and members not to use strong-arm methods against believers. In a front-page editorial in September 1976 the Party daily *Népszabadság* warned that some *apparatchiki* "still do not understand that the main dividing line is between supporters and opponents of Communism, not between atheists and believers. They want to take action against the influence of the churches instead of relying on ideological and educational work which, though demanding greater skill, is more productive in the long run."

The relationship has many ups and downs.

Szczecin's Bishop Stroba told me that for nearly thirty years the government had not given permission to build a new church in that rapidly growing Polish city.

"Now I have gotten approval to build one," he said, "but I need and applied for three."

In the fall of 1976 Cardinal Wyszynski and his bishops publicly accused the Gierek regime of "an official conspiracy to enforce atheism" and of violating its own proclamations of tolerance.

In a pastoral letter read from all pulpits, he said the government was practicing discrimination and harassing believers. "Leading positions in the professions," the letter charged, "are closed to those candidates, regardless of skills, talents, and qualifications, who do not profess atheism." Students who openly voice their religious convictions are subjected to "threats and blackmail." Children in schools, state homes, and summer camps are told not to wear crosses. Seminary students are called up for military duty in "violation of Church-State agreements." The Church, the letter concluded, "is under attack."

Yet, just a few months after that complaint, Cardinal Wyszinski and Gierek began meeting.

On the other hand, the Polish government censored a critical passage out of Pope John Paul II's first Christmas message.

In Romania the government started moving against the Catholic Church in 1975. The ministry of the interior issued an order that called for confiscation of all church archives of historical value. The purpose, it was said, was to give the

Romanian state possession and control of all old documents of "national cultural significance."

The more devious thinking behind the order, however, was that a church that cannot document its past and history will not have much of a future.

Yet, within a few months after that order, which covered old books, manuscripts, letters, drawings, seals, and engravings, the Ceausescu government started putting out feelers to the Vatican to improve relations, and Romania's one million Catholics reported that pressures on them had eased up.

Many Party officials in Eastern Europe actually believe that the Communist tradition of atheism is wrong, counterproductive, and out of step with the times.

"By spending years painting God as the devil," a Czechoslovak Communist party official once told me, "we put ourselves in the position of the devil in the eyes of millions of people who would otherwise support us. One cannot simply ignore, erase, or forget the heritage of human values that Christianity has contributed during the past two thousand years. As Communists we, too, have those values. Instead of destroying the foundation of civilization that created them, we should build on it."

When he said that to me many years ago, he was a member of a small minority of Communists. Indications today are that this minority is no longer so small and believers in Eastern Europe have good reason to hope that in the not too distant future it may even become a majority.

16

Food for Thought

Few countries in the world devote as much attention to culture; spend as much public money on art, literature, and music; or have brought forth as many famous and talented writers, poets, playwrights, composers, performers, painters, illustrators, sculptors, and film directors as the East European ones. Per population, they publish more books, train more young artists, and maintain more opera houses, ballet troupes, symphony orchestras, and professional theaters than the countries of Western Europe or the United States.

And few people anywhere seem more devoted, more appreciative, or hungrier for culture than the Bulgarians, Czechs, Slovaks, Hungarians, Poles, or Romanians.

Some of the statistics and facts are staggering.

Poland has forty-five thousand libraries, containing two hundred and sixty million books, of which nearly 150 million are checked out each year—more than West Germany, for example, a country with almost twice the population and which prides itself on being a nation of "poets and thinkers."

Budapest has more opera houses than New York, a city almost three times as large, and attending a performance rarely costs more than the equivalent of two dollars.

Prague boasts more full-time professional theaters than any city in Europe with the exception of London.

A medium-size Polish city—Wroclaw, population just under 600,000—has a symphony orchestra with a longer season and more concerts each year than any of the great major orchestras of the United States. And it is one of nineteen full-time professional orchestras in Poland. Wroclaw also has two theaters—Jerzy Grotowski's Thirteen Rows Laboratory and Henryk Tomaszewski's Mime—that are rated by critics as among the best and most significant in the world. Their tours abroad are always eagerly awaited theatrical events in such places as New York, Paris, and Munich.

The Polish government spends an average of fifty million dollars a year for the protection and renovation of the country's artistic and architectural heritage and has even formed a state-owned company with seven thousand employees that specializes in preservation and restoration work.

Some of the world's best-known film directors—a number of whom now work in the United States and Western Europe—come from Czechoslovakia, Poland, and Hungary. Their movies usually win prizes at the famous yearly festival in Cannes, and a number of them have also received Oscars in Hollywood. Among them are Milos Forman (*One Flew Over the Cuckoo's Nest*), Roman Polanski (*Rosemary's Baby*), Jan Kadar (*The Shop on Main Street*), Andrzej Wajda (*Ashes and Diamonds*), Vera Chytilova (*Daisies*), Jiri Menzel (*Closely Watched Trains*), and Jerzy Kawalerowicz (*Mother Joan of the Angels*).

When working and traveling in Eastern Europe it is almost impossible for me to arrive in Bucharest or Budapest, Warsaw or Prague without having a choice of a half-dozen concerts, several new plays, a couple of new art exhibitions, or a significant movie from which to select *every* day.

But there is another side to all this: government control and Communist party restrictions on culture and the arts, censorship, and even ugly police tactics to suppress not only works considered critical of the regimes or the Party line, but those which do not promote it.

To be sure, all the East European countries are freer, more liberal, and more tolerant, in their approach to literature, art, and music, than the Soviet Union. There the lofty ideal that all art should serve the people is but a cover-up for the demand by the Party and government that it should serve the interests and promote the aims of authority.

In Hungary and Poland, for example, one can buy modern, abstract paintings either from the artists themselves or from government-run art galleries that would be considered treasonous "anti-Soviet propaganda" subject to confiscation by the police in the USSR.

In 1968 I bought what is to me a very wonderful, totally abstract painting from a well-known Polish artist who in the meantime has become a personal friend. I took the painting to Moscow with me when I was assigned there and hung it in my living room. When I left Russia again permanently and my belongings were cleared through customs, there was trouble. The authorities, first thinking it was by an "underground" Soviet artist, attempted to take it away on grounds that this kind of art is "not approved." Only after much argument and proof that it was not the work of a Russian painter, and had been brought into the country by me, was it cleared for shipment. When I told my Polish friend about what had almost happened to his work, he couldn't believe it.

In Czechoslovakia Vera Chytilova made a new film in 1978. It is a very funny sex comedy called *The Apple Game*. The Communist *apparatchiki* in charge of Prague's Barrandov Studios objected to it because it contained no propaganda promoting the Party, but released it anyway. It has been playing to capacity crowds in the movie houses. In Russia such a film would never even have got past the cutting room and the censors, and although made in an allied Communist country, it will never be shown there.

One of Hungary's most famous composers was Bela Bartok, who died in 1945. He was a pioneer of modern, abstract, and atonal music. In Hungary he is honored and loved. Music academies and conservatories are named for him and hardly a day passes on which one of his works is not performed by some orchestra, opera house, chamber group, or soloist. But the sound of his music is so unharmonious and "unpropagandistic" that in the Soviet Union it is practically forbidden. In fact, while a correspondent in Moscow, a number of musician friends used to ask me to bring records and scores of Bartok's work back to them whenever I went on trips to Western Europe or the United States. The same holds true for Poland's greatest living composer, Krzysztof Penderecki.

And yet, literature and the arts are not really free in most of the East European countries.

There are Romanian writers who are banned, such as Paul Goma, considered his country's leading novelist.

Except for Vera Chytilova and Jiri Menzel, all of Czechoslovakia's leading film directors—Milos Forman, Jan Kadar, Jan Nemec, and Ivan Passer—have been forced to flee, and now work in America. The works of Czechoslovakia's two leading playwrights. Vaclav Havel and Pavel Kohout, are banned and both are hounded by the secret police as are such leading writers as Ludvik Vaculik and Jan Prochazka.

Pal Bandy, a professor of literature at Budapest University, once explained what is meant by freedom of the arts in the East European countries.

"All citizens," he said, "are free to create what they want, to the extent that their creativity is an individual activity which does not require the financial support of the state. Thus, the freedom of a sonnet-writing poet differs from that of a film maker.

"However, no work of art can be published which is anti-humanistic, profascist, or attempts to arouse readers and viewers against other races and people. Our philosophy is Marxism, and I understand the term freedom as meaning freedom according to our philosophy."

Obviously that leaves room for interpretation by everyone involved in producing art, literature, and music for public consumption, especially the censors.

There is censorship in all the East European countries, but the fact that it exists is in itself subject to censorship. Censorship is actually the biggest secret of all in Eastern Europe. Only once has news of it really leaked out: in the spring of 1978 when Tomasz Strzyzewski, a young Polish censor, defected to Sweden and broke the big secret.

Strzyzewski had worked for nearly three years in the local Cracow branch of the Office for Control of the Press, Publications, and Performances—the GUKPPW—as Poland's government censorship agency is called. When he could no longer stomach the work he was doing, he left Poland with his wife and their two small children, smuggling out seven hundred pages of regulations according to which censors must work.

Those rules are a highly classified document which only the four hundred officials of GUKPPW are supposed to see. They spell out what the government and Party consider Poles should read and see, and tell Polish writers what to print. The list of taboos is staggering. It includes the names of persons who are never to be mentioned except in an unfavorable context. Among them are some of Poland's most famous intellectuals, artists, and scholars.

According to the rule book, Polish media are forbidden to publish anything even slightly critical of the Soviet Union. Censors are under orders, for example, to cut out any references to the poor quality of goods imported from the USSR. The Russians might feel insulted.

One instruction says specifically that any mention of "hippies and the counterculture" is prohibited unless it is an "obviously critical" mention.

Anything unfavorable to the Communist party and its top officials must be censored. There are regulations on when interviews with government and Party officials may be published and when the official texts, released by PAP, the Polish Press Agency, may be used in newspapers and magazines.

There was a regulation concerning a new film by Andrzej Wajda, *The Man of Marble,* which deals with the Stalin era. Although the movie was released—after Party chief Edward Gierek himself had given approval—the censorship rules said there was to be no advance publicity for the film and no announcement in papers as to where it would be showing.

The censors' rule book, according to one Polish intellectual, "reveals the planned destruction of our nation's culture and the systematic attempt to cripple individual thought and freedom of information."

On the other hand, just a brief look at Polish literature, art, and the press, can leave no doubt that the censor-rules, like many other rules in Poland, are there to be broken. Or, as one Polish writer puts it: "Of course we have censorship. My job is to get around it." Perhaps that explains why what one *doesn't* get to read in East European newspapers, magazines, and books, is very often more important than what one *does.*

Knowing their own countries' histories, East European

leaders probably figure they have good reason for censorship and limiting freedom of the arts.

There are few areas in the world where poets, writers, artists, and musicians have been as political, as involved in society, as revolutionary, or as patriotic and independent-spirited, as in Eastern Europe; few, also, where works of literature, art, and music have served as the vehicles to arouse the people to action against whatever tyranny was their oppressor and suppressor, whether foreign or domestic. Political and social thought runs like a single thread through the arts of these countries.

Consider the composers: Hungary's Franz Liszt, Bela Bartok, and Zoltan Kodaly; Czechoslovakia's Anton Dvorak and Friedrich Smetana; Poland's Frederic Chopin and Ignace Paderewski. All of them were intensely patriotic nationalists and revolutionaries. Love of their homeland and their people, and the hunger for independence and freedom are the most important themes of their music.

Or take the poets, writers and playwrights. Hungary's Sandor Petofi was one of the leading lyric poets of the nineteenth century. But his poems, such as "Up, Magyar," were all deeply patriotic and served as inspirations to the rebels of the 1849 Hungarian Revolution in which Petofi himself, only 27 years old, was killed. Perhaps an even greater Hungarian poet was Mihaly Vorosmarty, whose intensely nationalistic lyrics served as the call for rebellion against Austrian and Turkish rule. In Czechoslovakia the novelist Jaroslav Hasek created the whole symbol of Czech passive resistance to military bureaucracy and foreign authority with his four-volume novel *The Good Soldier Schweyk*.

Poland's greatest nineteenth-century poet and dramatist was Adam Mickiewicz. He was a patriotic revolutionary and freedom fighter, especially against czarist Russian rule, to the last drop of ink in his pen. Arrested for pro-Polish, anticzarist activities while a student at the University of Vilnius in 1823, he was deported to Siberia and later Western Europe and never allowed to return to his homeland. In the Revolution of 1848 and again during the Crimean War he organized legions of Polish émigrés in France to fight for Polish independence. Virtually all his poems and plays are calls and appeals for Polish freedom.

Culture has always been the barometer of political freedom and progress in Eastern Europe. That is still its role today. Moreover, these great figures of the past, all honored by statues, monuments, squares, streets, and boulevards, are used as symbols of rebellion by today's artists and intellectuals.

The activities of a "Petofi Circle" of writers and students sparked the 1956 Hungarian Revolution against Stalinist oppression. Among its members were some of modern Hungary's leading poets and authors, most of them Communists. In Poland in 1968 censorship of an anti–czarist play by Mickiewicz at a Warsaw theater touched off student riots all over the country and provoked a serious political crisis. When the Russians invaded Czechoslovakia to crush Dubcek's government, Czechoslovaks decided to "Schweyk" the invaders, that is, just sit down and do nothing except make fun of them, instead of offering armed resistance.

So it is hardly surprising that dissent in Eastern Europe—the human rights movement—is largely a development that originated among and is led by the writers, artists, and intellectuals. And at no time in Eastern Europe's postwar history have dissent and political unrest been stronger, better organized, or more persistent than in the late 1970's.

Although there is a common thread, the human rights movement takes different forms, uses different tactics, and pursues different aims in the various countries.

Hungary, for example, is not only the country most tolerant of dissidents, but the one in which organized dissent, such as it is, has as its goal more Communism instead of less. Hungary's human rights activists are "new leftists."

They are a small but vocal group of youngish intellectuals whose aims are surprisingly similar to those of the "new left" in the West, that is, a form of "Marxist purity." But they, too, face troubles expressing their views openly. Best known among them are Andras Hegedus, a former prime minister of Hungary; Gyorgy Konrad, whose novels *The Visitor* and *The City Founder* were published in Western Europe and the United States long before they came out in Hungary; Miklos Haraszti and Tamas Szentjoby, both popular and promising young poets; Agnes Heller and Ivan Szeleny, both well-known sociologists, and Yvette Biro, a leading film critic.

They claim that a "soulless bureaucracy" has developed and is suppressing the spirit of genuine Communism. Their chief complaint is that Hungary's successful experiment with economic reform and "goulash Communism" have betrayed the ideals of Communism. The 1968 reform has made Hungary the most prosperous country in Eastern Europe, but according to the "new left" dissenters, it has caused wide inequality in the distribution of wealth and has encouraged corruption. They spare no effort comparing the humdrum lives of factory workers with those of the rich new managerial class. Worst of all, they say, the economic reform has fostered a "consumer mentality among the masses."

Hungary's "new leftists" first began making news in 1974 when the poet Miklos Haraszti was sentenced to a suspended eight-months prison term for sending manuscript copies of his book *Piece Rates* to a West German publisher.

He had been in and out of trouble with the authorities since 1969 when he first complained publicly about "creeping bureaucracy" in Hungary. His book *Piece Rates* reveals the unfavorable opinions of assembly-line workers in a large Budapest factory where he was employed for about a year.

Several months after his trial, some of his friends, notably Konrad, Szeleny, and Szentjoby, were arrested and questioned and their apartments searched.

Konrad, a social worker, is best known abroad for his novels. The first of these, *The Visitor,* is based on his experiences as a social worker and tells about bad housing conditions in Hungary. *The City Founder,* is a critical view of urbanization problems.

Szeleny, who studied in America on a Ford Foundation grant in the late 1960's, helped Konrad with the research for *The City Founder.* He is regarded as Hungary's leading expert on urbanization.

Szentjoby, a poet, made a name for himself in intellectual circles by staging happenings in Budapest which dramatized problems raised by Haraszti, Konrad, and Szeleny.

Closely connected to them also is Agnes Heller, a prominent sociology professor.

Their opinions and movement are obviously embarrassing to the regime of Janos Kadar. But unlike some other East European leaders, he has not hounded his dissidents. Besides some comparatively mild police harassment, Kadar has left them pretty much in peace while at the same time encouraging them to leave the country. They have done that—for a while. Agnes Heller went on a teaching fellowship to Australia, Konrad on a study grant to the United States, and Miklos Haraszti and his wife to West Berlin.

There Haraszti still dreams of some utopia, still argues that Hungary's "goulash Communism" benefits the bosses more than the workers. He remains a Communist who is disenchanted by the departure Communism makes from the ideal and by the way the system operates in his country.

In Romania, on the other hand, the dissident movement was inspired by the 1975 Helsinki Agreement on European Security and Cooperation. This was the document signed by the United States, the Soviet Union, and more than thirty European countries with the aim of formally ending the cold war. It contains an important section, sometimes referred to as Basket Three, which guarantees the protection of human rights in all the signatory countries. What Romania's dissenters—and those in Bulgaria, Czechoslovakia, and Poland—demand is that their own government honor and uphold the human rights promises that it made by signing the Helsinki agreement.

The movement began with one forceful and very outspoken man, novelist Paul Goma, aged 45, a Communist whose troubles with the Romanian Communist regime go back nearly thirty years. Now living in France, he has sometimes been called Romania's Alexander Solzhenitsyn.

First arrested for his political activities as a high school student of sixteen, he was again jailed in 1956 while attending Bucharest University and served a two-year sentence followed by four years of "banishment at hard labor." In 1966 his first published works appeared, including portions of his first, autobiographical novel, *Ostinato*. Though neither that book nor those which followed were ever published in his homeland—only in the West—Goma gained stature as one of Romania's leading writers and served as editor of the literary weekly *Romania Literara*. In 1972 he went to France and West Germany for a year of study and work. On returning home he found that he had lost his editor's job and had also been expelled from the Communist party in a rather odd fashion: the authorities told him that irregularities had been found in his original membership application and that, as a result, he had never even been a member. From then on Goma was prevented from getting any kind of work, literary or manual. He lived with his wife and baby in the mountains, sixty miles from Bucharest, on contributions from relatives and royalties from his books published in the West.

In February 1977, fed up, Goma drafted an "open letter" accusing President Nicolae Ceausescu's regime of violating the Helsinki Agreement and of failing to protect such human rights as freedom of movement and travel, free circulation of ideas, and freedom of the press. Prominent Romanian artists, musicians, and intellectuals signed it.

For the next eight months Goma and the other signers of the letter were subjected to crude police harassment. Their telephones were cut and their homes cordoned off, and they were roughed up by secret police agents masquerading as gangsters. Goma himself was expelled from the Romanian Writers' Union, arrested, and held without charges for six weeks. During that time he was personally beaten by Romania's deputy minister of the interior.

Finally, in November 1977, Goma and most of the other signers of the letter were either forced or allowed to emigrate.

But the protest they began in Romania had left a seed which bore fruit in a very violent coal miners' strike and in a strong human rights movement among the 1.8 million members of Romania's Hungarian ethnic minority who, backed by neighboring Hungary, claim that their human rights are also being violated by the Ceausescu regime.

In Bulgaria, too, there were signs in 1978 of intellectual unrest, based on demands that the government stick to what it signed in the Helsinki Agreement.

Though its authors are unknown, a document called Declaration 78 began circulating there and reached the West. Its six-point program protests against violations of human rights, censorship, and restrictions on freedom of the press, the arts, and religion. It demands a higher standard of living and more social security, the establishment of independent trade unions, and opening of the country's borders to allow freedom of movement and the right to travel.

Communist propagandists try to give the impression that

dissenters and human rights activists are the scum of the earth. "Human shipwrecks," "alcoholics," "illiterates," "bandits," "fascists," "counterrevolutionary plotters," "mercenaries," and "agents of capitalist paymasters" are just a few of the derogatory terms used by the Communist media to describe them. Yet, among the protesters one usually finds Eastern Europe's most respected and internationally renowned writers, artists, scientists, and thinkers, not to mention an overwhelming majority who are themselves veteran and loyal Communists. That is especially true for Czechoslovakia and Poland where the dissident and human rights movements are the most widespread and effective.

The roots of protest and dissent in Czechoslovakia go back to the Soviet invasion of 1968, the crushing of Alexander Dubcek's reform policy, and the purge and persecution of tens of thousands of Dubcek supporters, liberal intellectuals, and reform politicians. All were—and remain—ardent Communists though they have been expelled from the Party.

In January 1977 these men and women put forth their views, and protested against the postinvasion regime of Gustav Husak in an organized and coherent form: a document called Charter-77. Basically it is a demand for human rights, a condemnation of their violation, and an appeal for upholding the Helsinki Agreement.

Its authors and original signers included nearly one hundred writers who have been black-listed by the government-owned publishing houses since 1968 and who have been circulating their works illegally and underground through a form of self-publishing called the Padlock Press. Among them were the playwrights Pavel Kohout and Vaclav Havel, both of whom have scored Broadway triumphs in America; the novelists Ivan Klima and Ludvik Vaculik; former Czechoslovak foreign minister Professor Jiri Hajek, and a number of former high-ranking government and Party officials such as Frantisek

*Russian tanks move into Prague,
Czechoslovakia, August 1978*

Kriegel, Milan Huebl, Zdenek Mlynar, and Jaroslaw Sabata.

The authorities have used every imaginable kind of police pressure short of mass arrests to crush the movement, but it continues to grow. More than a thousand leading Czechoslovak citizens—the men and women who ran and guided the country during the 1968 "Prague Spring"—have signed Charter-77 and identified themselves with it.

What's more, these dissenters are picking up strong support from the public at large.

Take the case of the construction workers who have been building Prague's new subway system since the early 1970's. In the fall of 1977 they were told to attend a mandatory meeting after work at which the only point on the agenda was the planned firing of a well-known and well-liked coworker who, before becoming a common laborer, had been a top-level Communist party official under Dubcek. His "crime"? Signing Charter-77.

At the meeting he was told to "defend" himself. He did by quoting from Charter-77 itself—the first time that the more than five hundred workers in the hall had an opportunity to hear some of the points of the document that the Party press had labeled "the work of spies and foreign agents." Subsequently two Party officials took the rostrum and demanded that the man be fired. But when a vote was taken, the overwhelming majority insisted that he be kept on the job.

There are other incidents like that.

The Czechoslovaks have always been resourceful in dealing with invaders and home-grown oppressors, either by totally ignoring them and going on with life as usual, or by making fools of them, by "Schweyking it." One of the funniest forms "Schweyking" ever took was during the 1968 invasion when Czechoslovaks removed and mixed up all the street and road signs in order to confuse the Russians. Charter-77 activists have been trying new variations on that old Czecho-slovak theme.

One example was a Prague theater performance starring the actor Petr Oliva, one of the few artists and intellectuals who support the Husak regime. Seventy human rights activists had bought tickets to the performance in a block of seats. When Oliva came on stage, they all got up in a group and marched out—to the deafening applause of the remainder of the audience.

Forming protest groups of any kind on the streets is forbidden. Thus, one day in 1977, when a prominent signer of Charter-77 was called for questioning at the secret-police headquarters on Prague's busy Bartolomejska Street, more than one hundred dissenters passed back and forth in front of the building, as "innocent pedestrians," until his release.

On another occasion a group of youths entered the low-ceilinged, underground passageway connecting one side of Wenceslaus Square with the other, and released scores of brightly colored balloons. Attached to each one, and within easy reach of all pedestrians in the underpass, was a mimeographed copy of Charter-77.

By far the most significant and effective human rights movement in Eastern Europe has been Poland's Committee for the Defense of the Workers, or the Social Self-Defense Committee, as it has been called since the beginning of 1978. It represents the first time that intellectuals in the Communist world have linked forces and made common cause with less privileged, ordinary citizens—the workers.

Dissent and protest have a long history in Communist Poland, going back to 1956, when demonstrations and riots that came close to a revolution finally put an end to Stalinist and "Moscow" Communist rule and brought Wladyslaw Gomulka back to power as Party chief. The country has hardly been quiet since then—witness the student demonstrations of 1968, the workers' strikes that toppled Gomulka and brought in Gierek in December 1970, the riots over price increases in June 1976. But all these upheavals had one thing in common. Either they originated among and were carried out by workers, or by intellectuals and students. Never, however, by both.

The Committee for the Defense of the Workers, established in September 1976, was the first attempt to change that pattern. It was formed to provide financial, medical, and legal aid to the workers, and members of their families, who were arrested and fired after the June 1976 price-increase riots in a number of Polish cities. Its fifteen founding members are all leading Polish intellectuals who represent a broad cross-section of views and philosophies, from "new left" Marxism to Catholicism. The chairman was Jerzy Andrzejewski, Poland's leading and most popular writer, whose first novel, *Ashes and Diamonds*, was a worldwide best seller in the late 1940's. Other members included Wladyslaw Bienkowski, a former member of parliament and the Communist party's central committee; Edward Lipinski, a famous professor of economics; the Reverend Jan Zieja, the canon of Warsaw's Saint John's Cathedral, and Jacek Kuron, an outspoken "new left" sociologist.

The committee collected and distributed thousands of dollars, publicized reports of police brutality and torture in connection with the demonstrations, and issued its own, illegally printed information bulletins about trials and imprisonment of the strikers. Most important, perhaps, it not only forced the government to give exact figures and charges about those being prosecuted, but eventually got the regime to back down so that only those workers guilty of real crimes such as assault and manslaughter were actually tried and imprisoned. Thanks to the committee's efforts, all those who had been fired for taking part in the demonstrations were rehired.

Its main work accomplished, the committee at first considered disbanding, but late in 1977 decided to reorganize and rename itself as the Social Self-Defense Committee, with much wider goals of protecting human rights in general. It has since been joined by a number of other dissident groups with fairly similar aims.

Thus far the Gierek regime has tread lightly in meeting this challenge to its authority. To be sure, the dissenters encounter police threats and harassment. Periodically some of them are arrested, then released. Their apartments are searched. They are shadowed. They are insulted in the official press. They are deprived of privileges, and some have lost their jobs. But there has been nothing—nor is there likely to be anything—like the much tougher approach in Czechoslovakia, not to mention the brutal repression, with years of imprisonment, used in the Soviet Union to silence dissent and protest.

What do the human rights activists really want and what do their movements mean for the future of Eastern Europe and for the rest of the world?

Certainly not a return to the kinds of governments their countries had before World War II, nor a return to capitalism. Those political leaders in the Western world who say they do are either misinformed or are fooling themselves and their voters. But they do want a different kind of Communism—the kind promised by Dubcek in Czechoslovakia in 1968. They want more democracy and more independence from Moscow without, however, leaving the Soviet bloc.

Adam Michnik, a young Polish intellectual and one of the founding members of the Committee for Social Self-Defense, puts it this way:

"The only policy for dissidents in Eastern Europe is an unending struggle for reforms, in favor of evolution, which will extend civil liberties and guarantee respect for human rights.

The example of Poland shows that pressure brought to bear on the government can bring significant results."

The nations of Eastern Europe are not captive. Neither are they free. They bear no resemblance today to the societies they were before they became Communist, but also no resemblance to what they were before October 1956 when rebellions and revolution rocked Poland and Hungary.

The Polish October, as it was called, and the Hungarian Revolution were, for all the drama, heroism, tragedy, and cold-war oratory that surrounded them, basically rebellions against Stalinism. The issue was not freedom versus Communism, but a different kind of Communism versus that which Josef Stalin had imposed upon the East European countries as well as his own people, a Communism based on military force, secret-police terror, and Moscow-trained *apparatchiki*.

Though Stalin had been dead more than three years when those rebellions started, his system still dominated political, economic, social, and cultural life throughout Eastern Europe. It was a two-track system: Soviet overlordship based on bayonets and tanks, on the one hand, and supported, on the other, by local "little Stalins"—the "Moscow" Communists— who subjugated their own citizens as cruelly as Stalin had the Russians.

The upheavals in Poland and Hungary changed that system and set forces in motion all over Eastern Europe, though at a cost of many thousands of lives.

Yet the demands of 1956 remain as valid—and in a sense as unsatisfied—today. They were made again in Czechoslovakia in 1968, and crushed without mercy. They are the reform platform of East European intellectuals and workers now.

Among these demands are: an end to police power and censorship, the guarantee of basic human rights, economic reform and decentralization, better working conditions and wages, genuine trade unions, higher living standards, and, above all, a real voice so that government will be conducted with the consent of the governed.

Very few in Eastern Europe would want to take their country out of the Warsaw Pact or its alliance with the Soviet Union. But the vast majority do want changes in the spirit and the letter of their contract with Russia, for their hunger for national dignity has never been greater.

The fact that the demands remain the same does not mean, however, that Eastern Europe hasn't changed. Indeed it has, and is, for the better. But dissatisfaction persists because material improvements have not been accompanied by the kind of freedom and self-expression to which mature societies are entitled. Moreover, East Europeans are keenly aware that the ghost of Stalin still haunts the Soviet Union itself. Until they have genuine guarantees against the revival of repression and terror, there is always the danger that the ghost will come to haunt them too.

The social and economic aim can be said to be Communism. The political one is democracy. That is what dissent is all about in Eastern Europe—in fact, what Eastern Europe is all about.

Once the Western world accepts and understands that, it will be able to formulate and conduct a meaningful policy for coexisting with the ninety million people who speak unpronounceable languages and who inhabit the small chunk of real estate called Eastern Europe.

Recommended Reading

To compile a recommended list of books about Eastern Europe is a formidable task because there are so many and any selection tends to be subjective. Those I have chosen are the ones I find most suitable and most useful.

Eastern Europe

Blumenfeld, Yorick. *Seesaw: Cultural Life in Eastern Europe.* New York: Harcourt, Brace & World, 1968.

Brown, James F. *The New Eastern Europe: The Khrushchev Era and After.* New York: Praeger, 1966.

Brzezinski, Zbigniew. *The Soviet Bloc, Unity and Conflict,* rev. and enl. ed. Cambridge, Mass.: Harvard University Press, 1967.

Djilas, Milovan. *The New Class: An Analysis of the Communist System.* New York: Praeger, 1958.

Neuburg, Paul. *The Hero's Children—The Postwar Generation in Eastern Europe.* New York: Morrow, 1973.

Portal, Roger. *The Slavs: A Cultural and Historical Survey of the Slavonic Peoples,* trans. Patrick Evans. New York: Harper & Row, 1969.

Seton-Watson, Hugh. *Eastern Europe Between the Wars 1918–1941.* Hamden, Conn.: Archon Books, 1962.

————. *The East European Revolution,* 3rd ed. New York: Praeger, 1956.

Shub, Anatole. *An Empire Loses Hope: The Return of Stalin's Ghost.* New York: Norton, 1970.

Skilling, Gordon. *The Governments of Communist East Europe.* New York: Crowell, 1966.

Stavrianos, L. S. *The Balkans Since 1453.* New York: Holt, Rinehart & Winston, 1958.

The Cold War

Fleming, D. F. *The Cold War and Its Origins 1917–1960.* Garden City, N.Y.: Doubleday, 1961.

Herz, Martin F. *Beginnings of the Cold War.* Bloomington: Indiana University Press, 1966.

Bulgaria

Brown, James F. *Bulgaria Under Communist Rule.* New York: Praeger, 1970.

Czechoslovakia

Levy, Alan. *Rowboat to Prague.* New York: Grossman Publishers, 1972.

London, Arthur. *The Confession.* New York: Morrow, 1970.

Lewis, Flora. *Red Pawn.* New York: Doubleday, 1965.

Shawcross, William. *Dubček.* New York: Simon & Schuster, 1970.

Sterling, Claire. *The Masaryk Case.* New York: Harper & Row, 1969.

Szulc, Tad. *Czechoslovakia Since World War II.* New York: Viking, 1972.

Tigrid, Pavel. *Why Dubček Fell.* London: Macdonald, 1971.

Hungary

Barber, Noël. *Seven Days of Freedom: The Hungarian Uprising 1956.* New York: Stein & Day, 1974.

Poland

Bethell, Nicholas. *Gomulka—His Poland and His Communism.* New York: Holt, Rinehart & Winston, 1969.

Halecki, O. *A History of Poland: From the Foundation of the State in the First World War to the Present Day,* trans. J. R. Foster. New York: Knopf, 1966.

Roos, Hans. *History of Modern Poland.* London: Eyre & Spottiswoode, 1966.

Stehle, Hansjakob. *The Independent Satellite.* New York: Praeger, 1965.

Romania

Hale, Julian. *Ceauşescu's Romania: A Political Documentary.* London: George Harrap.

Ronay, Gabriel. *The Truth About Dracula.* New York: Stein & Day, 1971.

The Soviet Union

Dornberg, John. *The Soviet Union Today.* New York: Dial, 1976.

———. *The New Tsars: Russia Under Stalin's Heirs.* New York: Doubleday, 1972.

Smith, Hedrick. *The Russians.* New York: Quadrangle/Times, 1976.

East Germany

Dornberg, John. *The Other Germany.* New York: Doubleday, 1968.

———. *The Two Germanys.* New York: Dial, 1974.

Hangen, Welles. *The Muted Revolution.* New York: Knopf, 1966.

Steele, Joanathan. *Socialism with a German Face.* London: Jonathan Cape, 1977.

Yugoslavia

Auty, Phyllis. *Tito: A Biography,* rev. ed. Baltimore. Penguin, 1974.

Clissold, Stephen, ed. *A Short History of Yugoslavia, from Early Times to 1966.* New York: Cambridge University Press, 1966.

Doder, Dusko. *The Yugoslavs.* New York: Random House, 1978.

Photographs appear courtesy of:

Eastfoto: 43, 130, 156 (top right), 196, 229, 242, 255
Polish Tourist Agency: 12
New York Public Library Picture Collection: 89, 216
Sovfoto: 107
Wide World Photos: 156 (top left and bottom), 173, 268, 292

Maps by David Lindroth

Index

John Dornberg was born in East Germany and immigrated with his parents to the United States at the age of seven. He attended the University of Denver and, after two years of service in the U.S. Army, began living and working as a journalist and foreign correspondent in Europe.

Mr. Dornberg was formerly bureau chief for *Newsweek* in Vienna and in Moscow but now works as a free-lance writer and political analyst specializing in Soviet and East European affairs. In 1970 he was expelled from the Soviet Union for writing about the dissident movement there.

John Dornberg is the author of the highly praised *The Soviet Union Today* and *The Two Germanys* (both Dial). He now lives in West Germany.